Transport and Ethics

TRANSPORT ECONOMICS, MANAGEMENT AND POLICY

Series Editor: Kenneth Button, *University Professor, School of Public Policy, George Mason University, USA*

Transport is a critical input for economic development and for optimizing social and political interaction. Recent years have seen significant new developments in the way that transport is perceived by private industry and governments, and in the way academics look at it.

The aim of this series is to provide original material and up-to-date synthesis of the state of modern transport analysis. The coverage embraces all conventional modes of transport but also includes contributions from important related fields such as urban and regional planning and telecommunications where they interface with transport. The books draw from many disciplines and some cross disciplinary boundaries. They are concerned with economics, planning, sociology, geography, management science, psychology and public policy. They are intended to help improve the understanding of transport, the policy needs of the most economically advanced countries and the problems of resource-poor developing economies. The authors come from around the world and represent some of the outstanding young scholars as well as established names.

Titles in the series include:

Competition in the Railway Industry
An International Comparative Analysis
Edited by José A. Gómez-Ibáñez and Ginés de Rus

Globalized Freight Transport
Intermodality, E-Commerce, Logistics and Sustainability
Edited by Thomas R. Leinbach and Cristina Capineri

Decision-Making on Mega-Projects
Cost–Benefit Analysis, Planning and Innovation
Edited by Hugo Priemus, Bent Flyvbjerg and Bert van Wee

Port Privatisation
The Asia-Pacific Experience
Edited by James Reveley and Malcolm Tull

The Future of Intermodal Freight Transport
Operations, Design and Policy
Edited by Rob Konings, Hugo Priemus and Peter Nijkamp

North American Freight Transportation
The Road to Security and Prosperity
Mary R. Brooks

New Developments in Transport Planning
Advances in Dynamic Traffic Assignment
Edited by Chris M.J. Tampère, Francesco Viti and Lambertus H. (Ben) Immers

Transport and Ethics
Ethics and the Evaluation of Transport Policies and Projects
Bert van Wee

Transport and Ethics

Ethics and the Evaluation of Transport
Policies and Projects

Bert van Wee

Delft University of Technology, The Netherlands

TRANSPORT ECONOMICS, MANAGEMENT AND POLICY

Edward Elgar
Cheltenham, UK • Northampton, MA, USA

Published by
Edward Elgar Publishing Limited
The Lypiatts
15 Lansdown Road
Cheltenham
Glos GL50 2JA
UK

Edward Elgar Publishing, Inc.
William Pratt House
9 Dewey Court
Northampton
Massachusetts 01060
USA

A catalogue record for this book
is available from the British Library

Library of Congress Control Number: 2011925793

ISBN 978 1 84980 964 1

Typeset by Servis Filmsetting Ltd, Stockport, Cheshire
Printed and bound by MPG Books Group, UK

Contents

About the author

Bert van Wee is professor of Transport Policy at Delft University of Technology, the Netherlands, in the Faculty of Technology Policy and Management. In addition, he is head of the section Transport and Logistics. He has (the Dutch equivalent of) a Masters in Geography (Utrecht University) and a PhD in Economics and Econometrics (University of Amsterdam). After finishing his Masters, he worked for an engineering consultancy (AGV) from 1983 to 1990. From 1990 to 2003 he worked at the National Institute of Public Health and the Environment (RIVM) doing research in the areas of transport and the environment, focusing on scenario development, forecasting, modelling and policy analyses. Between 1999 and 2003, and combined with his work at RIVM, he held a chair in Transport, the Environment and Land Use, at Utrecht University (Faculty of Spatial Sciences). Since 2003, he has worked for Delft University of Technology. His research areas include land-use and transport interaction, accessibility, the environment/sustainability, evaluations and policy analysis, and large infrastructure projects. He has a strong preference for multi-disciplinary research, and thinks that contemporary transport problems can best be studied and reduced from a multi-disciplinary perspective. He is often involved in research and discussion in the Netherlands in the areas of large infrastructure projects, long-term policy documents, and policy evaluations, and is frequently invited to comment by the media (TV, radio, newspapers, and other written press).

Preface and acknowledgements

This book is written thanks to my faculty offering me a part-time sabbatical, in order to study 'something other' than my mainstream research focus (I hold a chair in Transport Policy). I chose the link between transport and ethics. What were the reasons for this decision?

A first motivation is my deep interest in multi-disciplinary research. After a (Dutch equivalent of a) Masters in geography, I have been professionally inspired by other disciplines, the most important being civil engineering, economics, psychology, environmental and managerial sciences. New job positions were the most important trigger for studying 'new' disciplines, but also my belief that both scientific progress, as well as the practical use of science, benefits from a multi-disciplinary (and in some cases an interdisciplinary) approach. In addition, ethics (and more broadly, philosophy) had been – up to undertaking the work that resulted in this book – almost completely absent in my research focus.

A second motivation comes from my experiences with Cost–Benefit Analysis (CBA). Although they are quite positive, I had the feeling that something was still missing. Part of my work relates to the *ex ante* evaluation of transport projects and policies. In most western countries mainstream economic reasoning is very dominant in *ex ante* evaluations of transport projects and policies, CBA being the most widely used framework for evaluation. I have supported the use of CBA in several roles, for instance in my work as a member of scientific committees, to check if CBAs for large infrastructure projects were made according to scientific insights and practical guidelines, but also by publishing on the strengths and weaknesses of CBA, and on options for further improvement. What has intrigued me for a long time is the strong resistance to, or even rejection of, CBA by some persons in (mainly but not exclusively) the practitioner community (such as some policy makers and members of interest groups). On the one hand, I cannot avoid the impression that for some it is purely the fact that they do not like the outcomes, and as a result reject the method of CBA out of self-interest. On the other hand, I think that some individuals do have good non-self-interest related reasons to debate the use of CBA for *ex ante* evaluations of transport projects and policies. However, they often were not able to make them explicit. Various discussions have given me the impression that ethical questions such as fairness or equity[1] were behind some of the feelings of discomfort experienced by some of those individuals, and I could well understand these feelings.

The third reason is the motivation to do 'something' in some form of collaboration with people from another group in our faculty, preferably a well-respected group that I had not collaborated with previously. In this context, our faculty has a very strong group in the area of philosophy.

This brings me to acknowledging the persons that, in one way or another, have supported me in writing this book. The first is Professor Jeroen van den Hoven of our faculty philosophy group, who from the very inception of my ideas gave me strong support in bringing my plans into practice, by advising on literature, databases for literature, and other information, and also by discussing the subject. I also would like to thank our former dean Professor Hugo Priemus, who encouraged me years ago to take a sabbatical. In addition, the dean at the time of writing this book, Professor Theo Toonen, as well as the head of department, Professor Margot Weijnen, in several ways encouraged me to take this sabbatical. Next are my section members, who allowed me to do this work and made no issue of my limited availability. I am grateful to all of them, and in particular to Dr Vincent Marchau, Professor Lori Tavasszy, Dr Jan Anne Annema and Dr Caspar Chorus, who took over parts of my tasks during the year of my part-time sabbatical. I am also grateful to the almost 100 respondents who filled in my questionnaire about transport and ethics as described in Chapter 2, as well as to the persons I interviewed for Chapter 7. Next I want to thank the secretaries, and in particular Trudie Stoute,[2] who supported me most generously by performing any secretarial tasks in general, and also in relation to the part-time sabbatical leave. For their comments on (parts of) the draft version of this book, I want to thank Neelke Doorn, Jeroen van den Hoven, Karen Lucas, Ibo van de Poel, Piet Rietveld and Sabine Roeser. For correcting my English I want to thank Geoff Dudley. I want to thank all the persons who spontaneously sent me literature relevant for my sabbatical, including Jan Anne Annema, Rutger Beekman, Arjan van Binsbergen, Enne de Boer, Neelke Doorn, Karst Geurs, Marjan Hagenzieker, Gerard Hoekveld, Jeroen van den Hoven, Carl Koopmans, Patricia Mokhtarian, Ibo van de Poel, Piet Rietveld, Sabine Roeser, Behnam Taebi, Lori Tavasszy and Fred Wegman. I thank Marian Hagenzieker, Karen Lucas, Karst Geurs and Piet Rietveld for their contributions to joint papers based on parts of this book. I thank Peter Blok, Frank Bruinsma, Jeroen Klooster, Marianne Kuijpers, Henk Meurs, Rob Nieuwkamer, Sietze Rienstra and Erik Verroen for letting me interview them (Chapter 7). Finally, I thank Eric Molin for his data analysis (Chapter 7).

Abbreviations

CBA	cost–benefit analysis
CEA	cost-effectiveness analysis
MCA	multi criteria analysis
VOSL	value of a statistical life
WTA	willingness to accept
WTP	willingness to pay

1. Introduction

1.1 TRANSPORT AND SOCIETY

Transport is crucial for society: societies cannot function without the transport of people and goods. It enables us to participate in many activities at different locations, such as living, working, education, shopping and visiting relatives and friends. In addition, it allows us to transport goods, from the locations of mining of raw materials, via several production stages, culminating in the shops where people buy products, or even up to the final locations of use, such as houses or offices. On the other hand, transport carries costs, in terms of money, time, effort and negative impacts on society. In most western countries people spend 10 to 15 percent of their income on transport (Schafer and Victor, 1997). On average, and at the aggregate level (e.g. all persons in one country), people travel between 60 and 75 minutes per person per day, in almost all countries worldwide (Mokhtarian and Chen, 2004; Szalai, 1972; Zahavi, 1979). In addition to time and costs, it takes effort to travel. Cycling takes energy, and the cyclist can get wet, while driving a car over a longer period is tiring for many people, and switching trains, or changing from a bus to a train, is itself a negative experience for most people, not to mention the time it takes (Wardman, 2001). Transport also causes negative impacts on society, mainly due to accidents, emissions of harmful pollutants and CO_2, noise, the barrier effects of infrastructure for people, land take and fragmentation of nature.

1.2 TRANSPORT: A MULTI-DISCIPLINARY RESEARCH SUBJECT

Transport has been studied by many disciplines, including transport engineers, economists, psychologists, geographers, planners, environmental scientists and sociologists. First, a key reason for this wide variety of disciplines studying transport is the multitude of its important impacts on society, as presented above. Secondly, transport is, like land use, an *object* of study, not a discipline like economics or psychology. The object is also highly influenced by people, and can be studied from several disciplinary backgrounds, including economics, psychology, sociology and civil engineering. Thirdly, transport literally connects people, goods and activities, and therefore it is highly interwoven with spatial developments and general trends in society (including the economy), linking it to, amongst other disciplines, spatial sciences, economics and sociology.

As a result, mainstream transport journals are dominated by work from scholars with diverse backgrounds, as presented above. In addition, probably more than average in science, transport is highly interdisciplinary, though mono-disciplinary studies on transport are still very common. If I refer to mainstream transport journals, I refer to journals such as *Transportation Research Parts A–F*, *Transport Policy*, *Transport Reviews*, *Journal of Transport Geography*, *Journal of Transport Economics and Policy*, *European Journal of Transport and Infrastructure Research*, *Transportation*, *Transportation Science*, and the like, as well as to transport-related papers in spatial sciences, as published in journals such as *Urban Studies*, *The Annals of Regional Science* and *Environment and Planning (A–C)*.

1.3   ETHICS AND TRANSPORT

Ethics is defined as 'the discipline related to what is good and bad or right and wrong behaviour, including moral duty and obligation, values and beliefs and the use of critical thinking about human problems' (Beach, 1996: 2). Ethics differs from morality. Morality 'consists of a society's most general standards', whereas ethics 'are not general standards of conduct but the standards of a particular profession, occupation, institution or group within society' (Beach, 1996: 15).

Perhaps slightly surprisingly in mainstream transport literature, there is hardly any explicit literature on the ethical dimensions of transport, the major exceptions being social exclusion (see Chapter 4), distribution effects as recognized in economics (see Chapter 3), and some reflections on the mobility system or the car-dependent society from a sociological perspective (e.g. Beckmann, 2001; Khisty and Zeitler, 2001; Urry, 2004). Consequently, transport ethics has been largely ignored in the area of philosophy (Khisty and Zeitler, 2001). As a result, a literature search[1] in SCOPUS (in the social sciences and humanities section) using the search term 'ethics AND transport' in the title, abstract or key words, and selecting 'all years', resulted in 50 hits, of which only 15 related to transport of persons and goods (and not, for example, the transport of substances via the blood through the body). Of that 15, about half were only vaguely related to the subject of this book. A search on 'ethics AND mobility' resulted in even fewer useful hits. Searches on 'transport' and 'mobility' in the *Stanford Encyclopedia of Philosophy* resulted in 32 and 38 hits respectively, of which only a few were useful. Additional useful literature can of course be found (and actually was found – see the references in this book) using keywords like equity, environment and social exclusion, but the message is that there is hardly any literature that explicitly deals with 'ethics and transport'. In this book, I argue that transport relates to many ethical issues, which are given scant attention in the transport literature.

1.4 AIM OF THE BOOK

The aim of the book is not to give a full overview of all ethical aspects of transport, but more to elaborate on a selection of ethical issues in order to make the reader aware of ethical aspects of transport and give them 'food for thought'. The target audience for the book is the researcher, practitioner and policy maker who belong to the mainstream transport communities. I would not argue that the book is not relevant for philosophers (philosophy is the dominant science that studies ethics), but the book is primarily written for the mainstream transport community. The aim is only to make this target group aware of the ethical issues of transport, not to convince them of what is morally 'right' and what is 'wrong', nor to provide solutions for all the 'problems' that I discuss.

1.5 POINTS OF DEPARTURE AND DEMARCATION

My first point of departure is to take the perspective of the *ex ante* evaluation of transport projects and policies. Another option could be to take the perspective of design.[2] The reason for taking evaluation as the point of departure is that this is generally broader in character. Design dimensions are normally also included in evaluations, but evaluations can be broader. For example, the designer of a public transport system can have dimensions such as distances from bus stops to train stations in mind, as well as speeds and travel times, capacity, comfort levels and construction costs. But she might not explicitly have to include emissions or barrier effects. These effects nevertheless are important from the perspective of evaluation.

As a result of this point of departure, I do not include areas such as the ethics of driving behaviour, and general philosophical and sociological reflections on mobility, hyper mobility, car dependency, etc. In addition, I also do not discuss moral aspects related to how far policy makers can go in the use of technology to change the behaviour of people, including technologies such as the alcohol lock, or advanced road pricing systems that could (at least theoretically) endanger privacy (for an overview of the links between philosophy and technology and engineering see Meijers, 2009).

It is important to realize that from the point of departure of *ex ante* evaluation for decision making, a distinction can be made between choices in which moral aspects are included, versus those in which they play no role (Morton, 1991). For example, the choice between two locations for a potential new railway station probably does not necessarily include moral aspects,[3] while the choice between speed levels on motorways probably does: a balance needs to be found, on the one hand, between travel time savings and maybe also the fun of fast driving, and on the other hand the environmental impacts and risks. In the case of moral decisions, utilitarian approaches (see Chapter 3) may not be as attractive as in non-moral decisions.

My second point of departure is linked to the aim of the book and its target group: this theoretical point of departure is the 'mainstream economy', as most often used, not only by economists, but also civil engineers, geographers and other disciplines studying transport. I do not present a sharp definition of what 'mainstream economy' is, but I refer to it as a collection of theories, including Random Utility Theory, neo-classical economics, welfare economics and the like, that dominate transport research – see, for example, handbooks on transport economy (Blauwens et al., 2008; Button, 2003, 2010) and handbooks such as the one on transport modelling (Hensher and Button, 2000). The choice of the mainstream economy as a point of departure does not imply that the ethical issues discussed in this book take this perspective, it implies that I have readers in mind who are familiar with the use of the mainstream economy, and related methods and evaluation practices, in transport research. In several chapters I will at least make clear that the choice of the mainstream economy has several ethical implications.

My final point of departure is that I have in mind western societies. I do not claim the book to be irrelevant for developing countries, but I did not dig deeply into the specific studies and discussions of third world countries.

A first demarcation is that in this book I focus on transport *in public space*, ignoring within-buildings transport, and transport over the territory of an industrial plant. A second demarcation is related to overviews of environmental and safety impacts. These impacts in themselves are relevant from an ethical point of view, but are only included in this book in a very limited way, because they are widely addressed in the mainstream transport literature. Besides, the aim of the book is to give food for thought on ethics and transport, not to present overviews of effects that are ethically relevant.

1.6 ORGANIZATION OF THE BOOK

This book is organized as follows. Chapter 2 describes a questionnaire-based research survey amongst members of the transport community in the Netherlands, aiming to find out the opinions and wishes of the target audience for this book in the area of transport and ethics. Chapter 3 explains the use and ethical aspects of Cost–Benefit Analysis in transport, nowadays in most countries the most used *ex ante* evaluation method in the area of transport. Chapters 4–6 discuss the '*what* question': what are the ethical aspects of specific subjects? Important issues for transport policies relate to accessibility, the environment and safety. Probably the most studied ethical subject related to accessibility is 'social exclusion' – this subject is discussed in Chapter 4. Chapter 5 then focuses on the environment, in particular on long-term sustainability, probably one of the most difficult-to-address environmental subjects from an ethical perspective. Chapter 6 then discusses safety. Chapters 7–8 focus on the '*how* question': how to do research and develop and use models from an ethical perspective? Chapter 7 discusses the ethics of doing research. Chapter 8 then discusses modelling transport from an ethical perspective. Finally, Chapter 9 finally summarizes the main conclusions, and discusses avenues for further exploring the links between transport and ethics.

2. The opinion of the target group

2.1 INTRODUCTION

As a first step, and before starting to research and write, I wanted to find out exactly what the target group for this book would wish to see covered in it. Consequently, I sent out a questionnaire and analysed the results. This chapter presents the methodology and results.

2.2 METHODOLOGY

I issued a questionnaire to researchers (scientific and others), practitioners and policy makers in the Netherlands. After a brief introduction, in which I announced my intention to write this book (including identification of the target group), I asked two questions:

1. What comes into your mind primarily when you think about 'ethics and transport'? Even if nothing comes into your mind, please say so.
2. Which subjects would you like to be covered by the book?

In order to find out if the respondents' background is related to the answers, I added a third question, in which I asked about the profession of the respondents (research/science/practice/policy making). I also registered the gender of the respondents, in order to find out if gender is related to interests.[1] In addition, I asked them to forward the email to other people who could also answer these questions. To avoid bias towards people who expressed an interest in the subject, I encouraged them to not solely select such persons.

The questionnaire was sent out to 177 people belonging to the target group, with whom I had previously (before sending out the questionnaire) had email contact (all of them less than a year ago, the majority of them less than three months ago). Only those with whom I have had many contacts over the past years were included, and thus people that I had only had contact with occasionally were omitted.

Although the questionnaire was sent to policy makers and practitioners, the majority of those who received it, were researchers, and within this latter group there was a bias towards scientific researchers. In addition, therefore, I gratefully accepted the offer of including a request for answering both questions (as presented above) in an electronic newsletter of the Dutch professionals' magazine *Verkeerskunde*, in January 2010. *Verkeerskunde* is the most well-known and distributed journal for professionals in the Netherlands. In addition, another recently established, but already well-known, professionals' journal, *Verkeer in Beeld*, offered to include the message in their electronic newsletter of 12 January 2010 (4100 addresses).

For several reasons, of course, due to the selection of respondents, the results are not fully representative of the transport community in general. Firstly, the email was limited to Dutch persons, while overall (general) interest in ethical issues might differ between countries, as does interest in specific issues. For example, based on the literature (see Chapter 4), it is my impression that in the Netherlands the issue of social exclusion is less obvious on the research and policy agenda than in, for example, the UK, France, Australia and the USA. Secondly, the answers of the persons in my network do not match those that a random sample of the whole transport community in the Netherlands might have elicited. Thirdly, it is very possible that persons with an interest in the subject respond more than the average. Fourthly, the choice of the subject might result in a 'positive' bias towards the subject, because people might not want to disappoint me, or might be inclined to answer in a 'politically correct' way. Fifthly, within the professional community not everybody reads *Verkeerskunde* or *Verkeer in Beeld*. It is possible that those who read the magazine are more than averagely interested in new developments in their professional area, and might be more open minded. This last point probably had hardly any impact on the results, because only 16 respondents reacted as a result of forwarding the email directly, or due to the requests in the electronic newsletters. The exact number of 'newsletter respondents' cannot be given, because, in the case of a few persons, it is unknown to which category they belong. The maximum here is six.[2] Despite the potential bias, the questionnaire provides a useful first impression of how the transport community, at least in the Netherlands, thinks about the subject.

Within the deadline of two weeks, the questionnaire was answered by 98 persons. As explained above, of those, 16 were as a result of forwarding the email and the electronic newsletter requests. The response percentage of the 177 initially emailed persons was 46 percent (82/177). This quite high response might be a result of the fact that the 177 persons to whom I sent the questionnaire belong to my personal network.

Eighteen respondents (19%) were female and 80 (81%) male. Seven

(7%) respondents were policy makers, 28 (29%) practitioners, 51 (52%) scientists, and 12 (12%) other researchers (mainly consultants). There was no significant relationship between gender or profession and response rate.

Reactions Not Included in the Analysis

Some respondents mentioned subjects that are not related to ethics according to general academic interpretations. For example, a respondent mentioned as an ethical subject: 'People waste a lot of time on travel'. One can argue that this is their choice, and so in itself there is no ethical dimension included. Another example: 'Thanks to cars terrorists can transport explosives'. Of course this is true, but is it an ethical issue? I excluded such issues from the analysis.

In addition, some respondents included general ethical issues, not linked to transport, such as general manufacturers' responsibilities, or general issues of equity, fairness, justice, that were not further specified. These reactions were excluded from the analysis.

2.3   GENERAL REACTIONS

A majority of respondents did not just answer the questions, but firstly gave a general reaction. These general reactions provided a lot of interesting information. Most introductions included very enthusiastic reactions on the initiative, like 'very good idea', 'very relevant subject' or 'this is a huge gap'. On the other hand, some respondents gave less enthusiastic reactions. For example:

- I am a mechanical engineer and we do not at all deal with ethics.
- Ethics, do you realize what you are getting into?
- This subject would not have come into my mind.
- I never explicitly thought about ethics before.
- I do not feel connected to the subject.
- We hardly discuss ethics on the work floor.

Nevertheless, these respondents did respond to the questions. Five respondents offered to meet and discuss the subject, while 14 respondents spontaneously sent suggestions for literature that could be potentially relevant for the subject (three of them even sent hard copies of literature).

2.4 RESULTS

Most people either did not at all explicitly distinguish between questions 1 and 2, or made explicit that their answers were equal. Consequently, the answers were analysed by ignoring the difference between the questions.

Table 2.1 presents an overview of the subjects mentioned at least four times.

The table shows that environmental and sustainability related items were mentioned by a majority of respondents. Subjects in this category include general subjects like air pollution, the health impacts of air pollution, the depletion of fossil fuels, climate change, trade-offs between environmental impacts and economic benefits, and the general item 'sustainability'. Other more specific items mentioned were biodiversity and the food production impacts of biofuels.

Safety was mentioned by 32 percent of respondents. Almost exclusively their answers – if further specified – related to road safety. Three persons referred to third-party risks.

The subject 'ethics of research, policy and politicians' was mentioned by 31 percent of the respondents. In most cases the respondents referred to the ethics of research. Some respondents only mentioned that independence of research is an ethically relevant subject, others were quite normative, referring to the 'evil caused by the manipulation of researchers'.

Table 2.1   Subjects mentioned by the respondents

Subject	Frequency (%)	Subjects/remarks
Sustainability, environment, energy	56 (57)	Sustainability: 39 Environment: 35 Energy: 12
Safety	31 (32)	Generally: road safety
Ethics of research, consultancy, policy makers, politicians	30 (31)	
Distribution effects, freedom versus impacts on others	28 (29)	
Social exclusion, rights on mobility	28 (29)	
Evaluation, cost–benefit analysis	19 (19)	
Wasteful goods transport	17 (17)	
Driving behaviour, car choice	16 (16)	
Privacy	14 (14)	
Wasteful passenger transport/ethics of unlimited travel	9 (9)	
Is pricing fatalities ethical?	4 (4)	

Within this category, five respondents referred to the ethics of policy makers, and asked questions such as: 'What to do if the Minister wants a policy maker to act in a certain way, even if the policy makers know that the policy will turn out "wrong", or the information provided is misleading?' One person referred to the ethics of politicians. One academic wrote: 'in the USA, scientific research is much more dependent on external finance than in Europe'.

'Distribution and freedom versus impacts on others' related items were mentioned by 29 percent of respondents. Distribution subjects relate to the question who benefits and who 'pays'. 'Freedom versus impacts' relates to the trade-offs between individual freedom (of travel, travel behaviour) versus negative impacts on others. Respondents mentioning freedom related items often posed questions such as: 'Should unlimited freedom of travel be the norm, at the cost of external effects?' Specific questions were also posed on speed limiters: 'Is it ethical to impose speed limiters?'

Social exclusion, and remarks related on a right to a minimum level of travel (or activity participation), were also mentioned by 29 percent of respondents, although the term 'social exclusion' was hardly mentioned. People related the item often to (a minimum level of) public transport and a low level of accessibility in rural areas.

Nineteen percent of respondents mentioned subjects related to evaluation and evaluation frameworks, either in general, or with respect to infrastructure projects. In the Netherlands, Cost–Benefit Analysis (CBA) is the official method of evaluating large national transport infrastructure projects. Not surprisingly, CBA was often mentioned by the respondents, with subjects including the utilitarian approach, the value of time, how to deal with un-priced effects, etc. Value of time related items (three respondents) related to questions such as whether it is ethical to differentiate between income class and motive. One respondent wondered how to deal with norms for safety levels, or how to protect people against high concentrations of pollutants or noise levels, if this will lead to 'expensive' measures.

Seventeen percent of respondents mentioned subjects that could be labelled as 'wasteful goods transport'. They posed questions such as if it is ethical to 'unnecessarily' transport goods. In this category, the Parma ham example was the most frequently mentioned (seven times) (pigs are transported from the Netherlands to Parma, Italy, and then the Parma ham produced in Parma is transported back to the Netherlands). Respondents also in general asked if it is ethical to transport goods all over the world, contributing to external effects like the depletion of fossil fuels, climate change and air pollution.

Driving behaviour, including car type choice, was mentioned by 16 percent of respondents. People mainly referred to anti-social ways of driving vehicles (speeding; or more generally not driving in correspondence with traffic rules), but also to car type choice, SUVs being mentioned as examples four times. More specifically, the respondents wondered if it is ethical to buy a specific type of vehicle, in particular a (big) SUV, if its use negatively influences the safety of other persons, for example those who drive small cars. One person even wondered if it is ethical that a person with a high income is able to buy a safer car than a person with a low income.

Privacy items were mentioned by 14 percent of respondents. Privacy was often linked to road pricing, and the registration of person-related variables in questionnaires, but also to body scans at airports.

Items labelled as 'wasteful passenger transport' were mentioned less often than 'wasteful goods transport', but were still referred to by 9 percent of respondents. Examples include long-distance commuting, long-distance holidays and frequent flying.

Finally, 4 percent of respondents posed the question of whether it is ethically sound to price human lives. One could argue that this is a sub-category of 'evaluation frameworks', because price tags for fatalities are often used for CBA. Because the respondents themselves did not link pricing to CBA, it was considered as an independent category.

Twelve respondents made remarks, or posed questions related to, pricing in general or the official policy of the Dutch government (at the time of sending out the questionnaire – February 2010) to replace current taxes on cars (yearly tax, tax on new cars) by a kilometre-based charge, mainly referring to the fact that the implications will vary for different groups of people (e.g. with respect to income, profession, region within the country). In the event, this policy was later abandoned.

A few respondents made remarks about the limited possibilities for translating ideas about ethics over time and space. This means that what societies consider to be (un)ethical can change over time, and between countries or world regions.

A small minority of respondents explicitly distinguished between questions 1 and 2. The clearest examples of people who answered question 2 differently from question 1 are listed below:

- I would like to see a comprehensive overview of the ethical dimensions of transport.
- I would like to see a vision on transport and ethics.
- I would like to see which different definitions of ethics exist.
- Child-friendly transportation planning: are the interests of children included in decision making?

Table 2.2   Subjects that are significantly more or less often mentioned by respondent groups

Result	Significance
Women mentioned social exclusion more often than men	$p < .10$
Men mentioned ethics of research, consultancy, policy makers and politicians more often than women	$p < .01$
Researchers mentioned distribution effects, freedom versus impacts on others, more often than practitioners and policy makers	$p < .01$
Researchers mentioned social exclusion more often than practitioners and policy makers	$p < .05$

Gender and Profession

In order to find out if a relationship exists between gender or profession on the one hand, and answers on the other hand, Chi square tests were made for answer categories that allowed for these tests. In the case of gender, this was straightforward. In the case of profession, a clustering was made to allow for statistical testing by making the distinction between researchers on the one hand (scientific and non-scientific; 63), and practitioners and policy makers on the other hand (35).

Table 2.2 gives an overview of the subjects taken from Table 2.1 that were mentioned significantly with more frequency by specific respondent groups. Note that due to the low numbers, less frequently mentioned subjects are less likely to have differences between respondent groups.

Table 2.2 shows that despite the quite low number of respondents, and the large variety in answers, four relationships seem to be statistically significant, though one of them only at the $p = .90$ level. Firstly, women mentioned social exclusion more often than men ($p = .90$). This seems to be in line with common wisdom that women have more interest in 'soft' social issues than men. Secondly, all but one respondent who mentioned subjects related to the ethics of consultancy were male. It is possible that the difference between men and women is not related to gender, but to responsibilities held for employees: only two of the women who responded had senior staff positions. In this context, maybe people with staff responsibilities have experience with the dilemma of ethics of research. For example: how would you deal with a situation in which you do not have enough work for your colleagues and so need to

Table 2.3   Ideas of respondents – international dimensions of transport

---

The violation of human rights in third world countries, like Nigeria, for the extraction of oil

Solar energy could increase changes for development in third world countries

Scrapping old ships in Asia

Can western countries ask people in third world countries not to buy and use cars, when they themselves have done so without limit?

Wars to guarantee supply of oil

Table 2.4   Ideas of respondents – companies related items

The role of oil companies

Work conditions of truck drivers

Car producers: do they respond only to consumers' wishes, or are they responsible for their market behaviour?

The general responsibilities of companies, in this case related to transport

---

fire them, unless you accept that work does not allow you to be as independent as you would wish? Of all males that mentioned this subject, at least 14 (out of 29) had senior staff responsibilities. Because no question was related to staff responsibilities, it was not possible to replace the dependent variable of gender by staff responsibilities. Thirdly, distribution effects and freedom related items were mentioned more often by researchers than by policy makers and practitioners. This could relate to the idea that the subject is more of academic relevance than of (direct) policy and practice relevance; so that policy and practice with respect to transport is often related to the reduction of negative impacts (environment, safety, congestion). Fourthly, social exclusion was mentioned more frequently by researchers than by policy makers and practitioners. It is possible that this subject also receives more attention from researchers (and probably even more so from academics) than practitioners and policy makers.

It is also interesting to note that people wrote down in their responses many ideas and subjects. Examples, often combining two or three reactions, are listed in Tables 2.3–2.6.

Table 2.5   Ideas of respondents – choices and behaviour related items

---

Is travel behaviour a fundamentally different category of consumption
when compared with other goods?

Is it ethical that we can buy cars that allow us to speed?

Is it ethical to fly and compensate for CO_2 emissions?

Is the transport of living animals ethically sound?

A lot of transport related problems are the result of choices of people and
firms. Transport comes at the bottom of the list of choices
(after all other choices have been made)

For hobby reasons I have a classic car using unleaded fuel. Is this ethically
OK?

Table 2.6   Ideas of respondents – policy related items

Stop preaching that mobility is bad, but reduce externalities

European transport policy: should truck drivers from different countries
have equal positions?

The level of training for drivers' licences

One would expect that safety research would be divided amongst fatality
categories more or less equally to the fatalities themselves. But relatively
less money is spent on pedestrians and cyclists compared to cars

Is it ethical to impose speed limiters?

Is it ethical that people are more or less without limit allowed to park their
vehicles on the streets?

The revenues from tickets (speeding, parking, etc.) should be used to
improve road safety

Safety: is it fair that a rich person can buy a safer car (SUV) at the expense
of a poor person driving a small car who would fare worse in an accident?

Differences in safety norms between cars and trains

Are traffic rules fair; do people perceive them as fair?

2.5 CONCLUSIONS

The general impression is that many people, at least in my network, like the subject of 'ethics and transport'. This is not only expressed by the response rate, but also by the positive introductions of the responses, and the sometimes quite long answers (up to about 1200 words). Subjects of interest mentioned over ten times include 'sustainability/environment/ energy', safety, the ethics of consultancy and policy making, distribution effects, social exclusion, evaluation of transport policies (including Cost–Benefit Analysis), 'wasteful' goods transport, driving behaviour, car type choice, and privacy. Women are significantly more interested than men in social exclusion, and significantly less in the ethics of consultancy and policy making. This might not be the result of gender differences, but rather of differences in staff responsibilities: the subject was often mentioned by male persons with staff responsibilities, while only two of the females had such responsibilities. In addition, researchers have a significantly higher interest in distribution effects and social exclusion than practitioners and policy makers.

An important question is: should the results be the dominant factor for the selections of subjects in the chapters that follow? On the one hand, one could argue the answer is: yes, because the respondent group are members of the target group. On the other hand, what if – according to the literature – important subjects are not mentioned (or only hardly mentioned) by the respondents? Would that imply the subject is not of interest, or maybe even not of any relevance? It is possible that people simply did not think of a subject, but might still have had significant interest in it if prompted. In this context, I considered a second round, in which I would ask the respondents to what extent they would consider subjects to be relevant. In the event, I decided against this, for the reason that the results matched fairly well the ideas I had prior to the survey concerning which subjects were relevant for the target group. Based on both the results and my initial ideas, therefore, subjects that are covered by the following chapters include both the '*what* question' (social exclusion, the environment, safety) as well as the '*how* question' (ethics and doing research, CBA).

3. How suitable is CBA for the *ex ante* evaluation of transport projects and policies?

3.1 INTRODUCTION

Transport policy implies making choices, for example with regard to budget allocations for infrastructure in general, choices between categories of infrastructure (e.g. rail, roads, airport, harbours), choices between options for a specific infrastructure extension, such as a new motorway or railway line, to be built, and – given the choice between a new motorway or railway line – alternatives for that road or railway line. In addition, implementing non infrastructure related policies implies making choices, examples being pricing policies, setting (new) standards for emission levels of vehicle categories, or safety regulations for vehicles. Furthermore, even deciding not to build any infrastructure, or not to change any policy, is a choice in itself. On what basis then should decision makers make their decisions? Because of all the choices to be made, there is a huge need for *ex ante* evaluations of choice options.

Very generally speaking, several categories of indicators (outcomes of interest; evaluation criteria) can be distinguished. Often a distinction is made between three categories of indicators (often labelled as 'dimensions'): economic, environmental and equity indicators, as introduced by the World Bank in the 1990s (Serageldin and Steer, 1994). Based on this categorization Feitelson (2002) conceptualized important categories of trade-offs between those dimensions (Figure 3.1).

Trade-offs between efficiency (as part of the economic dimension) and equity are an important category of trade-offs. In the area of transport, it is generally recognized that optimal welfare will result if prices are set so that marginal costs equal marginal benefits. In the case of roads, this implies that welfare is maximized if marginal prices of road use equal marginal costs, including marginal external costs such as congestion environmental costs. Fixed costs, such as the costs of road construction, should then be ignored. But many people will consider it to be unfair if all tax payers would have to pay for roads: why not let the road users pay? A

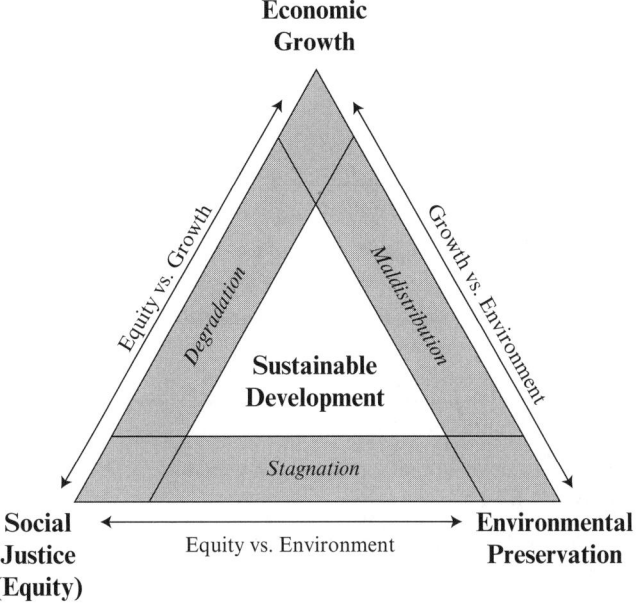

Figure 3.1   A trade-off approach to sustainable development (Feitelson, 2002)

'solution' for this dilemma could be to set fixed car taxes (new cars and/or on a yearly basis) covering infrastructure costs – most countries do have fixed costs on cars. For a further discussion on equity and efficiency in the area of transport, see Rietveld (2003).

An important question is: how are we to evaluate potential options for future transport projects and policies? Cost–Benefit Analysis (CBA) is nowadays a very popular *ex ante* evaluation method in many countries (Bristow and Nellthorp, 2000; Grant-Muller et al., 2001; Hayashi and Morisugi, 2000). In fact, it could be said that this method has prevailed from the time that the French engineer Dupuit (1844, cited by Thomopoulus et al., 2009) applied CBA to evaluate the impacts of a railway project. Whilst other techniques have been developed and used, to date they have not been used as often as CBA (Thomopoulos et al., 2009). Research into the use of *ex ante* evaluation frameworks shows that CBA is often used, at least at some stage of the evaluation (Odgaard et al., 2005; Thomopoulos et al., 2009). If costs and benefits for all individuals are included, the literature often makes this explicit, using the term Social Cost Benefit Analysis (SCBA), though a lot of literature also uses the term CBA in the case of an SCBA. In this book, I will use the term CBA when referring to SCBA.

Table 3.1   Sample questions related to CBA for transport policy options

---

Is each euro of equal 'value'? Is the euro of a rich person who is willing to pay €1 million for a trip into orbit of equal value to the euro of an orphan schoolgirl who is willing to pay for her daily trip to school by bus?

Should we try to maximize the 'benefits' of all persons, or focus on those who are worst off, for example low income categories?

How useful is utility, expressed in the willingness to pay, as the indicator of primary concern?

Do distribution and equity effects matter? And if so, how should they be included in *ex ante* evaluations?

Is it correct that we value one tree now to be of equal value to a (small) forest in 100 years?

Is it a problem that the democratic principle of 'one man one vote' does not apply in CBA?

Do only the *changes* that result from policies matter, or do absolute levels also matter?

Do only the outcomes of a CBA matter, or is the process also relevant?

Is a CBA useful if options to reduce social exclusion need to be compared with road infrastructure investments?

Many proponents support the use of CBA for the *ex ante* evaluation of transport policy options. But is it always that straightforward? Several questions can be raised (see Table 3.1).

These questions can hardly be answered without ethical considerations. Though this book does not try to come to conclusions about what is right or wrong, but rather aims to stimulate the reader to think about ethical issues (see Chapter 1), in the case of this chapter this is a bit problematic. This is because I have contributed to several CBA evaluations of transport infrastructure projects in the Netherlands, and also to discussions about the strengths and weaknesses of CBA, resulting in several publications.[1] As a result, in this chapter's introduction, I think I should be explicit about my position with respect to the use of CBA as a method to *ex ante* evaluate transport infrastructure projects. My position is that it is highly defensible to use the method, especially in the case of *ex ante* evaluating more or less comparable transport infrastructure projects, mainly for the practical reason that it may contribute to a 'better' quality of decision making. By 'better' I mean that it is likely that the politicians responsible for decision making might be 'more satisfied' with their decision (see Section 3.2). The alternative of the Multi Criteria Analysis (MCA) might also be an attractive *ex ante* evaluation method, but due to the difficulty of setting weights to evaluation criteria and the higher risk of double counting, MCA has some severe drawbacks (Eijgenraam et al., 2000; see also below). Would it then be an option to not try to *ex ante* evaluate the pros and cons of alternative choice options? I think the answer is 'no'. We need such an evaluation for reasons of quality of decision making. Not having a systematic assessment of the dominant pros and cons of a project has – at least in the Netherlands – resulted in decision making that has caused a lot of frustration among politicians, partly because of major inconsistencies in partial evaluations (e.g. economic only versus environmental only impacts) and highly debatable assumptions made in the related research (see Annema et al., 2007; De Jong and Van Wee, 2007). On the other hand, I think many challenges still remain to improve the quality and position of CBA (e.g. Van Wee, 2007b), and current practice may benefit from a – at least to some extent – structured and consistent *ex ante* evaluation. Nevertheless, some of the basic assumptions of CBA may be discussed from an ethics point of view.

This chapter not only discusses CBA itself, but also the context in which a CBA (or another *ex ante*) evaluation is made. Before the CBA itself is carried out, a process has resulted in the selection of alternatives to be compared, and after a CBA, a decision is made for which the CBA may – but does not have to – be inputted. Note that these three phases ('before CBA', 'CBA', 'after CBA') first of all do not necessarily need to be sequential, and that more complex structures of phases do exist. For example, preliminary outcomes of CBA can fuel the discussion on alternatives, or can lead to modification of alternatives (Annema et al., 2007). A decision also can be made even before the CBA is finished, or an informal decision can be made before any discussion on alternatives has started, let alone the *ex ante* evaluation of these alternatives. Because of these overlapping phases, and because all three phases include ethical aspects, this chapter is not limited to CBA only, but also briefly discusses process issues leading to alternatives and decision making.

This chapter is about CBA and transport, but many discussions also could apply to the use of CBA for *ex ante* evaluations in other areas.

The remaining part of this chapter is organized as follows. Section 3.2 will briefly discuss the concept of the quality of decision making, because CBA (as well as any other *ex ante* evaluation method) aims to contribute to this quality. Section 3.3 will explain what a CBA is, and why it is so popular in many countries. Section 3.4 will give an overview of the theoretical underpinnings of CBA, and discuss the question, what is 'optimal welfare'? Section 3.5 will discuss the question, from an ethical point of view, of criticism of current practice with respect to CBA. It should be emphasized that many more criticisms could be raised against CBA than those discussed in this chapter. This chapter is limited to ethics related critics, and discusses the subject from the point of view of ethical theories. Finally, Section 3.6 elaborates on the implications of the findings of this chapter for CBA practice.

3.2 QUALITY OF DECISION MAKING

In the case of *ex ante* evaluations, such as in the area of transport, a very important question is: how do we express the quality of decision-making processes? Or, more specifically: the quality of the input of research for decision making. (It is not within the scope of this book to discuss the quality of the whole decision-making process, and certainly not the quality of the decision itself.) For reasons of readability, I will refer to the quality of decision making (or its process). The answer depends on the perspective one takes. To give a few examples: from a technocratic utilitarian perspective, that is sometimes followed by economists, one may argue that the quality of decision making is higher if the decision is more in line with what could be labelled as 'first best', from whatever perspective (e.g. a broad welfare perspective). A utilitarianism based perspective holds that utility should be as high as possible. A rule based perspective could hold that the decision is best if it is made according to the 'right rules' (see Section 3.5 for a further discussion on these perspectives).

A practical rule of thumb could be that the quality of public decision making is higher if the decision makers make the choice they would have made: (1) if they had all (from their perspective) potentially relevant choice options available; (2) if they were fully informed; and (3) if they were able to evaluate different choice options. This could be a valid rule of thumb under conditions of a high level of democracy. Ideally, a researcher would like to empirically test what the decision makers would prefer to have available for making their choices. Such research is quite complicated, and probably depends on the place (country or regions), time, subject area (transport, education, defence, etc.), and specific case, and even differs between persons (decision makers). To explain the importance of cases: what a decision maker might need in the case of the choice between two routes for a new motorway might vary from what she needs if she were choosing between rail or road infrastructure, or between additional money to reduce social exclusion versus new infrastructure, or between policies to reduce CO_2 emissions. I *assume*, partly based on a lot of policy related research in the area of transport, that the decision maker at least wants to have insights into:

- Effects in real terms, both the pros and cons. Effects include all effects, and in cases where a policy aims to change a target indicator (e.g. CO_2 emissions, fatalities), effects on the target indicator are of major importance.
- Effects expressed in monetary terms if appropriate (in the eyes of the decision makers), and if generally acceptable methods to do so exist.
- Insights into who are the winners and losers, and how much these gain or lose (distribution effects).
- Insights into any values, in addition to those evaluated as a result of the bullets above, that might be relevant for the choice to be made.

In addition to including what the decision maker needs, one could argue, for process related reasons, that outcomes of interest for actors other than decision makers should also be included, even if the decision makers are not interested in these.

Trade-offs

Decision making implies trading-off pros and cons. In some cases, this is relatively unproblematic, especially if the pros and cons all relate to the same group of consumers, and their willingness to pay is known. But in many cases people, organizations, and decision makers cannot avoid a trade-off, although it may often be difficult to compare factors. The outcomes of interest that are often difficult to compare in the case of transport related decisions could, for example, include risks (expected accident levels), quality and quantity of the natural environment, travel time gains, CO_2 emissions and their impacts, and exploitation benefits for transport companies. Some of the concepts that follow are related to such difficult trade-offs.

3.3   CBA: AN OVERVIEW[2]

Basically, a CBA is an overview of all the pros (benefits) and cons (costs) of a project. These costs and benefits are as far as possible quantified and expressed in monetary terms. Costs and benefits occur in different years within the time horizon of the CBA. To deal with this, they are presented as so–called *net present values*, implying that – even after a correction for inflation – it is better to have one euro or dollar now than in, for example, ten years' time. The discount rate is used to express this valuation. Final results are often presented in summarizing tables. Results are expressed in one or more main indicators, such as the difference between costs and benefits, the return on investment, and the benefit-to-cost ratio. Almost every handbook on transport economics pays attention to CBA in transport (see, e.g. Blauwens et al., 2008; Button, 2010).

There are several explanations for the popularity of CBA in the *ex ante* evaluation of infrastructure projects and its role in decision making. Firstly, most of the costs and benefits are relatively well known, at least theoretically. Investment, maintenance and operation costs can be derived from data from projects constructed in the past, or from tenders. The most important benefits are travel time savings, both for travellers and freight transport. Models are generally used to estimate (changes in) the demand of passengers, or volumes of goods transport that will benefit from a new project. In addition, in the case of passengers, the travel time savings per trip can easily be estimated by comparing travel times with and without the proposed infrastructure project, using changes in network characteristics. Next, the so-called Value of Time (VOT) is used to express shorter travel times in monetary terms. VOT is higher for business travel and goods transport than for commuting, and leisure travel has the lowest value of time. VOT differs between modes, income classes and some other characteristics of travel and travellers (e.g. Gunn, 2001). Because VOTs are income dependent, there is an equity issue related to using different VOTS for different income categories (Grant-Muller et al., 2001). Another moral dilemma might occur with respect to the question of travel time, and whether or not its valuation should be based on real-world driving speeds of road vehicles. For example, should travel time changes which result from speeding be included?[3] One could argue that speeding is an offence or even a crime, and related travel time savings should not count. But what to do then, if at the time of decision making, there were to be a discussion about whether or not to increase maximum speeds on motorways? Maybe the morally right thing to do is to not count travel time gains due to speeding, unless the policy decision to increase maximum speeds could be made. In that case, a sensitivity analysis could show the impact of the choice in question. Note that in the past much more research has been carried out on the VOT for passengers than for goods transport, especially for rail freight transport, making VOT estimates for rail freight transport relatively uncertain. In contrast, there is far more debate about the indirect and environmental effects and effects on nature. Direct effects result from transport benefits, as a result of a reduction in generalized transport costs, while indirect effects are additional to direct effects (see Vickerman, 2008).

The second reason for the popularity of CBA is its often-assumed 'neutral' characteristic, as opposed to its main competitor, Multi Criteria Analysis (MCA). In an MCA, effects are presented and weighed using weights per effect. Setting the weights is not at all value free, and no generally accepted method to set weights exists (contrary to CBA where the willingness of consumers to pay sets most weights). It is therefore much easier to manipulate the final outcomes of an MCA compared to a CBA. Note, however, that CBA is also not completely value free, for example because of the use of the utilitarian concept, the assumption that price tags should be based on consumer preferences, and because several methodologies exist to obtain these price tags, the choice often having a major impact on the outcomes. In addition, the models to estimate the transport effects can be manipulated (which of course is also true for MCA). Nevertheless, there is a broad consensus on CBA as being much more value free than MCA.

Note that the travel time savings, often the most important benefits of infrastructure projects, are not fully expressed in a country's Gross Domestic Product (GDP). Travel time savings for business trips and goods transport lead to higher productivity and lower costs, and have an impact on GDP, but if a commuter can leave home later because commuting times are reduced, or because it takes less time to travel to a relative, GDP is not affected. In CBA, it is common to include all welfare relevant effects, implying that all benefits for consumers are included, even if they are not expressed in GDP.

Next to travel time savings, additional travel (induced demand) is an important category of benefits of transport infrastructure projects, the benefits of which are generally estimated using the so-called rule of half.[4] Other benefits of rail and tolled road projects might be the exploitation gains of the company operating the service or road section. In addition to travel time gains, environmental and safety impacts are also relevant in *ex ante* evaluations. Note that changes in safety levels and environment impacts might be both positive and negative, implying that safety and environmental changes can be listed both under the costs as well as under the benefits.

The Importance of the 'Right Boundaries'

For CBA (as well as for other evaluation methods) the spatial and temporal system boundaries are of crucial importance. If the spatial boundaries as used are too tight, relevant effects might occur outside the area under consideration. In the case of infrastructure changes, all non-marginal effects at the network level should be included. Using too tight barriers might also result in 'closed partiality'. Impartiality is a concept strongly related to justice. To evaluate the ethical dimensions of a decision it may be valuable to ask oneself what an impartial person would think about the decision options. Sen (2009: 123) distinguishes between open and closed impartiality. In the case of closed impartiality, the procedure of making impartial judgements invokes only the members of a given society or nation. In the case of open impartiality, the procedure of making impartial assessments can (and in some cases, must) invoke judgements, among others, from outside the focal group, to avoid parochial bias. Sen concludes that assessment of justice demands engagement with the 'eyes of mankind'.

> [F]irst, because we may variously identify with the others elsewhere and not just with our local community; second because our choices and actions may affect the lives of others far as well as near; and third because what they see from their perspectives of history and geography may help us to overcome our own parochialism. (Sen, 2009: 130)

Closed partiality can have several limitations:

- *Exclusionary neglect*: it can exclude the voice of people who do not belong to the focal group but whose lives are affected by the decision of that group.
- *Inclusionary incoherence*: inconsistencies can potentially arise in the exercise of closing the group when the decisions to be taken by any focal group can influence the size or composition of the group itself.
- *Procedural parochialism*: 'closed impartiality is devised to eliminate partiality towards the vested interests or personal objectives of individuals in the focal group, but it is not designed to address the limitations of partiality towards the shared prejudices or biases of the focal group itself' (Sen, 2009: 139).

In the case of too tight boundaries, the lives of some people would be ignored in the *ex ante* evaluation. An example could be people in third world countries whose living environment might change, due to climate change or the depletion of fossil fuels. Temporal boundaries are relevant for several reasons. One of them is that only after the opening of a new infrastructure project can the benefits be realized, whereas construction costs precede benefits. So, most costs precede benefits, and count relatively strongly due to discounting. In addition, due to the generally used discount rates, longer construction periods can significantly reduce the benefits of a project. It is important that a relatively long time horizon is included in a CBA. It is generally recognized that, in the case of new infrastructure, the time horizon should be at least two or three decades from the start. Note that benefits in the very long term hardly affect the net present value, due to the generally used discount rates. One can debate if all effects should be discounted (and at which discount rate) – this will be discussed in Chapter 5.

3.4   WHAT IS OPTIMAL WELFARE?

Pareto and Alternatives

The most often cited optimum for welfare is the Pareto optimum, which says that the optimum is reached when nobody can increase his welfare, unless someone else's welfare decreases. A big problem occurs here in that the conditions are seldom met in the case of many practices, including those concerning transport projects or plans. Consequently, it is almost impossible to do anything in the transport system without having losers. Let us assume the example of building a ring road around a town in order to reduce noise nuisance and air pollution, and to increase safety levels. In all likelihood there will be people living in the outskirts of town that will face increasing noise levels due to the new ring road. Would a Pareto optimum then imply that the new ring road should not be built? This is questionable, because due to increased car ownership and car use levels, people living along the current roads will be losers. So, there will be losers anyway. Alternatively, in the case of regulations to further decrease the emissions levels of cars, the persons that will buy new cars, in all likelihood will lose if the new cars are even one euro more expensive, due to the technical changes as a result of the new emissions regulations. Thus, I would argue, as have many others (e.g. Hausman and McPherson, 2006), that in real-world cases, the Pareto principle is of limited use. Note that the Pareto optimum has strong links with the ethical ideas of Kant (see next section).

People have long since recognized these problems, and developed alternatives for this dilemma. Probably the most frequently cited and used alternative is provided by Hicks (1939) and Kaldor (1939). They state that what matters is a 'potential Pareto improvement', which describes how some method of redistribution is possible. The winners should be able to, in one way or another, redistribute the gains to the losers. One way of doing this (but not the only one) is seen in the principle of willingness to pay (WTP). If the WTP of the winners is larger than the decrease in welfare of the losers, a potential Pareto improvement is the result.

One can easily see the link between the ideas of Hicks and Kaldor, and CBA. Their perspective is particularly useful to legitimate the use of a CBA: there can be losers whose losses are lower than the gains of winners. In that case, choosing for the particular policy option is OK, provided that potential compensation is possible. Because price tags in CBA are mainly based on consumers' WTP, Hicks and Kaldor offer a solution for the dilemma of the Pareto optimum.

This principle has been criticized because it is not clear why one would advocate a project in which the winners could hypothetically compensate the losers, as, in practice, the losers may be much worse off if actual transfers do not take place (Varian, 1992, cited in Rietveld et al., 2007). In addition actual compensation could be attractive, but may easily violate the efficiency criteria. Rietveld (2003) gives several reasons why compensation might be problematic from an efficiency point of view:

1. If implementation takes place, the cost of compensation may be high.
2. It is often difficult to determine the adequate level of compensation.
3. Compensation may have adverse incentives. Rietveld gives the example of compensation for road-pricing charges that would make the original incentive to change behaviour disappear.
4. Compensation usually has a lack of focus because it is extended towards certain groups, and does not address differences within groups.
5. Compensation may be problematic because the resources for compensation cannot easily be mobilized.
6. A lack of trust on the part of interest groups vis-à-vis the public sector may hamper agreement on compensation.
7. The practice of actual compensation may lead to a culture where everybody is calculating whether she will get a fair piece of the pie.

In addition, transport measures can lead to so-called indirect effects (effects outside the transport sector, in the wider economy), that are difficult to address, as a result of which, compensation is cumbersome (Rietveld et al., 2007). For a discussion on equity, including compensation issues, see Rietveld (2003) and Rietveld et al. (2007).

Consequentialism and Utilitarianism

Utilitarianism is a theory within the wider family of consequentialism. Consequentialism is 'the view that normative properties depend only on consequences' (*Stanford Encyclopedia of Philosoph*, n.d.). Utilitarianism, more specifically, act consequentialism,

> is the claim that an act is morally right if, and only if, that act maximizes the good, that is if, and only if, the total amount of good for all, minus the total amount of bad for all, is greater than this net amount for any incompatible act available to the agent on that occasion. (*Stanford Encyclopedia of Philosophy*, n.d.)

Utilitarianism was developed by Jeremy Bentham and John Stuart Mill. An important question is: what is the indicator to be used in the case of 'the good'? Audi (2007) considers happiness as the final indicator. In practice, happiness is quite difficult to use as an indicator if one has to come to judgements or evaluations. In economics utility is generally used as the indicator to be maximized (or at least, evaluated).

CBA is strongly related to consequentialism and utilitarianism because it assumes that all pros and cons can be expressed in terms of utility. More specifically, it aims to express these pros and cons as much as possible in monetary terms. Utilitarianism is a powerful ethical view or theory in cases of public policy, because it means that ethical questions can be answered by straightforward calculation (Hausman and McPherson, 2006). Thus Hansson (2007: 163) states that CBA is 'the only well-developed form of applied consequentialism'.

3.5   THE LINK WITH THEORIES ON ETHICS AND JUSTICE: CRITICS OF CBA

Several reasons exist to challenge CBA and its utilitarianism foundation. Briefly summarizing them, there are, at least, the following categories of criticism:

1. Utilitarianism could be useful for some evaluative purposes, but not for all. In other words, the area of application is limited.
2. Selecting the indicator to be maximized is not without dispute. This could be welfare, but other alternatives exist.
3. Distribution effects and equity are ignored.
4. Some effects are difficult to express in monetary terms.
5. There is more to be considered than utilitarianism. Other – in some cases competing – theories exist.
6. There is more to be evaluated than welfare. Other values may also be relevant.
7. Not only humans matter.
8. In utilitarianism, poor people count less than rich people.
9. The choices of people are not always based on reason.
10. CBA evaluates changes in welfare and ignores absolute levels.
11. Not only the outcomes of choice options matter, but so does the process of selecting/defining/designing options.

Before discussing these criticisms, it is important to emphasize that this section focuses on specific criticisms, and so not all the pros and cons of the use of CBA from an ethical perspective are considered. It is also important to realize that even if such a broader perspective were to be chosen, there is the risk of bias if one presents an overview of the literature: it is possible that philosophers who criticize CBA are more likely to publish about the moral dimensions of its use, when compared with those who do not.

The Limited Area of Application

Utilitarianism might be a useful theory to evaluate some choice options, but not all. For example, for questions such as how to think about euthanasia or abortion, utilitarianism is probably not the most helpful theory. For example, no reasonable person would support a policy of slaughtering persons because the benefits of the use of donor organs for people who would otherwise die are greater than the losses of the people to be killed. In the case of *ex ante* evaluations of transport policy options, it is questionable if such moral dimensions should be put into the equation. I think that if the *ex ante* evaluation considers choice options for road or rail extensions, the criticism is of limited relevance. But in the case of selecting policy options to reduce social exclusion (see Chapter 4), it might become relevant. This is especially true if budget allocations are the subject of study, which involve comparing quite 'incomparable' allocations of a Ministry of Transport, such as policies to reduce social exclusion and high speed rail extensions. In this case, using CBA can be criticized because of its utilitarian assumptions. To the best of my knowledge, in practice, CBA is not (or hardly) used for such comparisons.

Philosophers and others have often criticized utilitarianism as a theory to measure welfare, and theoretically elaborated on the concept of welfare (e.g. Daly, 2007). However, they have paid much less attention to the problem of how to measure and judge welfare (Bognar, 2009). This might explain part of the popularity of utilitarianism as a theory for measuring welfare, because it allows for calculations and consequent judgements.

The Indicator to be Maximized

CBA assumes what type of welfare should be maximized or optimized in one way or another, for example by maximizing benefits minus costs, or optimizing the benefit–cost ratio. It is questionable if all *ex ante* evaluations should focus on maximizing an indicator at all, and if so: which indicator? Utilitarianism is not the only theory that could be useful for *ex ante* evaluations, though it is quite popular in the area of transport. The most powerful ethical criticism of utilitarianism is that it is insensitive to inequality of utility (Roemer, 1996). Roemer gives the example of the utility pairs of two persons of (1, 99) and (50, 50). The pairs have equal outcomes (and therefore from a utilitarian perspective they are socially indifferent), but are very unequal. Roemer gives an overview of alternatives. One category of theories comprises the egalitarian theories. Important in this category is the question *what* should be equalized. What egalitarians have in common is the premise that citizens must be treated as equals in some respect (Sen, 1992). In the case of evaluation it is then important to have a view as to how an individual's overall advantage is to be assessed. Utilitarianism concentrates on individual happiness or pleasure as the best way of assessing how advantaged a person is, and how that compares with the advantages of others. Another approach assesses a person's advantage in terms of his or her income, wealth or resources. A third approach is the capabilities approach, which focuses on a person's capability to do things she has reason to value. The focus then is on the freedom that a person actually has. Consequently, below I will introduce the ideas of Rawls and Sen, two very influential philosophers famous for their egalitarian theories.

Rawls
Rawls' theory of justice (1971) differs from utilitarianism in two ways. Firstly Rawls argued that justice should focus not on welfare, but on the provision of certain kinds of goods he labelled 'primary' for all persons. Secondly, we should not strive for the maximum of the sum of some index. What matters is the minimum of a set of individual welfare levels, not the sum (as valued by utilitarianism). According to Rawls (and several others), utility is not interpersonally comparable. But there are certain 'primary social goods' that a person needs, and these can be compared. Rawls states that justice is reached if the people who are worst off have the highest level of primary social goods. Rawls calls this the 'difference principle'. Primary social goods according to Rawls are:

- Basic liberties, including freedom of association, liberty, and so on
- Freedom of movement and choice of occupation
- Powers and prerogatives of offices and positions of responsibility
- Income and wealth
- The social bases of self-respect.

Rawls states that the equalization of goods, with regard to the first two categories, must be complete, and is lexically prior to the distribution of the other primary social goods (Rawls, 1971, 1982, cited in Roemer, 1996). Note that primary social goods differ from economic resources and commodities. The only primary social good that is a conventional primary good is income (and wealth). Should then income be equalized?

An extreme position could indeed be the assumption that it is welfare or income that should be equalized. But equalizing welfare or income has hardly any proponents because it is assumed to be unfair. A simple example to illustrate this: consider two equal persons that only differ with respect to their preference for money versus time. Person one prefers to work 40 hours per week, person two 32 hours. Equalizing income would then be unjust. Roemer (1996) argues that what matters is that persons are free to choose their occupations and position, and the amount of time they work. I tend to agree, though of course complete freedom in these respects does not occur, for example an employer may expect a person to work for a minimum of, say, 40 hours a week, but offers a job which is officially for only 32 hours per week. In this case, the person may not be able to (instantly) change jobs if she would like to work less or more. In addition, if a job change implies a change of residential location, a lot of so-called transaction costs occur (such as the costs of finding and buying a new dwelling), as well as social displacements of the person and – if applicable – her household.

A problem may occur, as Pareto shows (see above), due to adopting the principle of equal primary social goods. What to do if an allocation exists that delivers a distribution of primary social goods giving everyone a higher index of those goods than at the equal distribution? For example, consider a society with two groups. Both have the same income levels. In this case, a policy could lead to an increase of income of both groups, but the incomes of people of one group doubles, whereas the incomes of people in the other group increases by 1 percent. This is a Pareto improvement. But is it fair? And if not, should one be against the policy? And what should we think if the income of group one doubles, and of group two increases by 90 percent: is this undesirable because differences occur?

Sen

Sen (2009) disagrees with Rawls. He argues it is not welfare or the provision of certain kind of 'primary goods' that should be equalized, but what he calls 'capabilities', which lie between goods and welfare. Sen argues that 'the fit between a person's holding of primary goods and the substantive freedoms that the person can in fact enjoy, can be very imperfect because of the actual capabilities of people' (Sen, 2009: 64). Focusing on the actual opportunities a person may have, adopting the capability approach implies a radical change in the standard evaluative approaches that are widely used in economics and social studies. This does not mean that, according to Sen, income is irrelevant. He considers poverty as a capability deprivation. Nevertheless, he argues that income and wealth are inadequate ways of judging advantage. Why is income to some extent irrelevant? This is because the conversion of income into the kinds of lives that people can lead is influenced by several factors, including:

- Personal heterogeneities
- Diversities in the physical environment
- Variations in social climate
- Differences in relational perspectives. (This relates to the idea that people belong to communities. Sen gives the example of clothes: in a richer society people might need other, more expensive clothes to appear in public without shame than is the case in a poorer society.)

Sen also does not accept welfare as the relevant indicator for equality. One of the reasons of Sen's objections against welfarism is that it matters what the basis of welfare is. To give an extreme example (Roemer, 1996): the welfare a sadist derives from whipping another differs from the welfare derived from having enough to eat. In this example, the basis of welfare is not OK. In addition, it is not the goods themselves that (only) matter, but (also) the impacts on the quality of life. Goods are input for welfare. As a result, as far as the fourth category of primary social goods of Rawls is concerned (income and wealth), income should not be equalized, but distributed in such manner as to equalize the functioning that persons can achieve. As a result, a handicapped person will generally require more income than a non-handicapped person. Sen also refers to research into the area of happiness (see, e.g. Easterlin, 1973, 1974; Veenhoven, 1987, 1991), that shows that if people get richer in already quite rich societies, they do not (or hardly) become more happy. Consequently, evaluating outcomes of potential policies only in terms of incomes could be very limited because, certainly in rich countries, income increases might not lead to an increase of happiness. This underpins Sen's criticisms of welfarism.

Considerations of justice should not only include capabilities of individual capabilities, but also of group capabilities (Sen, 2009: 245). People belong to many different groups. It could be that a person is not capable of, for example, voting in the case of an election. But if her neighbour is willing to vote on her behalf, the person faces fewer restrictions compared to what would be the case without such a neighbour. The same could apply to travelling. For a person that is not able to drive a car, it could really make a difference whether or not she has a person in her social group that is willing to drive her.

Combining the ideas on primary goods, freedom and capabilities, Sen argues that there are good reasons for moving from focusing on primary goods to actual assessment of freedom and capabilities. Sen then links these ideas to institutions, arguing that the choice for institutions should not only depend on the nature of the society in question, but also on behaviour patterns that can be expected.

Implications for CBA

In my opinion, it would be worth experimenting with the *ex ante* evaluations of transport plans and policies in line with the ideas of Rawls and Sen. Additional evaluations could relate to primary social goods, to capabilities, or to the welfare or well-being of the least advantaged.

In the case of primary social goods, it is important to decide which trips or activities will be considered as primary social goods. It is beyond the ambitions of this book to come to a 'final' proposal, but I think that a certain level of access to schools, jobs, shops, family or friends, and health care facilities could be considered as more likely to be included in a list of primary social goods, than access to luxury holiday destinations or helicopter access to business parks for captains of industry. Of course, this may entail a huge element of subjectivity, as does the concept of paternalism. I do not want to suggest that certain categories of activities and related access to them should not count. I only want to state that the option exists to label some categories of activities, and related access to them, as primary social goods. I think doing so strongly relates to the concepts of access and accessibility, and exploring ways to include these concepts in *ex ante* evaluations of transport policy options could be of interest (see also Chapter 4 on social exclusion). Below I will use the word accessibility in referring to both access (the person's perspective) and accessibility (the destination's perspective).

In the case of capabilities as proposed by Sen, it also could be an option to include levels of accessibility in the evaluation. This is because accessibility strongly relates to the capabilities of performing activities at certain locations. A major question then becomes: whose accessibility? Who to compare? Again, I do not aim to come to a 'final' conclusion, but it might be worth exploring accessibility of groups such as disabled persons (in several categories), low income groups, or people that do not have access to a car.

A third option could be to focus on the least advantaged. This could be done by evaluating their welfare in the traditional way, such as that conducted in CBA. Alternatives could relate to accessibility levels (and related indicators) of the least advantaged, as described above.

A fourth option could be to focus on quality of life related indicators, happiness often being used in research (see Section 4.5: 'The Problem or Challenge'), but rarely in the area of transport, an exception being the study of Spinney et al. (2009) which studies the quality of life of elderly

Canadians, using contextually-derived time budgets that measure daily exposure to psychological, exercise and community benefits of transport mobility.

Distribution Effects and Equity are Ignored

Equity is studied in economics, though it is not considered to be a priority subject. In textbooks on economics it hardly plays a role – if at all (Akerlof and Shiller, 2009). Both economists and social psychologists study equity. Economists generally focus on the monetary values, while sociologists (and social psychologists) would also include subjective evaluations of transactions such as gratitude or thanks. When subjective elements enter into the evaluation of transactions, this becomes a theory of fair exchange (Akerlof and Shiller, 2009). Sociologists also include norms, which describe how people think that they and others should or should not behave.

In the *ex ante* evaluation of transport projects and policies, especially in CBA, equity issues are often ignored, but can easily play a role. One can think of impacts of potential policy options on income groups or regions. Rietveld et al. (2007) emphasize that it can be important to explicitly distinguish between intended and unintended effects on equity with regard to policies to support poor regions; for example, the provision of additional infrastructure is an example of intended equity impacts. On the other hand, policies with other aims, such as pricing policies, may have unintended equity impacts (leading to increases or decreases in levels of equality).

Rietveld et al. (2007) discuss equity issues related to transport. They state that if equity were to be explicitly included at the level of people (or even in the case of comparing regions), it is important to choose the level of aggregation: this can be individual or household. And in the case of the household level, one could argue that corrections should be made for the presence of children, because households with children need more money for an equal level of welfare. Equity could be explicitly included in *ex ante* evaluations using measures – well known examples being the Gini coefficient, the Theil measure, and the coefficient of variation. As an example to show that it is possible to express levels of equality, the Gini coefficient and the related Lorenz curve will be discussed here. Because it is easier to explain the Gini coefficient after the Lorenz curve, this curve will be explained first. The Lorenz curve graphically shows the cumulative distribution of a group of people (from 0 to 100%), ordered from a low to high value of an indicator, such as income, on the x-axis, and the value of that indicator for these groups of people on the y-axis (see Figure 3.2).

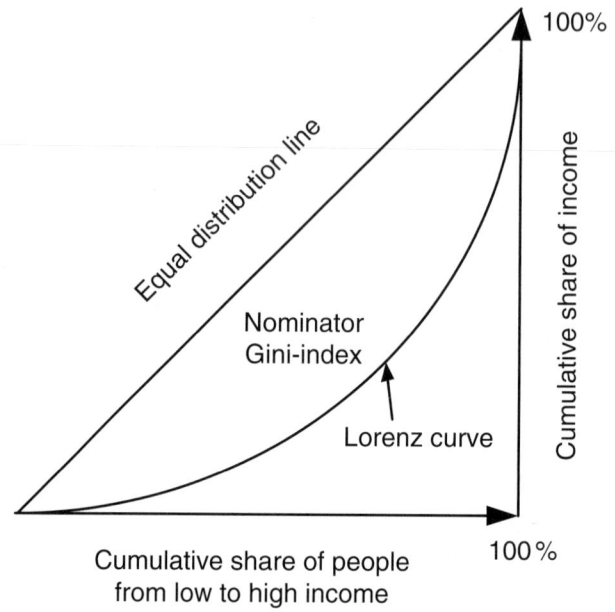

Figure 3.2   The Lorenz curve and the Gini coefficient

The Gini coefficient or index is the ratio of the area between the line that would result from a perfect equal distribution (in case of equal x- and y-axes the 45 degree line) and the Lorenz curve, divided by the triangle between this 'equal distribution' line, the x-axis and the y-axis. For the mathematical expression of the Gini coefficient, see, for example, Rietveld et al. (2007). Note that the Gini coefficient is generally used to express levels of equality in income distributions, but theoretically can easily be used for any other unit (such as primary social goods as defined by Rawls – see above – or vehicle miles travelled), as long as an interval or ratio indicator is used. Rietveld et al. further discuss the use of the Gini index (or alternatives like the Theil or Atkinson index) in a welfare function.

The use of equity considerations in the area of transport is complicated by the fact that it is not only income (or money) that plays a role, but also other outcomes of interest that matter, such as environmental pressure, travel time and accessibility levels. Of course, one could argue that such outcomes of interest could be converted into monetary terms, but this is not always straightforward (see below).

CBA is often criticized for ignoring distribution effects. Indeed, many applications of CBA do so (see e.g. Rietveld et al., 2007; Thomopoulos et al., 2009). However, it is important to realize that CBA does not exclude reporting distribution effects, for example over income classes or regions. Consequently, the criticism mainly relates to the use of CBA in practice.

It is not only the equality of distributions of a variable such as income that could matter, but also the value of each unit for distinguished (groups of) people. From a utilitarian perspective, the value of each benefit for each person counts equally. But for decision making, it may be of importance who benefits, and to what extent, together with who loses, and to what extent. Based on a literature review, Thomopoulos et al. (2009) give an overview of equity categories that could matter in *ex ante* evaluations of transport policies and plans, and considerations from an equity point of view – see Table 3.2. Note that such considerations, and the way to use them, are political choices.

In an overview of equity aspects of road pricing Levinson (2010) distinguishes many kinds of equity effects, related to population, spatial, temporal, modal, generational, gender, racial, ability, cultural and income issues. Several of these effects add to those of Thomopoulos et al. or could be seen as special cases of more general equity effect categories. Probably the two most important distinctions that are made from a distributions or equity perspective are distinctions between income classes and regions. This is especially the case if low income categories or poor regions 'lose', and high income categories or rich regions 'win'. This may be politically relevant.

Some Effects are Difficult to Monetize

CBA aims to express (preferably) all effects in monetary terms. However, some effects, such as construction costs or travel time savings, are easier to express in monetary terms than others, such as nature, aesthetics or social cohesion. As a result, decision making may be biased by the tendency to focus on easy-to-measure user impacts (Litman, 2001, cited in Weisbrod et al., 2009; Mackie and Preston, 1998). For a discussion on extending monetary values to less easy to monetize indicators, see Weisbrod et al. (2009) who conclude that the variation in monetized values is due less to imprecision in measurement, than to fundamental (including methodological) issues about whether to use damage compensation, impact avoidance costs, stated preferences, or behavioural valuation perspectives to define those values. In addition to valuation problems, the *value* of changes in distributions, for example over income classes or regions, is inherently difficult to express in monetary terms – it is mainly a political preference that matters.

A specific case of monetization relates to so-called 'irreplaceable things', such as irreversible effects on nature. Thus, some things are replaceable, others are not, and so irreplaceable things may be valued more highly than

Table 3.2   Equity types and principles found in the literature

Equity types	Features
Horizontal equity	Comparable individuals, groups or regions should be treated in a comparable way
Vertical equity	Disadvantaged individuals, groups or regions deserve protection. People should be burdened according to their ability to contribute, and this may lead to schemes where tax may be progressive
Territorial equity	Results from the notion of individual equity, when it is projected on relatively homogeneous regions, and the need to get similar funds for (public) transport
Territorial cohesion	Refers to balanced development of human activities across the EU
Level playing field	Transport sectors should be treated in similar ways according to taxation, payment for the use of infrastructure, etc.
Transport users should pay their way	This concept is usually interpreted in terms of average costs implying that the collective of all transport users exactly pays for the aggregate costs
Individuals that are negatively affected by policies need to be compensated	This principle has its starting point in the status-quo situation, and implies that winners have to compensate losers
Egalitarianism	All individuals are treated equally, making the same contribution, disregarding their financial (or other) ability
Spatial equity	Refers to the geographical location of an individual, group or region affected by a transport infrastructure project
Social equity	Refers to the impacts on personal, economic or social characteristics of an individual, group or region
Solidarity	It is anticipated that an increased focus on solidarity issues will be facilitated by setting the EU transport policy in the context of the wider EU cohesion policy

Source: Thomopoulos et al. (2009).

replaceable things (Morton, 1991). A mainstream economist supporting the welfare maximizing paradigm could argue that this distinction is not relevant: if things are irreplaceable, and are valued positively, the fact that they are irreplaceable is expressed in the willingness to pay of consumers, or the values of decision makers. But let us link the concept of irreplaceable things to democracy in the sense of majority voting. Suppose in a country there is a debate about giving up an irreplaceable nature area to build a new motorway. For decades, a majority has voted against building the motorway. But after a certain election 51 percent of members of parliament support the decision to build the motorway. Would it then matter if the nature area was an irreplaceable thing? One could argue that the choice to build the motorway is made democratically. But what if there is a fair chance that after (one of the) next election(s) a majority would regret the decision? From a longer-term perspective, one could also argue that it matters that the nature area is an irreplaceable thing.

Note that the problem of monetizing difficult to monetize outcomes of interest is a problem which is typical for CBA, but the real problem is that in the case of decision making the incomparable outcomes of interest need to be compared anyway (see Hansson, 2007). This would also be true in the case of an MCA or score card based *ex ante* evaluation, or if no *ex ante* evaluation were made at all.

Other Theories

In addition to utilitarianism, ethical literature gives several theories that could – at least theoretically – be of interest for the *ex ante* evaluation of transport policy options. Below I will briefly reflect on some of them.

Deontology

> The word deontology derives from the Greek words for duty (deon) and science (or study) of (logos). In contemporary moral philosophy, deontology is one of those kinds of normative theories regarding which choices are morally required, forbidden or permitted. In other words, deontology falls within the domain of moral theories that guide and assess our choices of what we ought to do (deontic theories). (*Stanford Encyclopedia of Philosophy*, n.d.)

Consequently, it is not the outcomes that matter, nor the virtues of persons. Deontology rejects the idea that there is an overarching principle that could be used for integration (and thus evaluation) or prioritization. Nevertheless, in case-specific circumstances priorities may occur. Darwall (2003) gives the example of a person who promised to do something of low importance, but finds herself placed in a position to give another aid without which a person may die. Keeping the promise would cost a person's life. The twentieth-century English moral philosopher W.D. Ross (cited in Morton, 1991: 12–13) developed a common-sense ethical theory referred to as 'intuitionism' based on eight obligations:

- Keep promises
- Act justly
- Express gratitude for services rendered
- Do good deeds towards others
- Avoid injuring others
- Make reparations for wrongdoing
- Avoid lying
- Improve oneself.

Ross recognized these obligations can conflict, and concluded that we need practical wisdom to determine which duty is the one we ought to fulfil. One of the most influential deontologists is the eighteenth-century philosopher Immanuel Kant, who developed the principle of the Categorical Imperative. For reasons of clarity, I do not give the original (I think, difficult to understand) formulation, but an easy one: 'Act in such a way that you always treat humanity, whether in your own person or in the person of any other, never simply as a means, but always at the same time as an end' (Kant, cited in Audi, 2007: 9). This extraction to treat persons not merely as means, but also as ends in themselves implies that everyone matters and matters equally.

The concept of duties as proposed by deontologists could be relevant for the evaluation of potential transport policy options. For example, one could argue that society has the duty to provide a certain level of access to activity destinations for most – if not all – members of society. The consequence could be that *ex ante* evaluations should include at least some kind of evaluation of accessibility levels. The options as described above could be helpful. In addition, the government might have made promises in the past, for example to a specific region or city, such as the promise to (not) build a new motorway.

Kant's idea that people should never be used as a means could be interpreted as meaning that it is immoral that some people should lose in order that others win. This interpretation links Kantianism to the Pareto optimum (see above). Strictly applying the Pareto optimum is highly problematic, as explained above. Nevertheless it could be worth including explicit information on losers, as already mentioned before in this section.

Contractarianism

The idea of contractarianism is that 'whether an action is right or wrong depends on whether it accords with or violates principles that would be the object of an agreement, contract or choice made under certain conditions by members of the moral community' (Darwall, 2003: 21). 'The moral theory of contractarianism claims that moral norms derive their normative force from the idea of contract or mutual agreement' (*Stanford Encyclopedia of Philosophy*, n.d.). As explained above, strictly applying this principle in the case of many future options for transport policies is problematic, since there are almost always people who lose, and who would therefore not sign a contract unless they are compensated. Using contractarianism as a point of departure could lead to the idea that, in *ex ante* evaluations at least, it should be made explicit who the losers are, and what they lose. The question of whether or not the results are ethically unacceptable is a matter of decision making, not of *ex ante* evaluation.

Values Matter

A utilitarian approach may be too limited, because in addition to maximizing the sum of utility over all persons, values could matter as well, with freedom probably being one of the most important values. Hausman and McPherson reflect on the issue of freedom of choice. They argue that from a libertarian point of view not only do the outcomes matter, but also the process. In other words, 'one does not respect freedom by forcing people to do what they would have chosen to do, and one does not respect rights by forcing on people risks that they would voluntarily have chosen to impose upon themselves' (Hausman and McPherson, 2006: 267). To give an example: a person could decide to accept a job offer at a location one hour from her home. It could really make a difference if this is the job she voluntarily has chosen, compared to a situation where this job is the only job available for her. In the latter case there is not an element of freedom of choice. The same applies to many other choices for activities and related destinations. The concept of freedom in *ex ante* evaluations could be included by evaluating policy options via accessibility indicators, such as the accessibility of activity destinations of several kinds of activities within certain time limits, or weighted by travel time or generalized transport costs for the trips to be made, or via person based, or logsum based accessibility indicators (see Geurs and Van Wee, 2004a, for a review of accessibility indicators).

Sen (2009: 225) has argued that at least the quality of life, of the well-being and freedoms of people, should be included in moral evaluations. Looking merely at the means of living is too limited, we should also look at the lives that people manage to have, as well as the freedoms they have to choose their ways of living.

In addition, more values exist. In this context, Nagel (1987) wrote a very influential chapter on values. He distinguishes five fundamental types of value that give rise to basic conflict:

- Specific obligations to other people or institutions
- Constraints on action deriving from general rights that everyone has
- Utility
- Perfectionist's ends or values
- Commitment to one's own projects or undertakings.

Special obligations can be manifold, varying from obligations of parents to their children, to commitment to a political party. Constraints derived from general rights that everyone possesses could follow from constitutions, but also from general normative ideas of justice. Utility is related to welfare. According to Nagel, utility is an extremely important factor in decisions, particularly in public policy. Perfectionist's ends or values refer to the intrinsic value of certain achievements or creations, apart from their value to the individuals who experience or use them. Nagel gives the example of the intrinsic value of scientific discovery or artistic creation. Commitment can imply choices to be made that one (a person, a government, an organization) would not have made without commitment (Morton, 1991). Commitments can be either agent-centred (in the sense that the reasons for action they provide apply primarily to individuals whose actions are in danger of infringing general rights), or personal. Commitments should not be confused with self-interest, because self-interest aims at the integrated fulfilment over time of all one's interests and desires, and self-interest therefore is broader than commitments.

Audi (2007) presents what he calls 'basic values'. These are, at least: hedonic values, moral values, intellectual values, aesthetic values, spiritual and religious values, social values, emotional values and athletic values. 'Basic' means that a value is not reducible to any other value or to combinations of others, nor can its realization be combined with that of others. Note that Audi's concept of values is broader than that of Nagel. Several of Nagel's values relate to what Audi calls 'moral values'.

If we, for example, take the values of Audi as a point of departure, an *ex ante* evaluation could explicitly check if other values are at stake, such as moral values, intellectual values, aesthetic values, spiritual and religious values, social values and emotional values. From the perspective of *ex ante* evaluations of transport policy options, I now briefly discuss aesthetic, religious and social values. Theoretically, some of these values could be included in a CBA, such as aesthetic values. But in practice methods to express aesthetics in monetary units are still in their infancy. I think that if aesthetic values are of minor importance for the decision maker (or other actors involved in the decision making), it doesn't really matter that science does not (yet) have adequate methods to value aesthetic values. But if these values are of major importance for decision making, or even the primary goal, as in the case of a landmark bridge, CBA would probably not be the preferred method of *ex ante* evaluation, or at least would, provide an incomplete evaluation. Religious values probably hardly play a role. On the rare occasion that they do play such a role, this probably is because new infrastructure is planned on a religious location. If the procedures for selecting policy options are sound, religious interest groups probably will express their objections against related proposals. In this case, religious values could be included in the evaluation. To some extent, social values are probably strongly related to accessibility, a subject that is discussed at several places in this section, and will be discussed also in Chapter 4. But social values can include more, such as forced relocations due to new infrastructure, cultural diversity, and safety impacts. For an overview of social effects and impacts of transport, and the way they can be assessed and are assessed, in the UK and the Netherlands, we refer to Geurs et al. (2009).

Values and duties can lead to altruistic behaviour. If so, it is complicated to include those in CBA. This is because it is difficult to distinguish the utility of the person who behaves altruistically from the utility of those who benefit from her behaviour. On the one hand, double counting could easily occur (the same utility is counted twice), on the other hand, if additional benefits for the altruistically behaving person exist, these should be included. It is beyond the scope of this book to further discuss how to include (specific forms of) altruistic behaviour.

The main conclusion of this discussion on values is, firstly, that some values could be covered by adding specific accessibility indicators to *ex ante* evaluations, and, secondly, that an explicit check could be made on the relevance of values for the *ex ante* evaluation, and related decision making, other than utility related values.

Not Only Humans Matter

CBA takes human beings as a departure point. Impacts on other species and nature are included from the humans' perspective (if at all); for example, the willingness to pay for nature conservation can be, and sometimes is, included in CBAs. But one can debate if the human perspective is all that matters. Several philosophers have argued that there is an ethical dimension that could be relevant, in addition to the human dimension – see, for example, Jamieson (2003). One could argue that even if human beings were to become extinct, it matters if the planet is in its current state, compared to a state of much pollution, complete deforestation, and huge levels of erosion.

Rich People Versus Poor People

Taking changes in utility as the main indicator for evaluations, CBA is an undemocratic evaluation method, in the sense that the principle of 'one man one vote' does not apply. Rich persons – *ceteris paribus* – per person have more influence on the outcomes of a CBA than poor people, because of their higher income and related willingness to pay. When applied to the evaluation of transport infrastructure extensions, a potential ethical problem occurs because of the use of the concept of the value of time (VOT – see Section 3.3). The VOT of higher income groups is higher than of low income groups. As a result, higher income groups score better in CBA than lower income groups (e.g. Mackie et al., 2003). As a reaction, the so-called 'equity value of time' was introduced in virtually all cost–benefit analysis used in the US and abroad. The equity value of time is based on an average income level (Morisugi and Hayashi, 2000, cited in Martens, 2006). In addition, another problem occurs with the straight-forward summing up of the willingness to pay (WTP) in the case of individuals, which is that the marginal utility of one monetary unit decreases with wealth. In common language: for a person on a minimum wage, an increase of – for example – 100 euros per month, adds more to her utility (and probably well-being) than for a person earning one million euros per year. Hausman and McPherson (2006) cite Bradford DeLong, who explains that a policy of maximizing net benefits coincides with a utilitarian policy, if and only if each individual's utility is weighted inversely proportionally to each individual's marginal utility of wealth. This implies that a rich person needs more money for an additional increase of his utility.

Choices and Reason

As explained above, price tags used in CBAs are often based on the WTP of consumers. For several reasons this method has been criticized in the literature. Firstly, people not only base their choices and behaviour on reason, but also on passion and impulse (e.g. Sen, 2009; Sunstein, 2005). People may, for example, over-eat and over-drink. Sen speaks about the 'weakness of will'. If this is the case, then it can be questionable if behaviour always is useful to express utility, welfare or well-being. Sen argues that these departures from rational choice do not, in themselves, suggest that the idea of rationality should be modified (Sen, 2009: 177). In addition, it is questionable if this subject is relevant for *ex ante* evaluations of potential future transport policies. In the 1980s the Dutch professor of psychology Michon argued that car use to some extent could be considered as behaviour subject to addiction. The same could apply to travel behaviour in general. But to the best of my knowledge, such ideas have not been widely discussed in academic literature, so that the scientific basis for this point of view is probably (still) weak. I consider such questions, therefore, as maybe a subject of academic research, but currently not a reason to criticize current CBA practice in the area of transportation. Secondly, according to Sen, who refers to Adam Smith, people do not make decisions based only on their self-interest, but also on sympathy, generosity and public spirit, and doing so is very productive for society. This is very likely to be true, while probable related behaviour is included properly in a CBA, via the willingness to pay and demand curves. Sunstein (2005) also notices that people might base preferences on altruism (see also above), but its valuation is ignored in evaluations. Thirdly, preferences can be based on false beliefs (MacLean, 2009), and if beliefs are false, price tags based on revealed preferences, as well as (in some cases) stated preferences, could be wrong. False beliefs can result from people being poorly informed, and because of people's 'weakness of will' (MacLean, 2009).

Absolute Levels are Ignored

It is important to realize that a CBA evaluates the *changes* due to policy options, not the absolute levels that result from policy options. This contradicts the use of welfare indicators that need *absolute* levels of indicators (see above); for example, if one is interested in the number of people with an income below a certain level, the *changes* in income do not matter. It is possible, of course, to report the number of people below such a level as an addition to a CBA. Then a combination of a CBA and an MCA might result. It is also possible to report and evaluate the change in the number of people above or below a certain absolute level of an indicator.

The Process Matters

In line with the ideas of Sen, I think it is not a good idea to substitute public deliberation with CBA, firstly because preferences can be influenced by arguments and deliberation. Secondly, people may value their role in decision making, regardless of the outcomes. Sen therefore argues that not only the result of choice matters, but also the process of choice. In his discussion, leading to the conclusion that not only the consequences of choice matter, but also the process, Sen refers to what he calls the 'social realizations'. Social realizations are much more inclusive than only the outcomes, and can include a broad view of the realizations, including the nature of the agencies involved, the processes used, and the relationships of people (Sen, 2009: 219). As a result, utilitarian ethics is restrictive because it does not include the wider social realizations. An example of literature explicitly discussing ethics in decision making in the area of transport is McKay (2000), who discusses incorporating the ethical principles of differing values, equal consideration, equitable participation, distributive justice and emphasis on non-quantifiable factors, into the decision process. She examines these five principles through the evaluation of the decision to build the Red Hill Creek Expressway in the region of Hamilton-Wentworth in Ontario, Canada. She concludes that the process failed to consider these fundamental principles in the decision-making process. Without these principles, the decision will inevitably become mired in the responses of competing stakeholders.

Other Critiques of CBA

The main purpose of this section is to discuss CBA from an ethical perspective. Extending the scope beyond these ethical criticisms we find that some methodological criticisms exist. The four most common methodological criticisms are, first, that the list of pros and cons may not be complete. The second is that it is difficult to estimate the quantitative changes in an outcome of interest that matters. The third is that the price tags to be used to value changes in quantitative indicators are not available, or highly debatable. Fourth, the quality of cost estimates is often poor, and these estimates are often manipulated by proponents of a project (Flyvbjerg et al., 2003a – see Chapter 7).

The general belief among proponents of CBA with respect to the first methodological issue is that if what is missing is of hardly any importance for the decision maker (and preferably also not for other actors), then this does not have to be a big problem. In other words, one should try to include all of the decision maker's relevant outcomes of interest, and maybe also what other actors consider to be important. If what is missing is of major importance, ignoring related outcomes of interest reduces the value of a CBA – at least additional information should be reported. Or maybe an MCA is the better alternative.

With respect to difficult to estimate changes in outcomes of interest, the idea is to develop methods to be able to do so, while as far as possible using methods to estimate changes from the consumers' perspective.[5] If these are not available, or cannot be developed, an alternative may be expert judgements. But there might be outcomes of interest that matter, but that are inherently difficult to tackle this way. These might in fact even be the aims of a project. For example, consider the idea of prestige: this was probably the main reason for the competition between the USA and the Soviet Union to be the first country to land a man on the moon. In such cases a CBA framework is of very limited value. What it can do is to value the pros and cons partially (for those outcomes of interest that can be quantified and valued), and then use the sum of benefits minus costs, and compare this difference to the 'difficult to estimate' outcome of interest, for example prestige or aesthetic values. Sometimes, changes in outcomes of interest are inherently difficult to estimate, due to a lack of insights in the probabilities that something might occur. An example is the probably small chance of catastrophic risks, for example extreme climate change (Posner, 2004; Sunstein, 2005). If nothing reasonable can be said about (changes) in the likely occurrence of catastrophic risks or other events, they are inherently difficult to include in a CBA. See for a discussion on these issues, Sunstein (2005) who compares the quite different positions of Posner (2004), Ackerman and Heinzerling (2003) and Burgess (2004).

If no (undisputed) price tags for unit changes are available, again the answer could be to try to develop them. For example, environmental economists have tried to develop methods to value the environment (e.g. Hanley and Barbier, 2009). The fourth criticism, the poor estimate of costs, is discussed in Section 5.3.

CBA is also criticized for making the decision, instead of supporting the decision-making process (Grant-Muller et al., 2001). One can discuss if this is a criticism of CBA or of its use – I would argue the latter is the best interpretation.

In addition, CBA is criticized because 'the area of greatest political interest – the impact of infrastructure on economic performance – is precisely the area of greatest technical weakness within the appraisal' (Grant-Muller et al., 2001: 250). Grant-Muller et al. (2001: 250) state that the wider policy impacts most often mentioned within transport appraisal are: 'improving accessibility, promoting economic regeneration and/or economic competitiveness. In the EU context, additional wider policy impacts include: reducing peripherality, promoting social cohesion, eliminating or reducing barriers such as border crossing costs, and promoting interoperability'. In other words: often a mismatch exists between the political reasons for supporting a project, and the – according to welfare theory – dominant benefits. Several of the impacts that are relevant for political reasons are difficult to estimate and express in monetary terms, or are related to distribution effects that do not make a difference at a national level (e.g. a more equal spread of prosperity). Note that the discrepancy between the political motivations of a project and the strengths of a CBA is a general criticism, and that several of the political motivations relate to ethical issues, including reducing peripherality and promoting social cohesion.

Hansson (2007) gives a list of ten problems with CBA, some of which are related to those discussed above, and some of which will be discussed in Chapter 5. Here I discuss two of the more important other criticisms. The first is that if CBA were to be applied to both privately as well as publicly funded infrastructure, an inconsistency might appear: in the case of publicly financed infrastructure all pros and cons would matter, including impacts on, for example, the environment, whereas in a case of publicly funded infrastructure, only the pros and cons for the private investor would matter. This would cause bias against publicly financed projects (Hansson, 2007). A solution to this problem could be that, even in the case of privately financed infrastructure, a CBA including all relevant effects should be made (independently), and presented to public decision makers deciding on the project. Note that in many countries private parties do not have the right to simply construct infrastructure – public decision making is needed for such a private decision. Secondly, a problem occurs because the future is often difficult to predict, but such predictions (or better: forecasts) are needed, certainly for transport infrastructure decisions if a consequentialist framework, like a CBA, is used for the *ex ante* evaluation. Note that the same problem also occurs in the case of an MCA.

A Categorization of Critics

Critics of CBA, as discussed above, can be categorized both from an ethical perspective as well as on other grounds. A first distinction is between 'real critics' and 'opportunistic' critics. The latter category includes criticizing CBA simply because one does not like the outcomes. I have discussed criticisms of CBA over the past decade or so with many people, and found that some people simply criticize CBA only because they dislike the outcomes, in combination with decision making not favouring their 'preferred project'. In those cases, I often had the feeling that if the outcomes and decision had reflected the preferences of the persons involved, they would have considered CBA to be an adequate framework for *ex ante* evaluation. In the remaining part of this section, I will ignore such critics, because they fall outside the scope of this book.

'Real critics' include: (A) content related critics; and (B) process related critics; Content related critics include: (A1) critics of CBA as an

Table 3.3   A categorization of criticisms of CBA

'Opportunistic criticisms'	• Disagreement with outcomes of CBA
'Real criticisms' content: CBA & input for CBA	• Missing outcomes of interest • Wrong quantitative assessment of values of outcomes of interest • Wrong valuation of outcomes of interest
process	• Position of CBA in decision making • Process of developing a CBA • Communication

evaluation framework itself and (A2) critics of the inputs for CBA. Process related critics include: (B1) critics of the position of CBA in decision making (either its formal – often institutionalized – position, or its not-institutionalized position); (B2) critics of the process of developing a CBA, including several forms of participation in such a process; and (B3) critics of communication issues.

With respect to the content related critics (both of CBA itself and of the inputs for CBA) there are three categories of criticisms:

- Outcomes of interest, that are relevant for at least one of the actors involved, are ignored.
- The quantitative assessment of the values of outcomes of interest is flawed.
- Outcomes of interest are valued 'wrongly'.

These criticisms can be raised both with respect to CBA in general, as well as at the level of a specific application of CBA (in the scope of this book, the *ex ante* evaluation of a transport project and policies).

Table 3.3 gives an overview of these categories of criticisms.

Most of the ethical criticisms, as discussed above, relate to not including potentially relevant outcomes of interests, and also to the valuation of those outcomes of interest that are included. For further discussions on the limitations of CBA, see, for example, Thomopoulus et al. (2009), Grant-Muller et al. (2001), Sagoff (1988) and Gardiner (2006).

MCA as an Alternative, or Combining CBA and MCA

If transport policies or projects that have important effects that are difficult to monetize need to be evaluated (e.g. nature effects, aesthetics, specific social effects, distribution effects), MCA may be an alternative.

Alternatively, a hybrid methodology combining CBA and MCA could be an option (e.g. Beuthe, 2002; Grant-Muller et al., 2001; Macharis et al., 2010). Not surprisingly, MCA has been used especially to assess project impacts if environmental or social effects are important (Lahdelma et al., 2000), or if explicit attention needs to be paid to the perspectives of distinguished stakeholders (Macharis et al., 2010; Thomopoulos et al., 2009). Note that MCA is also often criticized, mainly because of the subjectivity of weights to be used, the possibilities for manipulations, and its lack of robustness (e.g. Eijgenraam et al., 2000; Thomopoulos et al., 2009). It is beyond the scope of this book to further discuss MCA.

3.6 IMPLICATIONS OF ETHICALLY BASED CRITICISMS OF CBA

What then to do with the ethically relevant criticisms of CBA? This section will firstly discuss this question in general terms. Next, a checklist will be presented that can be used for *ex ante* evaluations of transport policy options, both in the case of a CBA, as well as for research into specific effects of such policy options, for example in the areas of accessibility, the environment and safety.

General Discussion

First of all, it is important to discuss if, in a particular choice context, a CBA is useful at all. I agree with Hausman and McPherson (2006), who conclude that a CBA might provide a reasonable basis for decision making in cases where the winners and losers are more or less equal in their ability to pay, and when it is clear who the winners and losers are, and to what extent they win and lose. In addition, it may be used where uncertainty about dominant consequences is limited, and where the kinds of reasons recommending different policies are widely understood. This implies that the usefulness of CBA is higher if the alternatives to be evaluated are more or less comparable, for example alternatives for road or rail extensions. Applying CBA for comparisons of, for example, investments in road, versus on-demand bus or taxi transport for isolated regions, can be more problematic, and at least requires a check on ethical dimensions.

A second conclusion is that most proponents of CBA do not claim that the outcomes of a CBA should be the only basis for decision making, and certainly not that the 'best' option (according to CBA results) should always be chosen. This is firstly because political preferences may occur, as a result of which some may value certain outcomes more highly than may be assumed by the price tags, for example a green party may value changes in CO_2 emissions more highly than assumed in the CBA. Secondly, specific groups in society could be linked to political parties, and winners and losers might be unequally distributed amongst those groups. As a result, democratic decision making does not have to lead to choosing the 'best' option, according to the outcomes of a CBA. Thirdly, and this is more a methodological issue, CBA can generate more than one outcome. For example, imagine the case of two choice options for a new rail line, A and B. A is more expensive and has more benefits than B. A has a bigger absolute difference in benefits minus costs, whereas B has a higher return on investment, or benefits-to-costs ratio. What then to do? Choices like these are also influenced by general concerns of government budgets and deficits, or the opportunity costs of other policies (projects and others) that could have been financed by the money not spent in the case of choosing B over A. Such comparisons at the government budget level are generally not included in CBAs of transport infrastructure projects. More generally, so called 'perspective problems' may occur in the case of CBAs, that is that CBAs are used for a particular decision, and do not include effects outside that decision (Hansson, 2007).

Thirdly, several of the insights of ethical theories can be interpreted as a plea for the inclusion of specific accessibility indicators, for example for specific groups of the population. An important question then becomes: how to evaluate the scores on such criteria? In addition, should these then be expressed in monetary terms and included in the CBA? At least two answers could be given. One is that accessibility can be expressed elegantly in monetary terms, using the so-called logsum of utility based discrete choice transport models (see, e.g. De Jong et al., 2007). Nevertheless, this means that several of the critics underlying the plea for the inclusion of these indicators are ignored – see above. The other answer could be that the scores on the accessibility indicators should be presented separately. I think the latter option is often the best one. Note that this is not a plea against using utility based accessibility indicators. The deployment of such indicators is a very elegant way to express accessibility in monetary terms, and is consistent with the valuation of other indicators as generally included in a CBA framework. I would argue that these indicators are of great use *as far as the valuation of accessibility from a utilitarian perspective is required.* However, their value is much less – if not absent – in the case of specific evaluations based on the ethical theories as described above. The relevance of accessibility, and accessibility indicators for specific groups of the population, is further discussed in Chapter 4, on social exclusion. In addition, *only* using these indicators

Table 3.4   A checklist linking ethics to ex ante *evaluations*

---

1. What is the problem or the challenge?
2. What are the choice options?
3. What are all the important pros and cons of the choice options?
4. Who are the winners and losers?
5. Can losers be compensated, and will they be compensated?
6. Do particular trade-offs exist?
7. Do irreplaceable things exist or not?
8. Should outcomes be maximized or not?
9. Does closed partiality occur?
10. Are additional values affected, and if so: which, for whom, and in which way?
11. Do (additional) considerations with respect to equity, justice or equality exist?
12. Are commitments or duties at stake?
13. Is a choice needed?

---

to express accessibility gives only limited insights into the accessibility consequences of choice options: they measure the utility of accessibility, not accessibility itself.

Fourth, a very fundamental conclusion is that it is not only the outcomes of the CBA that matter, but also many process related issues. Process matters *in itself,* regardless of its impact on the outcomes. In addition, the process could have an impact on the outcomes, for example because of the selection of policy options or their specifications.

If a CBA is to be used at all, this chapter has shown that several challenges exist for improvements from an ethical perspective. Based on these challenges, a checklist is derived that could be used to link the ideas of this chapter to *ex ante* evaluations in the transport sector. The checklist can be applied in the case where a CBA provides the evaluation framework, but also in the case of another evaluation method (such as MCA), as well as for at least some of the *ex ante* evaluation of the individual effects that are included in such an evaluation method. Table 3.4 summarizes the checklist. The first three questions and question 6 are general, and not specifically related to the inclusion of ethics in *ex ante* evaluations.

What is the Problem or the Challenge?

A first question to be answered is what the problem or challenge is. In the case of transport, problems or challenges often relate to accessibility (in its many forms – see Geurs and Van Wee, 2004a), to reducing travel times, or to the reliability of travel times, to an increase of transport choice options, or to environmental impacts, such as air quality or reduced emissions, noise or climate change, or to safety.

What Are the Choice Options?

A second important question to be answered is: what are the choice options that could be made? A problem might occur if, in an early stage, the list of choice options is too limited, as a result of which potentially interesting options are excluded. At an early stage, it might be of value to even include 'bad' options, if there are potential supporters of such an option, in order to make clear it is a 'bad' option. In this early stage of decision making, it is important to include potential actors that might have an opinion on the choice options, for at least three reasons. Firstly, these actors could come with potentially interesting choice options. Secondly, it is not only the outcome that matters, but also the process (see above). From a broad democratic point of view (see above), public deliberation is important in itself. Thirdly, not all policy decisions can be implemented in practice. Actors or institutions that are against a specific solution might follow legal procedures to avoid implementation. Involving important actors in the process might reduce future problems related to implementation.[6] I assume decision makers would like to reduce such problems.

What Are All the Important Pros and Cons of the Choice Options?

Thirdly, I assume a decision maker (as well as other actors involved) wants to know what are the important pros and cons of the choice options. I assume they want insights into effects in real terms, as well as expressed in monetary terms, if (in their eyes) appropriate and generally acceptable methods exist to identify these.

Who Are the Winners and Losers?

Next, I assume the decision maker wants to have insights into who are the winners and losers, and how much these win or lose (distribution effects). This question aims to explicitly include equity and distribution effects. Note that the question of who are the winners or losers, is more often related to the specific roles or activities of people, than to the persons themselves. Take the example of a policy that benefits car users at the expense of cyclists, for example reducing the width of a cycle lane. A person can drive her car on that road one day, but maybe the next day she is a cyclist.

Reporting winners and losers is relevant in itself. In addition, in the case of discussions about distributive issues, one may want to evaluate distribution effects. In that case, one can apply distributive weights, either based on an income dependent decrease of marginal utility, or on (potential) political preferences. The researcher can vary quantitative weights, and check the impact on the outcomes of the CBA. In addition, it is advisable to check if losers can be compensated.

Related to the distribution effects is the lack of a democratic level of a CBA. One could check what the outcomes of the evaluation of policy options could be in the case of a democracy, according to the 'one man one vote' principle. Which choice option would be chosen, if the choice was made based on this democratic principle? This check seems straightforward, but it is not. Firstly, data on individual persons (how many, who would win or lose?) are often not available. Secondly, it is overly simplistic to assume that people would only vote based on their own direct interests; for example, a person that does not benefit from certain policies herself – say, a bus service – might value living in a society that provides these options for others. Thirdly, there is the problem of who to include. Let us assume a project of regional importance. A democratic evaluation, including all inhabitants of a country, would almost certainly lead to a negative decision, because a lot of tax payers lose a small amount of money, whereas a small minority, that is, the people who live in the region under consideration or regular visitors, benefit. Consequently, including only the choice for the regional project would be cumbersome. It may be better to include *in general* the preference for regional projects: all regions could benefit from a certain amount of money to be spent on regional projects. But this is too general to be of use for specific projects. On the other hand, only asking people who live in the region under consideration, or visitors, may also be problematic, because traffic flows outside the region (and thus travel times and accessibility levels, as well as noise and air pollution) might change outside the region – and ignoring the people involved here would be problematic. The conclusion is that some check on the level of democracy could be of interest, but could be difficult to make.

Note that the implicit interpretation of the concept of democracy, as presented above, is not the only option available. There are multiple interpretations of the concept of democracy, the two most important being: (1) the traditional, more formal, interpretation in terms of elections and ballots; and (2) democracy as 'government by discussion', the latter interpretation being widely accepted in political philosophy (Sen, 2009). The latter interpretation emphasizes the importance of political participation, dialogue and public interaction. The two interpretations do not exclude each other. Open, free and fair elections are a *conditio sine qua non* for democracy. But government by discussion involves more than high quality elections. In order to reach a high level of government by discussion, requirements include free speech, access to information, and freedom to have a non-mainstream opinion. Related to this interpretation, Gutmann and Thompson (1996), cited in Resnik (2007), have developed the concept of 'deliberative democracy': 'Citizens in democratic, pluralistic societies should decide controversial matters of public policy by engaging in honest, open, fair, well-informed and reflective debates and by giving publicly defensible reasons for their views' (Resnik, 2007: 56). According to Resnik, the related role of science is to provide neutral input, assuming science as 'normative rationalism' not as 'social constructivism'.

A very difficult issue in democracy is the recognition that democracy has to be concerned both with majority rule and the rights of minorities. What to do if a majority prefers a policy option that might violate the rights of minorities? If constitutional rights are violated, then of course the answer is clear, but in several other cases there are no legal barriers to implementing the policy. What should then be done? The answer very likely will be case specific.

To conclude, because a CBA is inherently a non-democratic tool, a check of a CBA based on democratic principles could be useful.

Can Losers be Compensated and will they be Compensated?

The decision makers could be interested in knowing if losers can, and will, be compensated. Furthermore, if they are compensated, do they feel compensated in a satisfactory way?

Are there Particular Trade-offs?

In the case of some choices, specific trade-offs might occur. For example, some choice options could have about equal outcomes of interest, except for a trade-off between travel time savings and expected accidents. If so, the decision maker might be interested in the occurrence of these trade-offs, as well as in the specific details of them.

Are there Irreplaceable Things or Not?

The decision maker might be interested in knowing if there are any 'irreplaceable things' involved in (some of) the choice options.

Maximization or Not?

A next question to be answered concerns the matter of if one wants to maximize any variable. Again: if yes, then what variable? The first option is to maximize a variable that aims to include *all consequences* (which is in line with consequentionalism – see above). The maximization of welfare or utility is the most common approach. The second principle could be to maximize not all consequences, but a *selection of consequences.* Rawls' approach of primary social goods could be one, but also Sen's approach of maximizing capabilities is – at least theoretically – an alternative. I think that in practice maximizing welfare is an option with a lot of support. I am not aware of *ex ante* evaluations in the transport arena that maximize other variables, as proposed by Rawls or Sen. Nevertheless, it is good to be aware of other variables that could be chosen.

Does Closed Partiality Occur?

As explained above, to evaluate the ethical dimensions of a decision, it may be valuable to ask oneself what an impartial person would think about the decision options. In the case of closed impartiality, the procedure of making impartial judgements invokes only the members of a given society or nation. In the case of open impartiality, the procedure of making impartial assessments can (and in some cases, must) invoke judgements, among others, from outside the focal group, to avoid parochial bias.

Are Additional Values Affected, and If So: Which, for Whom and in Which Way?

It is also necessary to consider possible insights into any values, in addition to those evaluated by answering the questions above, that might be relevant for the choice to be made. An important question then is: which values matter? Based on this chapter (see what is written above about Nagel [1987], Rawls [1971], Audi [2007] and others), I assume important value categories could be:

- Freedom
- Equity/justice
- Specific obligations or commitments to other people or institutions (see also below)
- Constraints on action, deriving from general rights possessed by everyone

- Commitment to one's own projects or undertakings
- Aesthetical values
- Social values.

Note that utility and welfare are not listed, not because they are irrelevant, but because they are included already in the pros and cons.

The decision maker, in addition, might have personal values:

- Perfectionist ends or values
- Emotional values.

In the case that values are of importance, a next question is if any order could, or should, be made. Note that a context independent overarching order does not exist (see above), so this should be a case specific order.

Do (Additional) Considerations with Respect to Equity, Justice or Equality Exist?

One of the value categories is equity/justice. This category is strongly related to equality – see the egalitarian theories as discussed above. For this category of values, asking specific questions could be of value. A first question to be asked is whether one wants to equalize something at all (as assumed in egalitarian theories). If the answer is yes, the question is: which variable? Options again could be welfare, primary social goods, or capabilities.

Are Commitment or Duties at Stake?

Commitments can imply choices to be made that one (a person, a government, an organization) would not have made without a commitment (Morton, 1991). I assume that a decision maker wants to know explicitly if any commitment or duties could play a role in the decision to be made. In the case of transport, these can be political commitments, or duties such as promises to groups of people or regions. Commitments could also relate to the programme of the political party to which the decision maker belongs, or the government coalition.

Is a Choice Needed?

Above, a distinction is made between voluntary and non-voluntary (forced) choices. This is especially significant if important values are negatively affected; for example, if there are people that 'lose' in an, ethically speaking (for the decision maker), unacceptable way, the option might be not to choose. To find out if this is possible, it is important to know if a choice needs to be made at all.

The 'Best' Policy

Now that we have discussed the checklist above, an important question of course is: what is the 'best' policy? It is important to recognize the three generally accepted criteria required to answer this question: effectiveness, efficiency and equity. Effectiveness relates to the question of whether the policy leads to an improvement. For example, if a policy aims to reduce road fatalities, the first criterion is to test if the policy indeed leads to a reduction in fatalities. The second criterion, efficiency, relates to the question of at which costs the improvement is made. For example, a road safety policy can result in a reduction in fatalities, but the price to be paid could be, for example, €40 million per (expected) reduced fatality, whereas other policies costing €400 000 per reduced fatality have not been implemented (yet). So, the policy is not efficient, in terms of cost-effectiveness. The third criterion, equity, is related to the question of whether the policy is 'fair'. Maybe a cost-effective way to reduce road fatalities is to increase the age at which people can get a driving licence to 30 years. But is this fair? The checklist above mainly relates to equity issues. This, of course, is not surprising, because ethics to a large extent deals with questions of equity and fairness.

4. Social exclusion

4.1 INTRODUCTION

Questions related to social exclusion include:

- Does it matter if people are socially excluded due to voluntary versus involuntary choice?
- Is social exclusion only a problem for those excluded, or also for society?
- How to value a reduction in social exclusion? How to compare related policies? Is the willingness to pay of socially excluded persons an appropriate indicator for the value of a reduction in social exclusion?
- What is a reasonable minimum level of (possibilities for) participation in social activities? How much is it worth to avoid lower levels than this minimum?
- Does it matter if social exclusion is the result of public policies instead of 'autonomous trends'?

Answering these, and other related questions, is not at all straightforward. This chapter aims to discuss social exclusion from an ethical perspective.

Definition and Background

One of the most frequently studied ethical issues in mainstream transport literature is the subject of social exclusion. The term social exclusion 'emerged as an important policy concept in France in the 1970s in response to the growing social divides that resulted from new labour market conditions and the inadequacy of the existing social welfare provisions to meet the changing needs of more dispersed populations' (Luxton, 2002; cited in Rajé, 2003: 322). In the literature the term social inclusion can also be found, referring to the process away from social exclusion. Social inclusion can be seen as an overarching concept that can include policies (but not necessarily only policies) to reduce social exclusion. In the remaining part of this book I will use the term social exclusion, because this is the most generally used term. The term is also broader than social inclusion, and it covers the ethical problems best. I define social exclusion as *the fact that some people or population groups are excluded from a certain minimum level of participation in location based activities, whereas they wish to participate, and need to do so in order to maintain a reasonable quality of life within the society in which they live.* In the words of Rajé (2003: 322) who presents an overview of definitions and concepts related to social exclusion: 'it is a process, which is understood to be multi-dimensional, and prevents individuals or groups from participating in normal activities of their society. It is linked to inaccessibility of goods and services, which contributes to a feeling of not belonging'. An important element is, firstly, that those who are excluded would prefer to be included. In other words, there are barriers that prevent inclusion, income levels probably being the most mentioned barrier in literature (e.g. Sanchez, 2008), but not the only one (see below). A second element is that the barriers are beyond the control of the excluded persons. A third element is that there is some minimum level of participation. This minimum is very difficult to define – this in itself is an ethical issue! Below that level, people face social exclusion.

The general (normative) idea of both policy makers and scholars studying equity and fairness, is that a certain level of options to participate in activities (social activities, work, retail, medical services, education, etc.) should be available for everyone, regardless of factors such as their income or age, and also for people who do not have a car, or access to a car (or even do not have a driving licence). That a certain level of options to participate in activities is to be guaranteed is generally considered to be an ethical question. This level is threatened especially in remote rural areas. The combination of 'free market forces' and transport policies might result in a situation in which some individuals have access levels below that which is deemed to be 'fair'.

An important prior notion is that social exclusion has an absolute and a relative dimension. The absolute dimension is independent of the level of social participation of others in society (e.g. a community, a region, a country), whereas the relative dimension relates to differences between individuals, households or groups of people. The absolute level relates to sufficientarianism (see Section 4.6), whereas the relative level relates to equity considerations.

Aim of the Chapter

This chapter aims to discuss social exclusion from the perspective of the *ex ante* evaluation of transport plans and policies.

Academic Literature

For only about a decade has social exclusion frequently received interest in academic literature. The subject nevertheless is considered as very relevant, as expressed by the fact that at least two special issues of the well-respected transport journal *Transport Policy* were devoted to this subject. In 2003 the special issue 'Social Exclusion and Transport Systems' appeared (see the editorial of Hine, 2003, for a brief overview), while in 2009 there was the special issue 'International Perspectives on Transport and Social Exclusion' (see the editorial of Stanley and Lucas, 2009, for a brief overview). The growing attention paid to social exclusion literature results from the awareness that, increasingly, some population groups face social exclusion due to spatial-economic developments, leading to scale increases in shops, education and medical services (and as a result the disappearance of local shops and services), especially in remote rural areas, in combination with increasing car ownership levels and decreasing quality of bus services. People without access to cars, who live in areas without basic services and shops generally, rely on public transport for their access. But public transport often cannot survive without subsidies, and especially in many remote areas, public transport patronage has decreased significantly as a result of increased car ownership levels. Consequently, either subsidies need to be increased, or supply of bus services need to be cut. Policy makers in many countries and regions have chosen the latter option, resulting in increasing levels of social exclusion. Note that the spatial-economic developments are strongly influenced by changes in the transport system. Many complex relationships exist between (growing) car ownership and car use levels, increased supply of road infrastructure, and spatial-economic developments – see Figure 8.1.

Demarcation

Below, I will present the demarcation and resulting focus of the chapter. An important demarcation is that I include transport-related social exclusion only. People can also be excluded from activities for reasons completely outside the transport system, for example in South Africa in the era of apartheid, black people were excluded from several activities because of the colour of their skin. Such forms of exclusion are outside the scope of this book on ethics and transport. The term 'social exclusion' as used in this book refers to *transport-related* social exclusion.

Social exclusion is often linked to other concepts, such as poverty, social inclusion, well-being, happiness, psychological well-being, economic utility, inequality, equity, equality, isolation, participation, capability, community strength, community cohesion, social capital, car ownership, car availability, Forced Car Ownership, poverty, and many more. These concepts have their backgrounds in several disciplines, including sociology, psychology and economics. This book does not attempt to discuss all these concepts and their relationships to social exclusion. For literature on these concepts see, for example, Kenyon et al. (2002), Stanley and Vella-Brodrick (2009), Currie et al. (2009), Litman (2006) and Rajé (2003).

Some scholars have emphasized the importance of social exclusion from the perspective of participation in decision-making processes; for example, Hodgson and Turner (2003) discuss this subject referring to the work of Hamilton and Jenkins (2000), Turner et al. (1998), Grieco et al. (1989) and others, who show how the transport profession systematically excludes groups, such as women and low income groups, from the governance and management of the transport system. In line with the definition as presented above, this subject is not included in this chapter as a subject of transport-related social exclusion itself, though it is recognized as being a cause of how the transport system is designed and evolves in such a way that it can contribute to an increasing level of social exclusion.

The occurrence of social exclusion has an impact on methods to study travel and activity behaviour in terms of survey design and data collection processes. For example, Lyons (2003) concludes that it is likely that people who feel let down by society might not be very well represented within surveys, because they tend to be suspicious of scrutiny and officialdom. Such methodological issues are not included in this chapter, although again I recognize they do have relevance in terms of how data is collected and analysed for the methods we propose.

Lyons (2003) also elaborates on the impacts of social exclusion on society. For example, parts of cities can become no-go areas as a result of deprivation, inadequate provision of services, in turn causing the build-up of an intimidating, insecure and unwelcoming environment. Lyons concludes that this not only affects those living in such areas but also those who must now manoeuvre around such areas, or choose to travel through them using individualized motorised transport rather than walking, cycling or using public transport (these impacts are also not included in this chapter).

The chapter does not present an explicit theory for social exclusion: such a theory does not yet exist (Stanley and Vella-Brodrick, 2009). Nevertheless, Section 4.2 includes some ingredients that could be useful for such a theory.

The chapter does not extensively reflect on methodologies to measure levels of social exclusion, but only in so far as they are needed to understand the ethical issues of social exclusion. However, some reflections are included to make clear that research into social exclusion has only relatively recently received attention, and that, especially, defining quantitative indicators and measuring them using advanced methods, are relatively undeveloped (e.g. Priya and Uteng, 2009). According to Stanley and Vella-Brodrick (2009), Gordon et al. (2000) claim to be the first to measure social exclusion empirically. Indicators for social exclusion can partly be derived from accessibility literature (see also Chapter 3), because poor access to activity locations is a dominant factor contributing to social exclusion. For further reading into methodologies, a few examples of papers in this area are as follows. Wu and Hine (2003) present an approach to measuring changes in bus service accessibility; Schönfelder and Axhausen (2003) present activity spaces based methodologies to assess levels of social exclusions; and Mackett et al. (2008) present a tool to make transport policies more socially inclusive.

Structure of the Chapter

This chapter firstly presents the causes of social exclusion (Section 4.2). Next, Section 4.3 gives some examples of empirical literature on social exclusion. Section 4.4 discusses social exclusions related policies. Section 4.5 links the concept of social exclusion to ethics, using the checklist given in Chapter 3. Section 4.6 discusses egalitarian theories and sufficientarianism as candidate theories to evaluate social exclusion policies. And finally, Section 4.7 summarizes the main conclusions of this chapter.

4.2   CAUSES OF SOCIAL EXCLUSION

Transport-related social exclusion is highly linked to the concepts of access and accessibility. The term accessibility is often used for a locations perspective, as opposed to access that assumes a person's perspective. In other words, a location is accessible by persons, while a person has access to locations. Because of the strong links between access and accessibility, below I use the term accessibility for both concepts. Based on a literature review, Geurs and Van Wee (2004a) distinguish four components for the concept of accessibility:

- The land-use component reflects the land-use system, consisting of: (a) the amount, quality and spatial distribution of opportunities supplied at each destination (jobs, shops, health, social and recreational facilities, etc.); (b) the demand for these opportunities at origin locations (e.g. where inhabitants live) and; (c) the confrontation of supply and demand for opportunities which may result in competition for and among activities with restricted capacity such as job, labour force and school vacancies and hospital beds (Van Wee et al., 2001).

- The transportation component describes the transport system, expressed as the disutility experienced by an individual when covering the distance between an origin and a destination; included are the amount of time (travel, waiting, parking), costs (fixed and variable) and comfort-related variables (such as reliability, level of comfort, accident risk, etc.). This disutility partly results from the confrontation between supply of, and demand for, infrastructure capacity. The supply of infrastructure includes its location and characteristics (e.g. maximum travel speed, number of lanes, public transport timetables, travel costs). The demand for infrastructure relates to both passenger and freight travel.

- The temporal component reflects the temporal constraints, that is, the availability of opportunities at different times of the day, and the time available for individuals to participate in certain activities (e.g. work, recreation). Note that this temporal component enjoys a rapid increase in popularity among academics in transportation and geography (e.g. Schwanen and Kwan, 2008).

- The individual component reflects the needs (depending on age, income, educational level, household situation, etc.), abilities (depending on people's physical condition, availability of travel modes, etc.) and opportunities (depending on people's income, travel budget, educational level, etc.) of individuals. These characteristics influence a person's level of access to transport modes (e.g. being able to drive and borrow/use a car) and spatially distributed opportunities (e.g. having the skills or education to qualify for jobs near their residential area), and may strongly influence the total aggregate accessibility level.

For the purpose of using the concept of accessibility, the order of the components could be changed into: (1) *what* do people need (individual component); (2) *where* are the locations of activity needs (land-use component); (3) *how* to get there (transport component); and finally (4) *when* to go there (temporal component).

Because of the strong links between accessibility and social exclusion these components can be used to derive causes for social exclusion. Below, we reflect on those causes and their mutual interactions, starting with the transport system:

- *The transport system.* Important characteristics of the transport system from a social exclusion perspective relate to infrastructure (availability and locations of roads, railway lines, bus lanes, railway stations, bus stations, airports, etc.), timetables (in the case of public transport) and prices (e.g. costs of vehicles, parking, fuel and tariffs of public transport and airplanes) and other barriers, such as access to train platforms and high entrances of buses (the latter two being important for specific categories of disabled persons), safety and security (e.g. Stanley and Vella-Brodrick, 2009).
- *The land-use system.* Briefly summarized, the land-use system can be defined as the locations of activities and objects over space. The land-use system is partly the result of spatial planning. In the case of planning, the (planned) locations of shops and services may influence their accessibility and related levels of social exclusion. Indirectly, due to planning of new residential areas, governments may prevent the disappearance of shops and services because the number of customers will fall below the thresholds needed. As a result, land-use planning may have an impact on social exclusion levels.
- *The individual component.* Changing needs and wants of people can have an impact on their level of social exclusion. The same applies to changes in their constraints and capabilities. For example, a person may not be able to drive a car (safely) anymore, due to advanced age, illness or because she becomes disabled. Changes for the better can also occur. For example, due to an increase in income a person may be able to purchase a car, reducing her constraints.
- *The time component.* The level of social exclusion can change due to changes in the temporal match between the wants and needs of people, and the options for access provided by the land use and transport system. For example, the opening hours of local shops can be extended, allowing a person to do their shopping after work.

Note that the components interact: all four dimensions interact in all directions, and potential social exclusion as a result of one dimension can be compensated for by another dimension. For example, the disappearance of the last shops in a village can be compensated for by better public transport options to travel to shopping areas in a nearby town. Regardless of the impacts on social exclusion (or more generally: access to activity locations), at least the first three dimensions interact. The interaction between land use and transport has long been recognized and studied (e.g. Wegener and Fürst, 1999), as well as modelled (see e.g. the special issue on this subject in the journal *EJTIR* (*European Journal of Transport and Infrastructure Research*) – see Geurs and Ritsema van Eck, 2004, for the editorial). This interaction has even been explicitly mentioned in literature on social exclusion (Lucas, 2006). Another important interaction relates to increased car ownership levels (partly as a result of income increases), allowing people to travel further for shopping and services. But this has a downside. Lucas (2004) argues that increased car dependency has stimulated car-oriented patterns of development. These have reduced the viability of other transport modes, significantly contributed to poorer local environments and increased the exclusion of already disadvantaged segments of the population. She also concludes that in many parts of the UK it is now virtually impossible to carry out basic daily activities without a car (Lucas, 2006).

The four components and mutual interactions are not the only causes for social exclusions. In addition (experienced) security problems could be a reason for people not to participate in activities. It can relate to both the transport and the land-use component. Probably the most often found example is the insecurity felt by lone women.

> Many women would not travel at night in isolated areas such as unlit parks or even in those well populated areas such as the centres of many cities for fear of assault or abuse, and for fear of the subsequent cultural response that the victim was 'asking for it' simply by being in the 'wrong place' at the 'wrong time' (DETR, 1997; Hamilton et al., 1991). (Hodgson and Turner, 2003: 266)

In addition, the level of access of information about travel options and activities and their locations is also important, and has been mentioned in the literature as a potential factor contributing to social exclusion, as well as to increasing the level of social inclusion (e.g. Stanley and Vella-Brodrick, 2009).

4.3   EMPIRICAL EVIDENCE

Due to the fact that only recently has social exclusion received much attention in academic literature, the number of empirical studies into the subject is limited. Up to 2001 hardly any research had focused on the link between transport and social exclusion (Lucas et al., 2009). It is not the aim of this chapter to give a full overview of the studies into the area of social exclusion and transport, nor to review them, because this is not needed for reflections into the ethical issues of social exclusion. Nevertheless, below are some examples of the literature on social exclusion that are given as an illustration.

Maybe the most comprehensive research in the area of social exclusion is the Australian study described in Currie et al. (2009). The project is investigating associations between transport disadvantage, social exclusion, and well-being in Metropolitan, Regional and Rural Victoria, Australia. Preliminary findings as reported in Currie et al. (2009) show that the number of households that have Forced Car Ownership (FCO) is higher than the number of households without a car. FCO households were found to be highly car dependent (80% of trips were made by car). They also found that for households without a car walking dominates travel (58% of trips), emphasizing the importance of accessibility by foot. They also found that 8.2 percent of Melbourne residents have 'very high' needs for public transport but 'zero', 'low' or 'very low' public transport supply.

Loader and Stanley (2009) not only found that bus service improvements in Melbourne, Australia, were likely to reduce risks of social exclusion for significant numbers of people, but also referred to research of the Department of Infrastructure (DOI, 2003) that came to the same conclusion. In addition, the DOI found that 69 percent of Melbourne's bus users do not have a driving licence, 43 percent have very low household incomes (below $A500 per week in 2003) and 54 percent are students.

Lucas et al. (2001) conclude that between 1991 and 1999 the number of UK households living more than a 27-minute walk from a shopping centre doubled, from around 40 percent to 90 percent of all households. For a doctors' surgery the number of households living within that 27-minute walk dropped from 72 percent to 40 percent.

Cartmel and Furlong (2000, cited in Stanley and Vella-Brodrick, 2009) found rural youth to be more likely to experience social exclusion than urban youth, due to an inability to access basic activities such as health services, education and employment.

Social exclusion has often been linked to the concept of accessibility, and some researchers have explicitly studied the (empirical) link between social exclusion and levels of accessibility. For example, Scott and Horner (2008) calculated accessibility indices to investigate whether cities are designed in such a way that the locations of opportunities vary between socio-economic groups. They found that accessibility levels of those groups that are generally considered to be at risk of social exclusion, are not lower than average, people living in rural areas being the exception.

One of the few papers I found on the *valuation* of transport initiatives aiming to reduce social exclusion is the paper of Lucas et al. (2009), that assessed the value of four initiatives in deprived neighbourhoods in the UK. Their research focuses on local practitioners and end-users (survey and interviews). They found that for users the value of new bus services exceeded the value of simply getting from A to B, with additional benefits being related to safety, contacts and social amenities. The yearly benefits of the four initiatives ranged from £21,000 to £661,000. They referred to increasing car ownership levels amongst low income groups: between 1995/97 and 2005 car ownership among the lowest income groups increased from 34 percent to 47 percent. They interpreted this trend as an indication of the basic social and economic need to own and use a car in a highly mobile and affluent society such as the UK. The results suggest that an increasing proportion of people living on low incomes in the UK are finding it increasingly necessary to own and drive cars to maintain a basic lifestyle. Without a car they would be excluded from fully participating in everyday activities that the majority take for granted.

As described above, barriers to the use of transport facilities can have an important impact on social exclusion. Hine and Mitchell (2001) carried out research among the transport disadvantaged in the UK. They found barriers to be related to:

- The inaccessible design of buses, trains and stations
- The locations of bus stops and stations
- The unpredictable long waits (especially at night) for buses and trains
- Customer care and travel information
- 'Fare' experiences of travel (the costs of fares).

To summarize, the examples of studies above show, firstly, that social exclusion does exist. Secondly, social exclusion results from a combination of the components of accessibility as described above, mainly the transport and land-use system; these components are most often studied. Thirdly, Forced Car Ownership may result from (changes in) the land-use and transport system, to avoid or reduce levels of social exclusion. Fourthly, as far as the studies show trends, the general trend is an increase in social exclusion.

4.4   THE ROLE OF POLICY

Policies to Reduce Social Exclusion: A Recent Trend

Social exclusion related policies have been developed relatively recently, the UK probably being the leading country in this area – and even for the UK, Stanley and Stanley (2007) conclude that social goals in transport are insufficiently understood and poorly defined. Only since the late 1990s in the UK has policy awareness been growing on the links between transport and social exclusion (Lucas et al., 2009).

A 'Healthy' Social Exclusion Policy

Before digging deeper into the role of policies, it is important to stress that policies serve more goals than social exclusion only, and can serve goals related to accessibility in general, congestion, economic growth, regional economic development, safety and the environment. In addition, if a policy is developed to have impacts on social exclusion, and has positive results, this does not mean that, per se, governments will be advised to implement it. An important question is: what could be the alternative policies that would reach the same goals? In order to select the 'best' policy, competitive policies need to be compared with respect to the level of reaching the goals, together with other relevant impacts/pros and cons, costs, cost-effectiveness, support of important actors, implementation period, and legal and institutional barriers, etc. – see also Chapter 3. As discussed in Chapter 3, the three generally recognized criteria to select policies are effectiveness, efficiency and equity. For policy choices, it is not sufficient to only study the effects on levels of social exclusion of a candidate social exclusion related policy. This of course is important, but it is also important to know what the competitor policies could be, and how these policies perform on several criteria, including efficiency and equity related criteria. If at least the efficiency criterion is included in the selection, I call such a selection based on an economic foundation. My general impression of literature on social exclusion related policies is that the economic foundation of these policies is generally lacking. Few studies reflect on the quantitative benefits, or on questions of economic efficiency, Lucas et al. (2009) being an important exception. As a result, I think that major research challenges remain before, at least, an economically founded policy for social exclusion can be developed, let alone a policy based on all the criteria of relevance.

The Transferability of Results

Another warning with important implications for policy is related to the transferability of research results. Because of the lack of comprehensive theory on social exclusion, as well as the limited empirical basis and methodological weaknesses of the research carried out so far, I think we have to be extremely careful with respect to transferring findings to other areas or periods of time. I think transferability is therefore very limited. This can be seen as a plea for more empirical research using state of the art methods in the area of social exclusion, as well as for theory development.

An Overview of Policies to Reduce Social Exclusion

This section now continues with an overview of policies to reduce social exclusion. These policies may include (partly based on Stanley and Vella-Brodrick [2009], and the components of accessibility as presented in Geurs and Van Wee [2004a], as discussed above):

1.   Regulations and other policies governing provision of bus services
2.   Subsidizing public transport
3.   Other (non price related) initiatives to make public transport more accessible
4.   Land-use policies having an impact on locations of activities
5.   Policies to promote cycling
6.   Car related policies
7.   Providing or stimulating mobile services
8.   Policies reducing time constraints
9.   Policies to change the needs, capabilities and constraints of people
10. Information and communications technology (ICT) related policies.

This section below reflects on specific social exclusion related policies. Some of the policies were found in the social exclusion (relevant) literature.

Bus related policies (1, 2, 3)

Demand based bus systems could be useful in providing a certain level of public transport in rural areas, especially if demand is dispersed over time and space (Battellino, 2009). Such systems can be cheaper, and for environmental reasons they can be a better solution than running almost empty large buses. For a discussion of specific models for transport for the disadvantaged in New South Wales, see Battellino (2009).

Subsidizing bus transport reduces travel resistance for its users. A distinction can be made between object and subject related subsidies. Object subsidies (in this case general subsidies on bus fares) subsidize the object for all users, in this case all bus users, not only for those who might otherwise face social exclusion. In general, object subsidies are inefficient if only a small percentage of users are the target group it is hoped to subsidize. Subject subsidies (person or household related) can be more specifically related to target groups; for example, only those groups who might face social exclusion (e.g. low income groups) are subsidized if they use the bus. Other (non price related) bus policies include policies such as making public transport safer, and removing physical barriers such as access to railway stations and platforms, or barriers for categories of the disabled to enter buses.

Local land-use planning (4)

Lucas (2006) concludes that many planning decisions in the UK are taken out of the hands of local authorities by the private sector, and other more powerful public sector agencies with an influence over location decisions, such as the health and education sectors. These do not include transport and accessibility as essential criteria in their location assessments. She remarks that there are only a few mechanisms for directly addressing a lack of essential services within local areas through the land-use planning system.

Clustering the disadvantaged (4)

A land-use policy directly aimed at reducing social exclusion is proposed by Hine (2003), who argues that the nature of transport provision can be affected by the spatial distribution of disadvantaged travellers. He argues that these people can be distributed in a 'cluster' that may be more easily served by conventional public transport.

Cycling (5)

Cycling could significantly increase the area to be covered within a given time span compared to walking, and in many cases even compared to travelling by bus. More specifically, by cycling, persons or households could: (1) considerably decrease travel times for local trips; (2) increase the number of activities that can be reached in a certain period of time; (3) make inter-local destinations accessible; and (4) increase flexibility of travel (and related activity participation) compared to travelling by public transport, because cyclists do not face the restrictions of timetables.[1] Of course persuading people to cycle is not always easy, and not only infrastructure needs to be provided, but also the culture and attitudes towards cycling may have to change.

It is important to realize that people without cars often rely on slow modes. For example, the Australian research of Currie et al. (2009) found that households without a car rely on walking for a majority of trips (see above). As explained, cycling instead of walking could significantly increase the range in the case of slow mode travelling. However, implementing cycling policies is difficult because many countries do not have a cycling culture. In most western countries cycling has only a very low share in terms of trips taken and certainly kilometres travelled, Denmark and the Netherlands being the most obvious counter examples (for an overview of cycling literature see Heinen et al., 2009).

Car related policies (6)
These policies can, in at least two ways, have an impact on social exclusion. Firstly, the car can reduce social exclusion. Policies could relate to improving car infrastructure in general, or for specific target groups. An example of target groups related infrastructure policies is the provision of parking places for the disabled. Secondly, policies that make the car less attractive can increase accessibility levels and travel resistance for non-car users; for examples, reducing access for cars or pricing car use could reduce congestion levels, and as a result increase the speed of buses. Or car related policies could make cycling safer and faster, while in car-free zones walking is stimulated.

Congestion charging (6)
A specific category of car related policies is road pricing, congestion charging being a subcategory. Some authors have addressed the issue of congestion pricing in the context of social exclusion (e.g. Bureau and Glachant, 2008; Jones, 2001; Levine and Garb, 2002; Rajé, 2003). Rajé states that it is important to note that road user charging per se neither causes, reinforces or alleviates social exclusion. Its impacts depend on the design of the road user charging scheme. Furthermore, it even depends on how levels of social exclusion are measured. The issue is that the charges increase the monetary costs of travel, but reduce travel times, and in some cases might even reduce barriers for travel; for example, if due to area pricing roads near schools become less congested, maybe more children can to travel to school independently. Congestion pricing might also generate revenues that are used within the transport system; for example, a part of the revenue generated by the London congestion charging system is used for public transport. The positive impacts of revenue use for bus services can result in an overall reduction of social exclusion (Rajé, 2003). For Stockholm, Eliasson and Mattson (2006) also found using revenues for improving public transport would benefit women and low income groups the most. In the case of congestion charging, exemptions are possible, for example based on social grounds.

Providing or stimulating mobile services (7)
Especially in rural areas, where shops and services such as libraries or health care services have disappeared, mobile services could provide an alternative. If such services move around in a region, even within one day, they could be a more cost-effective policy option compared to stationary service provision.

Policies reducing time constraints (8)
The temporal dimension (as presented above) could also be influenced by policies. For example, policies could have an impact on the opening hours of shops and services. In addition, governments may try to stimulate employers to be more flexible with respect to working hours.

Policies to change the needs, capabilities and constraints of people (9)
These include target group related policies. For example, barriers for visually handicapped persons could be reduced, and infrastructure elements could provide route guidance.

ICT (10)
Increasingly, ICT provides alternatives for physical travel and locations based activities. Kenyon et al. (2002) suggest that ICT, especially internet based ICT, can increase accessibility as an alternative to physical mobility, and so reduce social exclusion. They use the concept of 'virtual mobility', which they describe as 'a shorthand term for the process of accessing activities that traditionally require physical mobility, but which can now be undertaken without recourse to physical travel by the individual undertaking the activity' (Kenyon et al., 2002: 213).

ICT is not only relevant as a substitute for physical mobility, it can also contribute to a decrease of social exclusion levels, due to increased possibilities to find jobs or (locations of) activities of preference, both in a formal way (searching for options) as well as in an informal way, via web-based contacts and networks ('communities') (Kenyon et al., 2002).

Process related policies
The development of the *system* related policies as described above could benefit from *process* related policies, including the formation of partnerships between transport providers, local authorities, and local service providers in areas, such as education and health (Stanley and Vella-Brodrick, 2009). Such process related policies could then result in system changes. In addition, the benefits of process issues, as discussed in Chapter 3, also apply to social exclusion policies.

Relationships between Policy Instruments and Determinants for Social Exclusion

The options for transport policies to reduce social exclusion, as presented above, can be categorized based on the policy instrument and determinants for social exclusion, as presented in Section 4.2 – see Table 4.1.

Table 4.1   Dominant relationships between determinants for social
*   exclusion and policy instruments*

	Reduce travel resistance	Supply and locations of activities	Reducing time constraints	People's needs, capabilities, constraints
Public transport policies	*		*	*
Cycling policies	*		*	*
Car related policies	*		*	*
Land-use policies	*	*	*	*
Policies with respect to mobile services	*	*	*	*
Policies related to reduce time constraints	*		*	*
Policies to cope with people's capabilities				*
ICT related policies		*	*	*

Table 4.1 shows that many relationships exist between the policies and the determinants for social exclusion.

Interactions between Policies

It is important to realize that interactions between policies can occur. A first category of interactions includes synergy effects, that is, the effects of the combination of policies could result in additional positive benefits. For example, cycling policies could particularly be attractive if (potential) activity destinations are within cycling distance. A second example is that specific ICT policies to reduce social exclusion could be linked to more general policies in the area of mobile services. A third example is the integration of transport planning and planning for service provision; for example, planning of locations for schools could be synchronized with the planning of bus services. The second category of interactions is that policies could compensate for (a lack of) other policies; for example, mobile services could be provided to compensate for the lack of stationary services.

The link between policies is also discussed in the literature. For example

Lucas (2006) stresses the importance of synchronizing policies in the areas of land use, transport, education, retail, housing and health. Currently, policies in these areas are developed more or less independently; for example, scale increases in medical services lead to larger hospitals at fewer locations. This may be cost-efficient from a health care perspective, but it comes at a cost of poorer access for some populations groups. I do not argue that therefore these scale increases should be stopped (or even reversed), but repeat (see also Chapter 3) that it is important to assess all the pros and cons of policy options, in order to be able to at least recognize the most dominant trade-offs, or if not, to be able to assess what the 'best' policy option is. Another example of synergy effects is given by Hine (2003) who concludes that information technologies allow for the use and development of demand responsive transport. As a result, journeys can be matched to the individuals. In addition, these technologies can make demand responsive transport cheaper.

4.5   DISCUSSION AND RELEVANCE FOR ETHICS AND EVALUATION

This section applies the checklist in Chapter 3 to social exclusion issues.

The Problem or Challenge

A very fundamental question to answer is: what anyway is the problem or challenge? To answer this question, at least the following questions need to be answered:

- How to express social exclusion?
- What is the policy goal; what level of social exclusion is unacceptable?

The first question relates to indicators for social exclusion, which are discussed here before going on to examine the question of policy.

Which indicator to use for social exclusion?
Several categories of indicators can be used to measure social exclusion. I distinguish between three categories.

Mobility based indicators   Indicators could relate to car ownership, car availability, car use, mobility expressed in kilometres travelled per mode per person or household, and trips per day. Such indicators can be expressed per person and per household. The outcomes can really differ, an example being car ownership levels. Consider a two person rural household owning one car. If one of them works and uses the car to commute, the other has no car available. Another example: consider a person without a driving licence (and so without a car). It could really make a difference whether she lives on her own, or together with a partner with a car. In the latter case the partner can, for example, shop for her, or drive her to destinations of her choice.

In the case of using mobility related indicators, it is not the average value that counts, but the distribution of population over indicator scores. In particular, those who are worse off (in absolute or relative terms – see above) are of interest from the perspective of a social exclusion policy.

Activity participation based indicators These indicators express activity participation, not mobility. Indicators could be the numbers of out of house activities per person per day (possibly by category of activities such as shopping, social contacts, recreation, sports, work). One could argue that what also matters is the substitution of travel by ICT. Thus thanks to ICT people may participate in activities that *potentially* could be location based (see above). In that case, activities such as e-shopping or e-learning could be included.

Accessibility indicators Contrary to activity participation based indicators, in the case of accessibility indicators, it is not actual participation in activities that is included, but rather the possibilities for these activities – see Section 4.2 for an overview of categories of accessibility indicators. For social exclusion, it could be interesting to add to the indicators as presented in Section 4.2, indicators related to *minimum* distance, travel time or generalized transport costs from residential locations to the activity locations. For example, the distance to the nearest supermarket, grocery, primary school or health care centre could be relevant. This category of indicators can also include not only the nearest choice options, but also a minimum number of choice options, an example being the distance at which at least three primary schools can be reached.

I think that to measure social exclusion, mobility related indicators can be helpful, but, at least theoretically, they are less attractive. The main exception probably could be car ownership or car availability indicators, because these, in a simple way, tell us a lot about possibilities to participate in activities. Person kilometres travelled could even be a misleading indicator. One could argue that the more a person travels, the more destinations are within reach, or the more likely it is she participates in activities.

However, it could be that a person *needs* to travel over long distances to avoid even higher levels of social exclusion. Take the example of Section 3.5 of the job offer that needs a one hour drive from a woman's home. If this is the only job she could get, it is probably a form of forced long distance commuting.

In my opinion activity participation based indicators are more useful in the context of social exclusion than mobility indicators, because they more directly link to what matters: activity participation. A difficult choice is: which are better in the context of social exclusion: real activities or options to participate in activities (accessibility indicators)? Both have their pros and cons. Participation in activities measures directly what people do. If a person theoretically has many activities within access, but does not participate in them, she could face social exclusion. Maybe the researcher overlooked a specific barrier for activity participation, or could think social exclusion did not occur because the person might voluntarily have chosen not to participate in activities. On the other hand, one could argue that the major issue is to ascertain that a person has a certain level of activities within reasonable access. One could see it as a form of paternalism to judge the level of use.

For evaluation purposes of options for future policies, accessibility indicators probably are most useful, for several reasons. Firstly, they express options for participation in activities, which as indicators have advantages over real activity participation as discussed above. Secondly, options measure an element of freedom of choice (again, as discussed above). Thirdly, real activity levels for future years are not available. This problem can to some extent be 'solved' by using a model that has activity participation related output indicators. But it is at least easier to calculate accessibility indicators. Data and models to calculate some categories of accessibility indicators are generally available. For example, the number of activity locations that can be reached within a certain time using a specific transport mode can be calculated using network and related Level-of-Service (LOS) data and activity locations data. It is also relatively easy to include distance decay, expressing the lower level of attractiveness of a more remote destination (see Geurs and Ritsema Van Eck, 2001). Also indicators, as proposed above, expressing the minimum distance (or time or Generalized Transport Costs [GTC]) that needs to be travelled to reach, for example, a grocery or health care centre, can relatively easily be calculated.

The minimum level of participation in activities
This chapter now moves to the second question to be answered to define the problem or challenge: what is the policy goal; what level of social exclusion is unacceptable? Following the definition of social exclusion

as presented above, a major ethically relevant discussion is what is the minimum level of participation in society (including participation in several activities) (e.g. Department for Transport, 2002) below which a problem exists that legitimates or necessitates policy. This, at least to some extent, is a political issue, and so a political choice. The choice may vary over place and time, and between persons with different political preferences. This section below discusses a few subjects that could be relevant to find an answer to the questions as raised.

Voluntary versus non-voluntary choice
An important question in the discussion of social exclusion concerns whether the exclusion is the result of voluntarily made choices or not (e.g. Loader and Stanley, 2009). Suppose a person has lived in a rural town since she was born, and suppose over the past two decades the schools, shops and services have all disappeared. Next, imagine another person who moved voluntarily to that same town recently. Both people could face the same levels of accessibility to shops, schools and services, and could be equally socially excluded. But unlike the first person, the second person faces social exclusion voluntarily. She might prefer living in the country-side, accepting the low level of accessibility. Would that make a difference? To make the discussion even more complex: take the case of two persons who have lived in the town since they were born. Person A has a high income and could afford to move to a bigger town or city, but chooses not to do so, while person B does not have the financial resources to do so. Does this mean that the same level of exclusion is to be valued equally negatively? Here, freedom of choice (see Chapter 3) is at stake. A further complication: suppose there are two persons, A1 and A2, both having the financial resources to move. But A1 has a mother in poor health who relies on person A1 to help, so preventing her from moving, whereas A2 does not have such family related constraints. Would that make a difference? I now turn back to the first comparison above. Let us take the person that moved to the town voluntarily. One could even debate whether she faces social exclusion at all. Indeed, accessibility to, for example, shops and services, is poor, but the choice is made voluntarily. In the introduction to this chapter I defined social exclusion as *the fact that some people or popu-lation groups are excluded from a certain minimum level of participation in location based activities, whereas they wish to participate* . . . The question is: how strong should this wish be? If it were very strong, she probably would not have moved to the rural town. Maybe she would have preferred to have a supermarket at close distance, but her wish is not strong at all, because she works in a city and can do her shopping after work. One could even debate if she then is socially excluded at all. The question then is: how

important should be the wish for participation in the definition in order to label the poor level of access as social exclusion?

Note that the importance of facing a situation of voluntary versus non-voluntary does not only apply to social exclusion, but – amongst other things – also to risk: voluntary risks are more acceptable than non-voluntary risks (e.g. Espinoza, 2009; Sunstein, 2005).

Is policy the cause?

Another subject of discussion is the question of whether it matters if social exclusion is the result of policy or not. Before starting the discussion, it is important to stress that it is not a 0–1 variable: policy almost by defini-tion is relevant for levels of social exclusion; for example, the choice for a liberal-democratic society affects the thresholds for shops to survive. Without fully discussing this subject, I limit this paragraph to direct policy interventions. Let us take the rural town of the example above. Let us then assume the town had only one shop, a small supermarket, which disappeared because it could not survive for market reasons. It also had a medical service centre, which disappeared because of changes in health policies. Would it from an ethical perspective make a difference that the supermarket disappeared because of 'free market developments' and the health centre because of policy changes? I now link this discussion to the discussion about voluntarily made choices above. Take the example of the person who moved to the town voluntarily. Suppose the health centre disappeared after she moved to town. Would it make a difference if the disappearance of the health centre were to be well communicated to the person before she made her choice to move?

Evaluation

Social exclusion is linked to broader concepts such as happiness and well-being (see Chapter 3). It is therefore relevant to study social exclusion, as well as policies in their wider context (Stanley and Vella-Brodrick, 2009). Stanley and Stanley (2007) argue that reducing social exclusion per se is not the ultimate policy goal, which should instead be expressed in terms of enhancing quality of life. This may theoretically be true, but the same applies to, for example, economic growth and policies aimed at increasing income. The relationship between income and happiness (or quality of life) is also quite fuzzy (Easterlin, 1973, 1974; Veenhoven, 1987, 1991). In addition, Preston (2009) emphasizes the link between social exclusion and quality of life. I would not categorically claim that research in the area of social exclusion should always be placed in a broader framework, but it might certainly be useful in several cases.

The broader links that can exist between social exclusion and well-being are shown by the concept of Forced Car Ownership (FCO) as presented by Currie et al. (2009). If low income households are forced to have a car, because otherwise they would be socially excluded, this can significantly affect their purchasing power in general. Perhaps research then does not necessarily label the households as being socially excluded, but to avoid social exclusion they may have to pay a high price. A specific example of the link between car related expenditures and income is shown by Priya and Uteng (2009), who focused on the costs of obtaining a driving licence in Norway. These costs are at least US$5800.

Participation and the process of policy making

For assessing the level of social exclusion, including both its negative impacts and potential solutions, it can be very beneficial to involve the persons for whom policies are developed – see also above and Chapter 3 for the importance of the process of selecting and evaluating policies. In the words of Stanley and Vella-Brodrick (2009: 94): 'There is a need for social governance goals: the ability of people to determine their own goals of social inclusion and well-being, rather than these requirements being assumed, as is commonly the case where accessibility to services is viewed as the required outcome'.

Choice Options and their Pros and Cons: Winners and Losers

This section combines a few of the questions as presented in Section 3.6. I assume the outcome of the first step (see above) is that a social exclusion problem exists, and that policy options to reduce the problem are to be discussed. The next question then is: which policy options are available? Section 4.4 presented a categorization of such policy options. It is beyond the scope of this chapter to discuss pros and cons of these options for several specific cases of social exclusion. Here, I discuss the idea that the final choice for a policy (that can include multiple policy options as presented in Section 4.4) could work out differently for different groups of individuals that face social exclusion. To illustrate this, let us assume a rural village without primary and secondary schools, shops and health care and other services. I assume there is a town at 10 km providing all shops and services the inhabitants of the village need. A first policy option could be to introduce (or improve) a bus service to the town or a taxi system. Children that need to travel to school (and their parents) probably prefer a bus service with a fixed timetable, preferably synchronized with school opening hours, or more specifically, with the start of the first and second contact hour. On the other hand, elderly persons might prefer an on-demand bus system, or even an on-demand taxi system, that brings them to, for example, the health care centre at the moment they have an appointment at that centre. This example shows that the policy option can easily work out differently for two groups of (potential) users. Could 'democracy' solve the problem in the sense that the dilemma can be solved by comparing the number of children that need to travel to school, and the number of elderly people without access to a car? Maybe. But do all persons count equally? The children might be able to cycle to school, but cycling to town could be more problematic for the elderly. On the other hand, maybe the elderly people without a car are rich and moved voluntarily to the village after retirement. One could argue that they can order a taxi and pay for it themselves.

This example is a plea to dig deeper into the problem – to not only list the winners and losers, but also to look at what lies behind these numbers. In addition, the example shows two more aspects of the broader discussion. The first is the idea that digging deeper into the problem might result in additional policy options. In this specific example, it might be that only a few children need to go to primary school, and parents can easily set up a voluntary scheme for driving these children to and from school. Or let us assume the vast majority of children involved are children that go to secondary school, and could easily cycle if the road to town were to be made safer. Then an option could be to narrow the lanes for motorized vehicles, reduce the maximum speed to 60 km/h, and mark a width lane for cycling, preferably in another colour of asphalt than the lanes for motorized vehicles.

The second aspect is the plea for participation of the persons that could face social exclusion, as discussed above: such participation could not only lead to additional policy options, but also to give better insights into what are the pros and cons of policy options for specific groups.

The third aspect is the idea of compensation for losers – see the checklist in Section 3.6. Perhaps the losers from policies, or those that benefit less than others, can be compensated by introducing related policies. The participation process as mentioned above could contribute to finding attractive policy options. For example, making the road to the nearest town more attractive for cyclists can be combined with on-demand bus or taxi services, but this solution makes the parents of the primary school children worse off. They can be compensated, giving them a fixed budget for fuel costs to compensate for their voluntary system.

Maximization or Not?

In the case of social exclusion it is arguable to say that maximization of utility, as generally defined and measured, is probably not the best thing to go for. Instead, it is better to go for certain minimum levels of access to activity locations for specific groups – see above. Note that the two options (maximization versus minimum levels of access) might not necessarily differ too much. This is because, from a utility perspective, the difference in utility to have one supermarket within reach versus none, is much larger compared to an increase from one to two supermarkets within reach. So, if the utility of having access to supermarkets is estimated well, the two choice options could lead to (more or less) the same conclusions.

A problem might occur if utility is based on willingness to pay (WTP) in the case of (potential) social exclusion of (very) low income people. Because of their low income their WTP for, for example, additional bus services, probably is low, simply because they do not, or hardly, have money for it. Consequently, using the WTP measure in order to evaluate the pros and cons of options to reduce social exclusion could be problematic.

Does Closed Partiality Occur?

Depending on the policy options and the spatial scale at which they are evaluated, closed partiality can occur. To illustrate this, I again use the example of a rural village without shops and services. Suppose the inhabitants of the village (or their democratic representation) could decide on options to reduce social exclusion. For reasons of simplicity I assume the only problem is access to a supermarket for daily goods. Let us assume the choice is between subsidizing a supermarket, or subsidizing a bus service to a nearby village that does have a supermarket, offering the same supply of goods, for the same price, as the supermarket to be subsidized in the village under consideration. I assume equal subsidies are needed for both options. The village probably prefers subsidizing the supermarket because they then have the same quality of supply at a closer distance. But what if subsidizing the supermarket were to lead to the disappearance of the supermarket in the other village, the inhabitants of which then face the same problems of social exclusion?

To make the example a bit more complicated, I assume a rural village with a supermarket, but no other services. Subsidizing a bus to a nearby town might bring other services within reach. But what then if some people will also do their shopping in town because it has a higher quality of supply of goods or lower prices? This could lead to the disappearance of the local supermarket.

In other words: evaluations should be at least aware of effects in the wider system, and not ignore them through focusing on too narrow an area of evaluation. This is a very general issue: changes in the transport and land-use system do not only have direct (first order) effects, but

– especially in the long run – can easily result in additional indirect (second or third order) effects – see the literature about land use and transport interaction as referred to in Section 4.2.

Are Additional Values Affected?

Several of the values as summarized in Section 3.4 could potentially be relevant for the subject of policy options for social exclusion. I discuss some of them below.

Freedom of choice and paternalism
A very fundamental discussion is whether or not to develop specific social exclusion policies at all. This is at least to some extent a balance between freedom of choice versus the broader advantages of such policies for society. Libertarians and others that highly value individual freedom might argue as follows: The real problem is not social exclusion itself, but the lack of income of the people that face social exclusion. Why, for example, should public transport be subsidized for everyone, only because some people cannot afford it, and as a result may face social exclusion? At least subject subsidies are to be preferred over object subsidies: make public transport cheaper only for those who cannot afford it, and as a result face a too high level of social exclusion. But even such subject based policies might be questioned. Why would policy makers decide for others that they should spend additional income on travel? This can be seen as a form of paternalism, which some people may prefer to avoid. If the real problem is a lack of income (or purchasing power) then change income taxes, or introduce other policy measures to compensate for this. In addition, let people decide if they spend the additional income or money on travel, or use it for other purposes, for example moving to another residential location, or buying a computer, or a holiday.

But this is not the only possible way to look at this subject. In Section 3.6 I referred to the concept of democracy as 'government by discussion'. This interpretation of democracy emphasizes the importance of political participation, dialogue and public interaction. If society adds value to democracy, in the sense of 'government by discussion', one may argue that society may put a value on the participation of persons in related activities. The link with social exclusion is of course only a loose one. But if social exclusion policies could lead to a higher participation rate in several activities, also related to democracy, this could be of value for society, and, as a result, be a reason for policies to reduce social exclusion. Another reason to look at the subject in a different way is that there might be what economists call 'external effects': effects the decision maker does not include in her choices. If people were to participate more in outdoor activities, this might induce external effects in several ways. Note that participating in outdoor activities is certainly not only linked to the example of bus travel. It could also be that people 'walk' more, using equipment to help the disabled, such as (adapted) bicycles for instance. External effects include, firstly, that if more people participate in local activities, it might result in more lively streets, more social contacts, more social cohesion, etc. which could be valued by society directly, and maybe indirectly if it reduced vandalism and crime rates, and if it increased mutual respect between people (partly based on Lyons, 2003). Secondly, people or institutions that are increasingly visited by the persons that do participate in the activities, thanks to the social exclusion policies, might benefit from the increased activity participation. The reverse side of the coin is of course that the money the people under consideration spend on these activities and related travel is not spent on the consumption of other goods or services, which should also be included in the equation.

A next value that could be of relevance is related to the potential right people have to be integrated in society. Sarewitz et al. (2003) give the example of the America Disabilitites Act (ADA). A CBA showed that

> fitting public buses with wheelchair access devices would be more expensive than simply providing, at public expense, taxi services for people with disabilities who did not have their own means of transportation. Yet the point of ADA was that people with disabilities deserved, as humans and citizens, to be fully integrated into our society, not marginalized from it. (Sarewitz et al., 2003: 810)

In other words, maximizing utility according to common practice in CBA would result in other outcomes than a decision based on the right of people to be integrated in society.

A specific category of values concerns those related to commitments or duties. It is possible that governments have moral obligations related to these values. For example, in the past the government might have made promises related to social exclusion; for instance the local school was not (increasingly) subsidized and did not survive, so by way of, compensation the government promised to improve travel options to schools in a neighbouring village or town.

Are Commitments or Duties at Stake?

Political commitments related to social exclusion can be made; for example, politicians may have promised to maintain the primary school in a village, or to preserve a bus service, or to reduce the barrier effect of a new segment of line infrastructure.

4.6 EGALITARIANISM AND SUFFICIENTARIANISM: A RELATIVE-ACCESSIBILITY APPROACH

As explained in Chapter 3, CBA has its theoretical underpinnings in utilitarianism. In this section, I present two other ethical theories that may be more useful to evaluate policies on social exclusion effects: egalitarianism and sufficientarianism, and illustrate the impact the choice for a theory might have on the evaluation of policy options presenting a simple case.

Egalitarian Theories

Egalitarian theories, including those of Rawls and Sen, are an influential category of theories on ethics, and are discussed in Chapter 3. If we apply Rawls (or egalitarian theories in general) to the evaluation of transport and social exclusion policy options, this firstly justifies the case for moving away from WTP for journey-time savings calculations of 'benefit', and towards improved accessibility to basic destinations (such as food shops and other daily activity centres, such as workplaces, schools and medical centres). Secondly, egalitarian theories are useful for encouraging a focus on the relative level of accessibility between different social groups, particularly those who may be at risk of social exclusion. From such a perspective, the benefits of providing bus services to remote rural areas with low income households would be valued more highly compared to the traditional way of valuing those services within the CBA method.

Sufficientarianism

Another competitor theory is sufficientarianism. While egalitarian theories focus on differences and not on absolute levels of well-being, sufficientarianism assumes that everybody should be well-off up to a certain minimum threshold: to what is 'sufficient' for their needs. In the case of 'weak sufficientarianism' it is important to improve the well-being of people who are below the threshold. In the case of 'strong sufficientarianism', *absolute priority* should be given to the improvement of well-being of people whose level of well-being is below the given threshold. Indeed, the lower their level of welfare, the more important it is to improve peoples' well-being (Meyer and Roser, 2009; see also Wolf, 2009). The concept of sufficientarianism therefore provides us with an ethical justification for seeking to determine minimum threshold levels of accessibility to key destinations, and targeting transport policies to improve these, at the social groups and areas which are worst off in this respect. An example of an

Table 4.2   Assumed effects of three hypothetical bus options (values
expressed in monetary terms)

	Fast bus	Slow bus	Bus service on demand
Costs (net present value)	80	80	80
Willingness to Pay	100	50	30
For high income groups	80	10	0
For low income groups	20	40	30
Benefits – costs	20	−30	−50
Potential accessibility of shops and basic services accessible	25	50	30
For high income groups	35	10	0
For low income groups	15	90	60
% of population below a certain threshold for potential accessibility of shops and basic services	40	10	0
For high income groups	0	0	0
For low income groups	80	20	0

operational criterion could be that households should have a shop selling food within reach of a certain non-care based travel time interval.

A Simple Case

I now present a hypothetical case to illustrate that the different ethical theories as presented above can lead to different policy conclusions. I assume a town with two population categories: half of the households have high incomes and one or two cars, the other half has low incomes and no cars. The town has no shops or basic services. To reduce social exclusion, three policy options are considered: (a) introducing and subsidizing a new fast bus service to the centre of a town 15 km away, providing fast transport with a low frequency of six times per day that costs €10 per return ticket; (b) a slow bus with a frequency of 12 times per day costing €5; and (c) an on-demand bus service only for a subcategory of low income groups: those with an income below the minimum wage level (unemployed, disabled, retired without pensions). It costs €5, and will bring people to the centre of the neighbouring town or any other destination in that town. Option (a) is especially attractive for high income households with only one car, and for only a minority of the low income group. Option (b) is attractive for all socially excluded, but hardly for high income, groups. Option (c) is only (very) attractive for its target group. Table 4.2 summarizes the assumed effects. For accessibility, I assume a (not further specified) potential accessibility indicator, including in the nominator the number of shops and basic services within access, and in the denominator (door-to-door) Generalized Transport Costs which include travel time (multiplied by income group specific Values of Time), costs and effort (including, income group specific preferences for frequencies, assuming low income groups have as strong a preference for high frequencies as high income groups). All effects are relative to the situation in the same year or period without the policies under consideration – I assume 'do nothing'.

A CBA would lead to the conclusion that the fast bus service is the only interesting option: benefits exceed costs, mainly because high income people value the service. An egalitarian perspective would probably lead to the conclusion that the slow bus is the best option: it reduces differences between population groups most because potential accessibility for the low income group strongly increases, and that of the high income group hardly (note that high income households own cars, and the slow bus services do not add much to their overall potential accessibility). The perspective of strong sufficientarianism would lead to the conclusion that the on-demand bus service is the best option: contrary to both other options nobody's accessibility level falls below the threshold in this case.

To summarize, in this hypothetical case the ethical perspective has a major impact on the preference order of the policy options.

4.7 CONCLUSIONS

The most important conclusions of this chapter are summarized below.

Social exclusion can be the result of several causes, related to land-use changes, changes in the transport system, changes in characteristics of the population, and changes in temporal dimensions such as the opening hours of services and their mutual interactions. In particular, interactions between (a) increases in car ownership levels, (b) spatial-economic forces leading to scale increases of retail, schools and services and other location patterns of shops, schools and services, and (c) the decline of public transport, especially in rural areas, have resulted in an increase of social exclusion, especially in rural areas, and for those not able to drive a car.

Many policies exist to reduce levels of social exclusion. Policies could relate to public transport and cycling, to land use, cars, mobile services, time constraints, the needs, capabilities and constraints of people, and ICT.

Social exclusion can be expressed in three indicator categories: (1) mobility based indicators; (2) activity participation based indicators; and

(3) accessibility indicators. The latter two are – at least theoretically – to be preferred over mobility based indicators.

Social exclusion has several ethical dimensions, several of which could legitimate policy interventions. But it is not at all straightforward to select 'the best' policy. One can even question if social exclusion policies are desirable at all – maybe income policies could be preferred over social exclusion policies. On the other hand, because social exclusion policies may have wider effects on society beyond their impact on (potentially) socially excluded people, there is an argument for policies in this area. If one decides to develop policies to reduce social exclusion, one has to answer the question of what should be a minimum level of participation in activity categories, or a minimum level of having access to activity locations. This is not at all easy. The answer could depend on whether or not people voluntarily face social exclusion, and on whether or not social exclusion results from policies.

Finally, this chapter has shown that the checklist for ethical dimensions, as presented in Chapter 3, could be useful in understanding the ethical aspects of social exclusion and related policies.

5. Long-term sustainability and transport evaluation

5.1 INTRODUCTION

Questions related to long-term sustainability and transport evaluation include:

- Is discounting OK in the case of CO_2 or effects on the natural environment?
- How to compare future generations with the current generation?
- How important is the current infrastructure for future generations?
- How to deal with the possible depletion of fossil fuels in the *ex ante* evaluation of transport policy options?
- Will the free market result in an optimum allocation of CO_2 emissions in the case of a cap-and-trade system? How useful is the resulting market price for the *ex ante* evaluation of transport policy options?

Societies benefit heavily from transport. The transport system allows people to carry out activities at spatially separated locations, and allows goods to be transported. The flipside of the coin is that transport causes negative impacts on society, with safety, environmental impacts and congestion being the most dominant effects. Negative impacts on the environment include CO_2 emissions that are a likely cause of climate change, and emissions of Particulate Matter (PM) – CO, VOC and NO_x – resulting in local air pollution. Road vehicles, trains and aircraft produce noise resulting in noise nuisance. Apart from emissions related impacts, infrastructure can often be a barrier for man and animals (see below). In addition, the presence of driving and parked vehicles negatively influences liveability, even when they are not using energy or emitting pollutants and noise – for example, where children cannot play on the street or travel to school independently. Furthermore, at the moment, the transport sector highly relies on fossil fuels, mainly oil, a non-renewable source of energy. In 2009 in the USA the share of the transport system in energy use was as large as 27 percent (Davis et al., 2010). The transport system also uses a lot of raw materials, And this is especially the case with current and potential future high-tech vehicles, that increasingly need rare raw materials. For example, future electrical vehicles will probably use Lithium-Ion batteries, and Lithium is only available in a few places worldwide.

Because of the high share of transport in emissions, and the high energy cost of non-renewable resources, the current transport system is often considered to be unsustainable. But what is sustainability? The subject of sustainability can be defined in several ways. One category of definitions focuses on intergeneration aspects, the famous Brundtland definition (WCED, 1987) being a well-known example. This defines sustainable development as 'Development that meets the needs of the present without compromising the ability of future generations to meet their needs' (WCED, 1987: 43). Other definitions, including that of the World Bank, focus on 'the right balance' between economic, ecological and social impacts, often labelled as 'People, Planet and Profit'. In this chapter, I will discuss ethical aspects of sustainability and transport, adopting the former definition. Not that the latter is of less importance, but the issue of balancing (categories of) impacts is discussed in Chapter 3.

The discussion about long-term sustainability and intergenerational conflict is of course a much broader discussion than one related to transport only. For example, it also plays a major role in discussions on nuclear waste (e.g. Taebi, 2010), which can be radioactive for thousands of years, which is much longer than the time CO_2 stays in the atmosphere. In this chapter I will discuss some thoughts on intergenerational justice in the area of transport, followed by the implications for transport decision making.

This chapter therefore focuses on long-term intergeneration sustainability. If one were to accept the 'People, Planet, Profit' approach of sustainability, one might wonder about the ethical aspects of People and Planet. The People dimension is, at least to some extent, discussed in the chapter on social exclusion (Chapter 4), as well as in the chapter on CBA (Chapter 3). I realize the environmental implications (Planet) are not widely discussed in this book. The reasons I focus on the long-term impacts of transport only are, firstly, that these are very difficult to deal with in *ex ante* evaluations in general, and more specifically in CBA, and secondly that they are often considered to have important ethical dimensions. This is not to say that more general ethical discussions on transport and the environment are of less value. On the contrary, some people argue that environmental ethics is a category of ethics in itself, and not 'only' a category of applied ethics. For a discussion of environmental ethics, including the discussion on (non-)anthropocentrism I refer to Light (2003). Another point of departure is that I focus on the content of intergenerational justice, not the related institutions. For literature on institutions, see, for example, the second part of the *Handbook of Intergenerational Justice* (Tremmel, 2006).

The remaining part of this chapter is organized as follows. Section 5.2 firstly gives an overview of the impact of transport on the environment. From the perspective of long-term sustainability, probably the level of energy use and CO_2 emissions are the most important impacts, but for reasons of completeness all dominant emissions will be briefly discussed. Section 5.3 then discusses transport infrastructure in general terms. Section 5.4 gives an overview of ethical literature on intergeneration issues, and links it to the transport sector, focusing on infrastructure, energy use and climate change. Section 5.5 discusses intergenerational justice. Next, Section 5.6 links the overview to the theories as presented in Chapter 3 (and in particular the checklist in Section 3.6), to the subject of transport and intergenerational ethics. Section 5.7 finally summarizes the most important conclusions of this chapter.

5.2 TRANSPORT AND THE ENVIRONMENT[1]

This section aims to give an impression of the transport sector's impact on the environment in general, and to make clear why transport is often seen as the most dominant sector negatively influencing the environment – because of its high share in emissions of several pollutants. Table 5.1 presents the share of transport in total emissions of several pollutants in the USA in 2008. It shows that in the USA the transport sector emits way over half of NO_x and CO emissions, and about one-third of VOC and CO_2 emissions. The share of SO_2 seems to be small, but emissions of ships at sea are excluded, because these do not occur within a country's boundaries, and are therefore not included in national statistics.

Table 5.1 Share of transport in emissions in the USA, 2008

Component	Share
SO_2	4.5
NO_x	57.9
CO	73.2
VOC	37.7
PM-2.5	0.2
PM-10	3.2
CO_2	33.2

Source: Davis et al. (2010).

Table 5.1 does not fully express transport's share in the health impacts of these pollutants since, on average, the distance between road traffic and the people exposed is much shorter than for other sources of pollution, such as power plants. Traffic emissions therefore have a greater than average health impact per kilogram compared to other emissions (Dorland and Jansen, 1997; Eyre et al., 1997; Newton, 1997). This is especially the case for road transport compared to non-road transport. The importance of the distance between the source and the receptor is demonstrated by the concentrations of pollutants as a function of the distance between a location and the road: the greater the distance, the lower the concentration. Bennett et al. (2002) have introduced the concept of the 'intake factor', being the intake of a pollutant by individuals and expressed in mass, divided by the mass of emissions. Evans et al. (2002) give an overview of studies on this subject and refer to the publications of Smith (1993a, 1993b), concluding that the intake of emissions of particulates from vehicles is ten times higher than those from a power plant. For further examples of this concept, see Marshall et al. (2003, 2005). To conclude, the share in emissions of different sectors is only a rough indicator of the share in effects. The impact of distance on effects should be included to give insights into the environmental effects of emissions, resulting in a relatively high share of road transport emissions.

Note that this overview includes environmental impacts, especially local air pollution, that is not of much importance from an intergenerational perspective.

5.3   TRANSPORT INFRASTRUCTURE[2]

This section aims to set the scene with respect to transport infrastructure. Over generations, countries have invested in transport infrastructure. To give an indication of the size of transport infrastructures in physical terms, Table 5.2 gives some characteristics for the EU 25.

The importance of transport infrastructures for society can be shown analytically. As already mentioned above, without transport modern societies would not be able to function. Expressing the importance of transport infrastructure by showing the share in added value, employment, expenditure and comparable indicators, can therefore be seen as too narrow. In fact, a multiplicative model to express the importance of transport infrastructure might add to a sum function model, splitting society into categories, with a total sum of 100 percent. Nevertheless, the sum function model gives some indication of the importance of transport infrastructure for society. Table 5.3 gives an overview of key indicators for EU 15 and 25.

Table 5.2   Selected transport network indicators, EU 25*, 2004

Indicator	Value
Length of road network	4734 (x 1000 km)
Length of motorway network	59 (x 1000 km)
Length of railroad network	198 (x 1000 km)
Length of inland waterway network	37 (x 1000 km network in use)
Length of oil pipelines	30 (x 1000 km)
Number of airports	88 (absolute number)

Note: * EU member states as at 1 May 2004.

Source: EU (2006).

Table 5.3   Some indicators for transport, EU 15/25

Indicator	Value
Number of jobs	
EU 25	8.2 million
EU 15	6.8 million
Percentage of household income spent on transport	
EU 25	13.8%
EU 15	13.9%

Source: EU (2006).

Transport infrastructure includes the physical infrastructures, such as roads and railroads. These infrastructures not only include the direct surface-related hardware (and in the case of the railways also the electricity supply), but also hardware related to management and safety. One can think of signs for rail infrastructure, dynamic signs for route guidance at roads, and ICT systems for air traffic management.

Each new generation inherits a certain level of infrastructure from previous generations – often still extremely useful. The heritage each generation receives is not only important because infrastructure is vital for societies, but also because transport infrastructure is very capital intensive: the construction of motorways and railroads in densely populated countries and regions is extremely expensive. Campos and De Rus (2009) compared the construction costs of 24 high-speed rail projects in operation worldwide, and found that the costs per km range from €9 million to €39 million, with an average of €18 million. As an illustration, the construction costs of the so-called Betuweline, a 160 km long dedicated rail freight line between Rotterdam harbour and the German border, are €4.7 billion, or about €30 million per kilometre. Urban rail projects are in general even more expensive. Flyvbjerg et al. (2008) compared per kilometre costs of 17 European projects. They conclude that these costs vary greatly, from US$16 to US$330[3] per kilometre. A third reason why the heritage of transport infrastructure is important is because changing infrastructure takes a lot of time. This relates to the infrastructures themselves, as well as to related land-use impacts. Due to the high construction costs, transport infrastructure networks have very high levels of sunk costs (costs which have already been incurred and cannot be recovered), leading to relatively slow dynamics. Building new transport infrastructures in densely populated regions is very complex because of the (lack of) availability of land and the impacts on the environment. This complexity also results in relatively slow dynamics, both with respect to the introduction of new types of infrastructure (in past centuries: rail lines, roads), as well as with respect to changes in the networks of a specific type of infrastructure. To make it even more complex, land-use changes have an impact on transport and vice versa, as conceptualized in so-called Land Use–Transport Interaction models (LUTI models – see below). These interrelations mean that changes in infrastructures lead to changes in land-use patterns. In addition, even if land use itself were not to be affected, infrastructure has an impact on location choices, because people might change their destinations (e.g. accept jobs further from their dwellings), and companies will buy and sell goods over longer distances.

Due to the large costs of transport infrastructures, and the limited dynamics, the risk of making 'wrong' decisions is relatively high. The phenomenon of *lock in* can occur relatively easily. In addition, due to the slow dynamics, transitions that need radical innovations at the system level are very difficult to realize. Let us assume a new type of infrastructure is developed, leading to low construction costs (compared to current infrastructures), low costs to operate, very low environmental pressure and hardly any risks. This system might be highly desirable. But the transition to the new infrastructure will be very difficult, and on a short to medium term (say up to 15 years) it may even be impossible. This is because of the huge sunk costs of current infrastructures, the very likely lack of space to construct a new network for the new system, especially in densely populated regions, and because of the large investments in current vehicle fleets.

One might argue that maybe in the future the importance of infrastructure could reduce, making the intergenerational dimension of infrastructure less relevant; for example, thanks to ICT people would not need to travel that much anymore. However, it is quite likely that this is a misconception. As explained in Chapter 1, on average people spend between 60 and 75 minutes per day on travel, all over the world, regardless of income levels. People nowadays spend as much time on travel as they did, for example, 30 years ago. This phenomenon is referred to as the theory of constant Travel Time Budgets (e.g. Mokhtarian and Chen, 2004), and can be explained by economic, but also by other theories, in areas such as biology, psychology, geography and cultural studies (e.g. Van Wee et al., 2006). The concept of Travel Time Budgets has been debated for decades (see, amongst others, Mokhtarian and Chen, 2004; Van Wee et al., 2006), but nevertheless seems to be quite a robust concept, especially useful for the long term and at an aggregate level (e.g. a country). This stability does not apply to goods transport. For goods, transport time is a cost factor, but there is no tendency to constancy. Consequently, from an intergenerational perspective it seems plausible to assume that future generations might travel as much as we do. Time spent on travel is of course an output indicator, which does not necessarily need to be equalized, or even discussed, from an equity perspective. What matters more from such a perspective is the level of opportunities to participate in activities at spatially separated locations. Here, the concept of travel time is only discussed to underpin the plausibility of the assumption that future generations will travel about as much as the current generation.

The main message of this section, therefore, is that the heritage of transport infrastructure is very relevant from an intergenerational perspective.

5.4 INTERGENERATIONAL DIMENSIONS OF TRANSPORT

This section discusses the most dominant dimensions of transport from an intergenerational perspective: infrastructure (including its impacts on land use), energy use, and climate change.

Transport Infrastructure: Intergenerational Relevance

What we leave for future generations not only relates to non-renewable resources, but also to man-made resources, such as buildings and infrastructures for transport, electricity and water. An important question is: why is transport infrastructure important from an intergenerational perspective? There are at least seven reasons.

A first *potential* reason is that in many countries most – if not all – transport infrastructure is in public hands. This is not to suggest that privately owned heritage is not relevant from an intergenerational perspective, but if the public sector is highly involved, one could argue it is even more important to include intergenerational issues in cases of the *ex ante* evaluation of policy options. On the other hand, one can debate how important ownership is – would it matter from an intergenerational perspective if, for example, airports or motorways were in private or public hands? A second reason is that transport infrastructure is strongly related to basic values, in particular the freedom to move (see Chapter 3). Probably we should safeguard such values for future generations. Thirdly, adequate transport infrastructure is of crucial importance for societies, both from an economic perspective, as well as from the wider societal perspective. Fourthly, transport infrastructure is very expensive. Long-term impacts of transport are very relevant for *ex ante* evaluations in the area of transport and related decision making for a number of reasons. Fifthly, transport infrastructure lasts for a very long time, at the least in the sense of the land take and the impacts of transport on the wider society, but also often the infrastructure itself. This applies to roads, railways, harbours, airports and metro systems. Many rail lines that western countries nowadays operate were already constructed in the nineteenth century. Most motorways in western countries were built more than three decades ago, often much longer. Motorways that were built before the Second World War, in countries like Germany or Italy, are still in use today. Maybe the rails themselves are replaced multiple times, as are the top layers of asphalt, but at least their locations remain the same. Furthermore, transport infrastructures shape urban and regional development. As a result, it would be logical to at least recognize the idea that transport infrastructure could easily have an impact on society for at least a century. Sixthly, as stated above, transport, more than any other dominant sector, relies heavily on fossil fuels, mainly oil. Consequently, we consume non-renewable resources, and therefore may leave future generations with fewer possibilities to fulfil their needs. Seventhly, building transport infrastructure often has long-term negative implications on communities and nature. These relate to the landscape, but also to barrier effects. Infrastructure can be a barrier causing long detours for people travelling, but also an impossible to breach barrier for some species. If species cannot survive, this may affect ecosystems. As a result of these seven reasons, an important question, therefore, is: how to deal with such long-term issues in decision making with respect to transport infrastructure?

Energy and Climate Change

The second issue I will discuss in this chapter is energy use and climate change. Because both are strongly related, I discuss energy use and climate change together. The intergenerational aspect of energy use relates to the availability of non-renewable (fossil) energy, and raises the questions of how much should be left for future generations and which level of use is acceptable from an intergenerational perspective. The intergenerational aspect of CO_2 relates to the question of what is an acceptable level of greenhouse gas (GHG) emissions and related climate change.

The depletion of fossil fuels will have strong implications for society, not only in the transport system. In this context, politicians may prefer to reduce climate change by reducing GHG emissions. The *general* ethical issue of climate change is briefly referred to in the introduction to this chapter. What could specifically be important for the link between climate change and energy use on the one hand, and transport on the other, is firstly that CO_2 emissions and energy use in the transport sector are rapidly increasing, more than any other large sector (OECD/IEA, 2009), and secondly, that transport may also in the future, more than other sectors, continue to rely on fossil fuels. For example, bio-fuels could be produced, but if so, using them as input for electricity production may be more cost-effective than using the same inputs to produce bio-fuels for the transport system. Electricity is already a dominant source of energy in industry, including offices and households, and if it is not it could be; for example, gas for heating could be replaced by electricity. The only category of transport that uses electricity in relatively large quantities is rail transport. At the time of writing this book, electrical cars seem to be a potentially promising alternative for internal combustion engine cars, but significant barriers still reduce large-scale applications. Barriers include range, battery prices, recharging equipment at home and in other places, recharging times, and perhaps cultural or psychological barriers. Even if these drawbacks are reduced, electricity might still not be an option for lorries and buses, not to mention aircraft, barges and sea-going ships. Thus the transport sector is vulnerable in the case of the depletion of fossil fuels, 'peak oil' or unstable production and export of oil.

Finally, transport, probably more than any other category of consumption, allows us to consume energy and emit GHGs in large quantities in a short period of time, flying being the most extreme option. A fully occupied Boeing 747-300 intercontinental flight of 10 000 km taking 10 hours, takes about 325 litres of jet fuel to transport one passenger (calculations based on figures derived from http://en.wikipedia.org/wiki/Boeing_747).

5.5   INTERGENERATIONAL JUSTICE

Introduction

Intergenerational justice hardly received any attention from philosophers until 1980. The reason why philosophers have probably long ignored the issue is that the impact of human beings on the planet was relatively limited (or not recognized) for a long time (Tremmel, 2006). A key difference between intergenerational justice and other forms of justice is its unidirectional dimension: future generations depend on actions of the current generation, not vice versa. In this way future generations are vulnerable. Because of this unidirectional dimension, ethical theory on justice should be extended to include intergenerational issues. Theoretically there are three options. Firstly, the concept of the 'circumstances of justice' can be extended so that unidirectional justice can be included. Secondly, intergenerational justice could be studied on non-contractarian grounds – future generations cannot sign contracts with the current generation (see Chapter 3 for a description of contractarian theory). Thirdly, we can decide that intergenerational relations are by their nature not subject to judgements of justice at all (Heyd, 2009).[4] I assume the last option is not to be preferred, and so that intergenerational justice is a relevant concept – see Section 5.6 for a discussion.

Intergenerational justice relates to six forms of capital: natural capital; artificial and financial capital (financial capital also includes intergenerational debt); cultural capital; social capital; structural capital (formal and informal rules and institutions); and human capital (Tremmel, 2006; Wallack, 2006).

Intergenerational justice can be made specific by defining: (1) the period of time to be considered; (2) the question of who to consider; (3) the question of for what does it exist (content – see the six forms of capital above) and; (4) the question of significance of responsibility for the future, compared with responsibility for the present.

It could be a problem to motivate people to accept responsibility for the future (Birnbacher, 2006). Thus even when intergenerational justice is made explicit, and people are motivated to accept responsibility for the future, it is very difficult to apply it in practice. This is mainly because of the high level of uncertainty about the future (e.g. Davidson, 2009), for example in terms of the number of people (e.g. Arrhenius, 2009), their incomes (or better: quality of life), preferences of people in the future (Bykvist, 2009), availability of natural resources and substitutes for their current use (which are partly related to the uncertainties with respect to [technological] knowledge), and finally the future state of the environment. All such uncertainties are not only problematic because of the uncertainties themselves, but also because of how to deal with them. To illustrate this, let us assume there is no uncertainty about the size of the future population (over time), and we are sure that the world population will double in, say, 50 years – should the rights on non-renewables then be distributed equally over generations (regardless of their size) or do their sizes count? Gosseries (2001; cited in Steiner and Vallentyne, 2009), for example, states that differences in population size do not matter, Steiner and Vallentyne conclude that they do: it is people who matter, not groups of people.

In this section, I will discuss intergenerational justice from the position of *ex ante* evaluations of transport projects and policies. It is beyond the scope of this section to discuss intergenerational justice in all its dimensions, and from the perspective of many theories *in general*. For such discussions, I refer to two books, the *Handbook of Intergenerational Justice*, edited by Tremmel (2006) and the book *Intergenerational Justice*, edited by Gosseries and Meyer (2009). The point I want to make in this section is that intergenerational justice may very well exist, and that, if it does, the conventional way of including long-term effects in CBAs of transport projects and policies, might at least be discussed, and may even be flawed. Despite the focused scope, I will refer to more general discussions on intergenerational justice, including some of the chapters in those books, if helpful for the purpose of this chapter.

Does Intergenerational Justice Exist?

How to deal with intergenerational dimensions of transport in the case of evaluations of policies and projects? An important underlying ethical question is: Does intergenerational justice exist at all? Almost all authors of the literature I have read in the area of intergenerational justice think the concept is valid and relevant (for an overview, see e.g. Tremmel, 2006; Gosseries and Meyer, 2009). This, however, does not mean that there is no dispute about this conclusion.

It is beyond any doubt that the choices the current generation make may have impacts on future generations. That in itself does not imply that intergenerational justice exists. In addition, the current generation should be responsible for its actions. Next, a person can only be blamed for not having avoided troubles she could foresee or expect (Birnbacher, 2006). Because current generations can be held responsible for their actions, and at least the depletion of fossil fuels and climate change can be foreseen, it is denfensible to conclude that intergenerational justice exists, at least in the areas of climate change and the use of fossil energy. In addition, it is without dispute that infrastructure is part of artificial capital, and so a subject to be included in intergenerational justice.

Probably the best-known philosopher who disagrees with this position is Professor Beckerman; (see, e.g. Beckerman, 2006). Beckerman concludes that justice assumes rights, and future generations cannot have rights because they do not exist yet. But he does conclude they have interests, and the current generation has a moral obligation to take account of our actions in terms of future generations. The discussion on the rights of people who do not exist is referred to as the 'Non-Identity Problem' (see e.g. Kumar, 2009; Meyer and Roser, 2009; Parfit, 1984; Schwartz, 1978).

Wolf (2003) discusses this issue, referring to scholars who honestly believe that intergenerational justice does not exist, because people that do not exist cannot have anything at all, including rights. Nevertheless, Wolf argues that scepticism about intergenerational justice is difficult to accept when one considers concrete cases and problems. It is beyond any doubt that the actions of the current generation can have impacts on future generations, examples being destroying swathes of nature and the depletion of non-renewable resources. But can our actions be harmful for other generations, and can they be unjust? Wolf quotes an example from Feinberg (1986: 154) that – in my opinion – quite convincingly leads to the answer 'yes'.

> A wicked misanthrope desires to blow up a schoolhouse in order to kill or mutilate the pupils. He conceals a bomb in a closet in the kindergarten room and sets a timing device to go off in six years. It goes off on schedule, killing or mutilating dozens of five year old children. It was the evil action of the wicked criminal six years earlier, before they were even conceived, that harmed them. It set in train a causal sequence that led directly to the harm.

This example shows that people who will live in the future will (then) have rights, and matter. But it does not imply we care about *potential* extra people. For example, if we save lives by making the transport system safer, we value the decrease in fatalities. But how about the (grand)children of the people whose lives are saved, those who will be born now that their (grand)parents lives are saved? Instinctively we do not (necessarily) value their lives, though there could be good reasons for doing so (Broome, 2005).

Which Theories to Use for Questions Regarding Intergenerational Justice?

Assuming intergenerational justice exists, and should be included in the *ex ante* evaluation of long-term policies (transport and other polices), an important question could be: which theories to use? First of all, it is important to understand that not all ethical theories (including those presented in Chapter 3) are equally useful. In general, according to Thompson (2009), liberal theories fail to adequately deal with intergenerational justice because of their focus on rights, combined with the lack of rights of people who do not exist. Another reason why (according to Thompson) liberal theories fail is that they only focus on the current generation. Thompson proposes a communitarian theory that looks at people as part of communities; communities – by definition – are transgenerational. Secondly, contractarian theories have the problem that contracts between generations – and certainly those who do not overlap – cannot be signed, and cooperation between generations is not possible.

Most theoretical literature on intergenerational justice I have found is based on deontology and more specifically on (egalitarian) theories on justice. The theoretical perspective one chooses may have an impact on the position taken in relation to intergenerational justice. I do not choose any position with respect to those theories, but rather repeat the aim of this section: I will discuss intergenerational justice from the position of *ex ante* evaluations of transport projects and policies. As explained above, the point I want to make in this section is that intergenerational justice may very well exist and that if it does, the conventional way of including long-term effects in CBAs of transport projects and policies, might at least be discussed, and may even be flawed. The question how then precisely to include intergenerational justice, in particular related to the depletion of fossil fuels, climate change and transport infrastructure, is beyond the scope of this book.

How to Deal with Intergenerational Justice? The Case of Non-renewable Resources

One important aspect of intergenerational justice and transport is the use of non-renewable resources. This includes energy (fossil fuels) and raw materials. Accepting that intergenerational justice exists, the next question then becomes: how to deal with it? This question is of relevance for the overall use of non-renewable resources, not only for their use by the transport sector.

Many philosophers refer to Rawls' theory of justice (1971) and his application of this theory to intergenerational justice. Rawls introduced the concept of the 'veil of ignorance'.

> To insure impartiality of judgment, the parties are deprived of all knowledge of their personal characteristics and social and historical circumstances. They do know of certain fundamental interests they all have, plus general facts about

psychology, economics, biology, and other social and natural sciences. The parties in the original position are presented with a list of the main conceptions of justice drawn from the tradition of social and political philosophy, and are assigned the task of choosing from among these alternatives the conception of justice that best advances their interests in establishing conditions that enable them to effectively pursue their final ends and fundamental interests. (*Stanford Encyclopedia of Philosophy*, n.d.)

Suppose parties do not know to which generation they belong . . . Thus the persons . . . are to ask themselves how much they would be willing to save at each stage on the assumption that all other generations are to save at the same rates . . . In effect then they must choose a just saving principle that assigns an appropriate rate of accumulation to each level of advance. (Rawls, 1971: 287, quoted in Wolf, 2003; see also Attas, 2009; Heyd, 2009; Wallack, 2006)

Later, Rawls argued that parties should make choices that are relevant from an intergenerational point of view, and should understand themselves to be choosing that principle they would want earlier generations to have adopted (Wolf, 2003). Others have built on the ideas of Rawls; for example, Attas (2009) proposes to base saving rates on the transgenerational least advantaged. Wolf (2009) discusses the theory of Rawls in the context of climate change related intergenerational justice, emphasizing that Rawls' theory was developed to be applied within a nation, whereas climate changes is global.

Accepting the guiding principle of just saving rates, the next question then is: which saving rate? Or maybe better: which principle for setting the saving rate? In ethical literature, many discussions on the 'right saving rate' can be found (see e.g. Attas, 2009; Heyd, 2009). Wolf (2003) argues that one category of setting saving rates could be based on the idea that sustainability is reached when we use resources at exactly the same rate at which we either replace them, or develop economic substitutes for them. The depletion of fossil fuels could be an example: if we could develop ways (technologies, institutions) to produce renewable energy sources (e.g. wind, solar, hydro-thermal based) in substantive quantities for prices comparable to, or lower than, oil based energy, then the depletion of oil is less problematic from this perspective. This, however, does not cover the issue that oil is a raw material for many more products, such as plastics, but it does tackle the energy content of oil and intergenerational issues.

In setting the 'just' saving rate several ingredients can be relevant (e.g. Wolf, 2003). Important ingredients are, firstly, population size, since it may change, having implications for the question of whether absolute or relative (to population size) saving levels matter. This subject is discussed in the ethical literature by many authors (see, e.g. Arrhenius, 2009; Gosseries, 2001, 2009; Parfit, 1984). Another ingredient is the availability of alternatives. One can think of alternatives for fossil fuels as discussed above. Thirdly, some goods are non-tradable, such as specific natural sites. The saving rate discussion therefore probably does not apply to such goods. Fourthly, maybe human well-being is more important than the level of resources or opportunities. Accordingly, the concept of 'stable welfare' could be attractive, either at a total level (the sum over all individuals) or at the average level (the sum divided by the number of people). But focusing on the average welfare may be problematic, since it ignores distributional issues, and so the distribution of welfare should be included in the analysis as well. A second problem with (average) welfare is that welfare and well-being are not the same. Fifthly, do we know what future generations will need, appreciate, value, etc.? After discussing such issues, Wolf (2003: 292) presents a definition for institutions and sustainability: 'Institutions are humanly sustainable if and only if their operation does not leave future generations worse equipped to meet their needs than members of the present generation are to meet their own needs'.

Note that this definition is highly inspired by the Brundtland definition of sustainable development, as presented above.

Although several philosophers have argued that contractarianism is not the best theory to discuss intergenerational justice, because contracts between generations cannot be signed, the Rawls-based idea of intergenerational justice can solve the 'contract problem' – it is based on the contractarian tradition in political philosophy: if people were able to design contracts with other generations, what then would the contract look like? But the idea of intergenerational justice can also be legitimated by utilitarianism. If we accept that there is no reason to assume that human beings of the current generation are worth more than people belonging to future generations, and we want to maximize utility from an intergenerational perspective, it would imply that we should include in the equation the utility of future generations.[5] A major problem then relates to discounting: should we discount options of future generations to meet their needs? If so, does this apply to all needs in an equal way? This issue is discussed in Section 5.6.

An important point can be made about what needs to be sustained. In line with the discussion on the difference between welfare and well-being, one could question the relevance of a certain level of resources. Sen (2009: 250) discusses this issue: sustaining living standards is not the same as sustaining people's freedom and capabilities to have what they value. Thus an important question to be answered is: what to sustain? I would argue that welfare can be used as a first indicator for well-being, freedom and capabilities. But because welfare is not the perfect indicator, I would also recommend an explicit check on the plausibility of using welfare in specific cases of choices to be made.

Another important choice to be made is the choice between an egalitarian position or a sufficientarian position, a choice that is already discussed in Chapter 4 on social exclusion. When applied to the concept of intergenerational justice this poses the question: should we focus on differences between generations (the egalitarian position) or on minimum levels of goods, or on satisfying the needs of future generations (a position based on sufficientarianism)?

A final remark on intergenerational justice and saving rates: most – if not all – the literature I have read on this subject implicitly or explicitly assumes that future generations will (in terms of income or welfare) be better off than the current generation. Included within this assumption is the reduced level at which future generations should be included in the equation. An increase in incomes may well occur, but does not necessarily have to be the case. If we look at history, and fluctuations of wealth over time and place, several examples of decreases in welfare can be found. If we discuss intergenerational justice from the perspective of natural resources, the time frame can easily be as long as a couple of hundreds of years. And within such a time frame decreases of welfare can occur.

How to Deal with Intergenerational Justice? The Case of Climate Change

A special case of intergenerational justice relates to climate change. Again, this discussion is a general discussion, not related to the transport sectors' emissions of GHGs only, but because of the high share of transport in GHG emissions, it is very relevant for the *ex ante* evaluation of transport projects and policies.

Climate change due to human activities very likely already occurs (see, amongst others, the reports of the Intergovernmental Panel on Climate Change – IPCC) and will likely occur in the long run (with changes happening from now until much more than a century from now), making it an intergenerational ethical issue. Hood (2003) states that 'climate change raises issues of equity and justice because it is expected that climate change will not affect all people or all countries the same' (Hood, 2003: 679). 'The same' firstly applies to measures to reduce emissions: depending on assumptions of equity, some nations should take more actions to prevent GHG emissions than others. For example, one may argue that it is fair that countries that are already responsible for a lot of GHG emissions should reduce such emissions disproportionately. Another aspect of 'the same' is the distribution of the burden of emissions reductions. A utilitarian approach assuming maximizing utility could lead to other outcomes than minimizing the impact on the least fortunate. This does not only apply to the distributional question of which nation should reduce GHGs to which extent (and when), but also to the overall level of the reduction of GHG emissions compared to a non-intervention policy. Let us assume that the world had a dictator that could decide upon the future level of GHG emissions. If she had a utilitarian approach to ethics, based on a world-wide willingness to pay (WTP) for reduced risks resulting from climate change (such as the risk of flooding), she would be willing to reduce GHG emissions that result in high flooding risks in Bangladesh to a much lower extent, compared to the support she would give an ethical approach based on the minimizing of the negative impact on the least fortunate. Note that it is highly questionable if it is ethically sound to apply the WTP approach to valuing human lives across world regions and over time – see Chapter 6.

Not only do the costs of measures and the distribution of the burden differ across countries (and probably even within countries) and world regions, but there is also the distribution over generations: the current generation might need to implement measures to reduce GHG emissions, and future generations benefit from these measures. This raises the question of how to value future generations as compared to the current generation. Some philosophers think we should care more about the current generation or those who live close to us in time, than about those who live in the more distant future, just because of their temporal distance from us. This position is called 'pure discounting' (Broome, 2008). An opposing view is that we should be temporally impartial. In that case discounting is not done (at least not for the reason of attributing less value to those who live in the more distant future). This is the view of, amongst others, Broome (2008). We discuss discounting in the next section.

The discussion is further complicated by technological changes. It would be too simple to say that all people, regardless the generations to which they belong, have equal rights on non-renewables, such as oil. This is because (future) technology might allow future generations to 'do more' with the same quantity of oil (e.g. Steiner and Vallentyne, 2009) – see also the different categories of capital as listed in the introduction of this section.

In addition to these ethical considerations, there is a concern that is relevant both from an ethical perspective, as well as from a more traditional economic perspective: the risk of catastrophe. There is a chance that temperature will rise much more than in the middle projections of the IPCC. If temperatures rose by more than eight degrees Celsius (the chances according to most studies being about 5 percent – Broome, 2008), the disruption could pose some risk of a devastating collapse of the human population, perhaps even leading to extinction. Any such event would be so bad that even multiplied by its small chance of occurrence, its severity could dominate all calculations of the harm that climate change could cause (Broome,

2008). Such a calculation would result in very high values of reductions of GHG emissions from a pure economic perspective. In addition, it would raise very serious, but very difficult, ethical questions.

How to Deal with Intergenerational Justice? The Case of Infrastructure

Contrary to the use of fossil energy and climate change, the discussion on transport infrastructure is transport specific, though several aspects also count for other infrastructures, such as electricity infrastructure.

The first issue I will discuss here is the issue of the value of infrastructure for future generations. It is of course very difficult to assess the value in this case. This is firstly because we are uncertain about future population size: the larger the population, the more people might benefit from the infrastructure the current generation leaves for the following generations. Secondly, we do not know what the transport needs of future generations might be. Assuming stable needs – translated in terms of infrastructure use per capita – over, let us say, five decades, would have significantly underestimated the value of airports or motorways in the 1950s, because nowadays people fly much more often than 50 years ago, but it would have overestimated the value of canals in that era, because of the mode shift from barge to roads. On the other hand, it is quite common to consider a period of only a few decades in *ex ante* evaluations such as Cost–Benefit Analysis. Consequently, even if we use longer periods, due to discounting the benefits over, for example, 50 years, this hardly matters (see Section 5.6). This implies an important question now is: How to deal with the estimation of the future value of infrastructure and discounting? A possible solution might be to do what-if analyses. Examples could include: what if future generations were to value infrastructure that we decide upon today, equally to the current generation (in absolute or relative [to income] terms, per person or in total)? What if the value were to increase according to the discount rate as assumed? We could base such what-if questions on analyses of historical value of infrastructures. A second solution could be to think of changes in infrastructure and its use over longer periods: how long were infrastructures in use (and to what level) in the past? Railway lines of the 1850s are often still in use, but horse tramlines of about a century ago are not. Thus, if infrastructure is not in use anymore, is it then useless? Horse trams were replaced by electrical trams, and therefore most of the investments in infrastructure were still of value. What would this imply for motorways and other roads, that are, in most countries, the most capital intensive category of infrastructure? If the current generation of road vehicles were to become obsolete, by what types of vehicles would they be replaced? If it were to be automated guided vehicles (AGVs), then the function of motorways would remain, but extensions to increase capacity would probably not have much value, because in the case of AGVs, capacity of motorways will increase multiple times. An even more difficult to value infrastructure category is airports. On the one hand forecasts under Business as Usual scenarios suggest aircraft forecasts exceed any other transport forecast (e.g. Schafer et al., 2009; WBCSD, 2004). On the other hand, if we run out of oil, or were to implement strict climate policies, air transport would probably be the most vulnerable category of transport (Gilbert and Perl, 2008).

An important question is: which quality and quantity of transport infrastructure should be left for future generations? In addition, how should quantity and quality be expressed? With respect to quality, one could argue that the infrastructure should on average be kept at a constant (and adequate) level of maintenance. This does not apply to each individual part of infrastructures, but rather at the network level. The 'constant level of maintenance' assumption could be criticized. For example, future generations might have better technologies or more money to maintain roads. If so, a future lower level of maintenance could be less problematic and less costly to improve. Another argument for the critics could be related to changes in vehicle characteristics and the use of infrastructure. What if future vehicles could be driven faster? Trains driven at 200 km/h require 'smoother' rail lines. Does this matter? Should the current generation therefore leave rail infrastructure in a 'smoother' state than it inherited the infrastructure from the previous generation? Or what if the current generation were to decide to use faster trains? This decision may or may not imply that the current generation will leave rail infrastructure in a 'better' condition. On the other hand, if in the future cars were to have better chassis, maybe less 'smooth' roads would result in the same level of driving comfort. It is also important to note that nowadays almost all western countries have speed limits on motorways. In this case, maybe we should not leave motorways in a 'better' condition than needed in order to drive comfortably at the maximum speeds as allowed. Because of such uncertainties I think that the 'constant level of maintenance' assumption could be a point of departure. But there can exist good reasons to leave this assumption.

The quantity of infrastructure to be left for future generations is probably even more difficult to address. A first question is: which quantity? Is it an absolute quantity, for example the number of kilometres of motorways or motorway lanes in a given country? How then to deal with changes in population size? Do they matter? The answer very likely is 'yes'. This is firstly because the higher the number of inhabitants, the higher the chances of covering the costs of infrastructure. Because almost all countries now have more inhabitants than in the past, the current generation should leave more infrastructure than it inherited. But on the other hand, if people are richer in the future, they can better afford building infrastructure in general. Even more specifically, if capacity is not fully used, an increase in population size would mean there are more people who can finance the same level (and thus costs) of infrastructure, so an increase in the size of the future population (everything else remaining equal) then could be a reason to leave less infrastructure for future generations. This is true from the perspective of equality of persons who are better off simply because there are more people to finance infrastructure. Secondly, the perspective of needs is relevant: the required level of infrastructure to fulfil transport needs (or better: needs to participate in activities at spatially separated locations or to transport goods), at least to some extent, depends on population size. An increase in population size, therefore, would imply the current generation should leave more infrastructure in order to allow future generations to fulfil equal transport needs.

Not only population size, but income changes and transport needs may be relevant for the question of the quantity of infrastructure which is to be left for future generations, while technological change may also be relevant. What if, for example, in 20 years' time road vehicle technologies will allow us to drive much closer to other vehicles, greatly increasing the capacity of motorways? Consequently, extensions of the motorway network that we consider now might not, or hardly be, of further use. Or what if a specific infrastructure type becomes obsolete? Leaving large quantities of it for future generations might even be valued negatively, for example because it could be a barrier, as dismantling it costs money, or because it could have negative impacts on landscape or nature. To summarize, it is extremely complex to take an ethical judgement on what is the optimum quantity of infrastructure that we should leave for future generations.

Combining both quantity and quality of infrastructure, it is important to realize that, thanks to the usual discount rates, according to CBAs, the value of infrastructure after a few decades is relatively low – see Section 5.6. One can debate if this is correctly expressing the intergenerational dimension.

5.6   APPLYING THE CHECKLIST OF SECTION 3.6 TO INTERGENERATIONAL SUSTAINABILITY AND TRANSPORT

This section discusses the relevant items of the checklist in Section 3.6, to the extent that they are not discussed in the sections above.

Sometimes multiple items of the checklist are combined for reasons of textual efficiency. The discussion is limited to energy, climate change and infrastructure.

What is the Problem or the Challenge? What are the Choice Options?

The depletion of fossil fuels as a problem is poorly recognized in strategic policy making, as well as in *ex ante* evaluations of transport projects and policies. With respect to literature on *ex ante* evaluations, an exception to this rule is the paper by Krumdieck et al. (2010) who present a method to express how risky society is with respect to oil availability ('peak oil') depending on – amongst other things – the level of necessity of activities. The subject is addressed more often in non-transport related literature, the first report to the Club of Rome (Meadows et al., 1972) probably being the best-known example. That report concluded that exponential demographic and economic growth is be sustainable, and would lead to environmental degradation and the depletion of fossil fuels and other non-renewable resources. In such studies the transport sector is also included.

Studies that specifically focus on the transport sector and its long-term energy use and emissions can be split into forecasting and backcasting studies. Forecasting studies start with the present, and then look at what might happen in the future under given assumptions of determinants for transport, such as demographic, economic, technological and spatial trends, often together with policies. Environmental indicators are often included, as is the energy consumption of transport. Examples of such a study are the world-wide outlook of the World Business Council for Sustainable Development (WBCSD, 2004), and the long-term forecasts of Schafer et al. (2009). Another category of studies into this subject is so-called backcasting studies. These studies set a certain target or set of targets for the future, and then look at how such targets could be met. An example of such a study is the OECD study into Environmentally Sustainable Transport (EST), carried out for a selection of countries at the national level. One of the targets in the EST study is a reduction of CO_2 emissions of 80 percent between 1990 and 2030 (see for an example of a country study, Geurs and Van Wee, 2004b). Backcasting studies, however, are rare. In addition, the insights they provide are generally not taken as a point of departure for (long-term) transport policy plans. Furthermore, they are even not linked to the *ex ante* evaluation of transport projects and policies. This also includes transport infrastructure plans – plans that are potentially relevant from the perspective of intergeneration sustainability. In my opinion this is potentially a serious problem. I think it would be better to explicitly check long-term plans, including infrastructure plans, for robustness: would we still have decided positively, under certain sets of plausible assumptions, with respect to the availability and price of fossil fuels, and the question of climate change (policies)? Insights into such robustness are first of all of interest from a general economic perspective (what are 'best' policies from a broad welfare perspective?), but also from the perspective of intergenerational justice. In addition, in the process of the selection of choice options for problems and challenges as generally defined, long-term implications for energy use and CO_2 emissions hardly play a role.

What Are All the Important Pros and Cons of the Choice Options?

As far as energy is concerned, probably the most important issue is that the problem of the depletion of fossil fuels is not recognized at all in the *ex ante* evaluation of choice options. To the best of my knowledge, I am not aware of CBAs for transport infrastructure (and non-infrastructure) projects that explicitly evaluate choice options from the perspective of the depletion of fossil fuels, and climate change (strategies). In addition, the potential value of infrastructure over more than a few decades is generally ignored. At best the 'rest value' of infrastructure after the time horizon of a CBA is roughly estimated. Furthermore, it is debatable if evaluation criteria such as climate change and the depletion of fossil fuels (and other natural resources) should anyway be traded-off or optimized – some have argued that the precautionary principle is the better choice (see, e.g. Gardiner, 2006).

Who Are the Winners and Losers – can Losers be Compensated, and will they be Compensated? Does Closed Partiality Occur? Are 'Irreplaceable Things' Involved or Not?

Because of the focus of this chapter, we only discuss these questions from the intergenerational perspective. Future generations might be better or worse off depending on the choices the current generation makes with respect to strategic choices for the transport system. As far as infrastructure is concerned, the intergenerational dimension mainly relates to the people that could potentially use the infrastructure in the future, to those who benefit from the use of others (e.g. consumers that can buy cheaper goods thanks to goods transport or shops visited by customers). Consequently, generally it concerns future generations living in the same region or country. As far as energy use and CO_2 emissions are concerned, the position of future generations living elsewhere, all over the world, is also at stake. This implies that because of these implications, and the lack of attention paid to energy use (and to a lesser extent CO_2 emissions), as addressed above, the risk of closed partiality is very large.

Fossil fuels and other raw materials can to some extent be considered as 'irreplaceable things'. However, some raw materials might be replaceable, and even fossil fuels might to some extent be replaced by non-fossil energy, such as wind and solar energy. Note that, as already stated above, it is important to realize that oil is not only used for energy, but is also a raw material for many other products, such as plastics. In addition, climate change induces changes that are more or less irreversible; for example, species can become extinct, in certain areas or at the global level, and ecosystems can become ruined. If raw materials and fossil fuels are to some extent 'irreplaceable things', and if climate change has effects on irreplaceable things, such as nature, it is questionable if discounting and trade-offs are valid from an ethical perspective.

As far as fossil fuels, raw materials and climate change effects are 'replaceable', an important question is: can these future generations be compensated? One could argue that we leave future generations with much more knowledge on (technical) solutions for increased energy demand and decreasing oil reserves, than we inherited from generations in the past. We might also leave ICT knowledge and related infrastructure for future generations, giving them electronic substitutes for travel. This could to some extent compensate for the depletion of fossil fuels and other raw materials.

All in all, with respect to energy and climate changes, important trade-offs between the current generation and future generations could easily occur. By ignoring intergenerational justice we might violate the options for future generations to be as well off as we are.

Equity: Will the Market Find the 'Optimum' in the Case of Cap and Trade?

An often defended economic line of reasoning with respect to CO_2 and other GHG emissions is that the best thing to do is to decide upon the maximum level of emissions that are considered to be acceptable, and then trade these emissions ('cap and trade'). The maximum level should be set by politicians, and is based on a trade-off between what is desirable from an environmental perspective, and what is acceptable from an economic or societal perspective. Trading therefore should result in an efficient allocation of GHG emissions. It is theoretically best to first set the cap at the world level, and then for all sectors (all sources of GHG emissions). However, due to a lack of a powerful and democratic organization to implement such a policy, regional policies, for example at the EU level or at the level of a selection of regions (e.g. the EU, Japan, Australia, USA) are more realistic. The current European Trading System for CO_2 is based on this principle. Another much more far-reaching example of such a line of reasoning is that of a Dutch structure of three advisory councils (of the Ministry of Transport, the Ministry of the Environment and the Ministry of Economic Affairs) on the future of transport and climate (Raad voor Verkeer en Waterstaat et al., 2008). It has a long time horizon (2050), focuses on long-term EU reduction targets, and covers the use of all means of transport. Note that cap-and-trade systems can be dynamic: in the future new caps can be defined. Note also that the price for CO_2 highly depends on demand and supply (the cap).

Would such a system be fair? In many cases it can be, but not necessarily in all cases. The main reason for considering such a system unfair is that an increased supply of options to consume fossil fuels and emit CO_2 can result in high(er) prices, resulting in perhaps unacceptably poor levels of equity. Let me give an extreme example: a trip into space. At the time of writing this book (2010) the first commercial trips to travel into space have been made. Such trips are extremely expensive, and involve an extremely high consumption of fossil fuels. Let us assume that the rich people in the world would greatly enjoy such trips, and that many of them are prepared to pay the high costs – even including the higher energy costs, due to a cap-and-trade system. Let us also assume that, as a result, the price for CO_2 will double. Is this fair? A lot of mainstream economists may answer this question positively: this is the result of the free market. If we do not like the outcomes, income policies are to be preferred. This answer is based on (a specific form of) utilitarianism, ignoring the difficulties (impossibilities) for world-wide (or even cross-country) income policies.

However, egalitarian theories, such as Rawls' theory of justice, would argue that the 20 percent or so of people who are worse off, lose significantly from the offer of the space trips: they are much worse off because they have to pay much more for energy related primary needs, such as heating and electricity and basic transport (maybe resulting in increased levels of social exclusion – see Chapter 4). Mainstream CBA evaluation frameworks would not cover such considerations of equity. What mainstream economies could include, is the so-called external costs of the decisions of people with expensive (or better: energy intensive) tastes: their choices (in this case for space travel) result in increases in costs for others, increases to be considered as external costs that can be included in the equation.

To conclude, I think it is advisable to at least consider multiple theories of justice in order to come to a moral judgement of options for supply under cap-and-trade systems.

The Importance of Discounting

As explained in Chapter 4 and Section 5.3, in CBA future benefits and costs are discounted to express them in the currency of a base year. In addition, a risk premium is often added to the discount rate to express the negative valuation of risk. Discount rates are generally between 3 and 5 percent (in real terms, after correction for inflation), risk premiums in the order of magnitude of 2–3 percent.

Before discussing the importance of discounting and discount rates, I first give an overview of the reasons to discount at all:

1. *Markets and tastes*: People now value one unit of a currency higher than the same unit in a future year, even after correction for inflation. This is also expressed in interest rates in money markets. For economists, this often is the most important – if not the only – reason to discount. But there are more reasons, as explained by Broome (2008).

2. *Diminishing returns*: Economists often assume an increase in per capita income for the future. The added value of additional income decreases if income increases ('diminishing returns'). In other words: the more goods a person already has, the less valuable are further goods. It is therefore logical to discount if one assumes in the future per capita incomes will increase: future income increases add less to future welfare.

3. *Prioritarianism: an ethical reason*: According to an ethical theory called 'prioritarianism' a benefit that comes to a rich person should be assigned less social value than the same benefit would have if it had come to a poor person (see e.g. Sunstein, 2005). Prioritarianism is an egalitarian theory (see Chapter 3). Note that this theory contradicts utilitarianism in that the latter concludes a benefit has the same value no matter who receives it. If we expect people in the future to be richer than the current generation, this could be a reason for discounting, according to prioritarianism. Note that this reason is highly related to the previous reason of diminishing returns. The main difference is the theoretical underpinning of the same conclusion, that if in the future people are richer, discounting makes sense.

Nevertheless, discounting is criticized because of underestimating the importance of future generations (e.g. Bromley, 1989; Gardiner, 2006; Koopmans, 2010; Pearce, 2007; Portney and Weynant, 1999). Similarly, the position of Rawls on intergenerational justice (see above) also leads to important criticisms of discounting: we probably would not want our ancestors to have discounted our interests using the discount rates we generally use in CBAs.

Table 5.4a   The importance of discounting: the correction factor for
*   future currency*

Year	Discount rate (%)									
	1	2	3	4	5	6	7	8	9	10
1	0.9901	0.9804	0.9709	0.9615	0.9524	0.9434	0.9346	0.9259	0.9174	0.9091
2	0.9803	0.9612	0.9426	0.9246	0.9070	0.8900	0.8734	0.8573	0.8417	0.8264
3	0.9706	0.9423	0.9151	0.8890	0.8638	0.8396	0.8163	0.7938	0.7722	0.7513
4	0.9610	0.9238	0.8885	0.8548	0.8227	0.7921	0.7629	0.7350	0.7084	0.6830
5	0.9515	0.9057	0.8626	0.8219	0.7835	0.7473	0.7130	0.6806	0.6499	0.6209
6	0.9420	0.8880	0.8375	0.7903	0.7462	0.7050	0.6663	0.6302	0.5963	0.5645
7	0.9327	0.8706	0.8131	0.7599	0.7107	0.6651	0.6227	0.5835	0.5470	0.5132
8	0.9235	0.8535	0.7894	0.7307	0.6768	0.6274	0.5820	0.5403	0.5019	0.4665
9	0.9143	0.8368	0.7664	0.7026	0.6446	0.5919	0.5439	0.5002	0.4604	0.4241
10	0.9053	0.8203	0.7441	0.6756	0.6139	0.5584	0.5083	0.4632	0.4224	0.3855
15	0.8613	0.7430	0.6419	0.5553	0.4810	0.4173	0.3624	0.3152	0.2745	0.2394
20	0.8195	0.6730	0.5537	0.4564	0.3769	0.3118	0.2584	0.2145	0.1784	0.1486
25	0.7798	0.6095	0.4776	0.3751	0.2953	0.2330	0.1842	0.1460	0.1160	0.0923
30	0.7419	0.5521	0.4120	0.3083	0.2314	0.1741	0.1314	0.0994	0.0754	0.0573
40	0.6717	0.4529	0.3066	0.2083	0.1420	0.0972	0.0668	0.0460	0.0318	0.0221
50	0.6080	0.3715	0.2281	0.1407	0.0872	0.0543	0.0339	0.0213	0.0134	0.0085
60	0.5504	0.3048	0.1697	0.0951	0.0535	0.0303	0.0173	0.0099	0.0057	0.0033
70	0.4983	0.2500	0.1263	0.0642	0.0329	0.0169	0.0088	0.0046	0.0024	0.0013
80	0.4511	0.2051	0.0940	0.0434	0.0202	0.0095	0.0045	0.0021	0.0010	0.0005
90	0.4084	0.1683	0.0699	0.0293	0.0124	0.0053	0.0023	0.0010	0.0004	0.0002
100	0.3697	0.1380	0.0520	0.0198	0.0076	0.0029	0.0012	0.0005	0.0002	0.0001

This section now continues discussing the importance of discount rates. Tables 5.4a and 5.4b show the importance of setting the discount rates. Table 5.4a shows the factor by which one unit of a currency in a future year should be multiplied to value it in terms of the base year. Table 5.4b is the inverse of Table 5.4a, and shows how many units of currency are needed in a future year to have an equal value to one unit in the base year.

Tables 5.4a and 5.4b show the importance of discounting and setting the discount rate. Table 5.4a shows that even a relatively low discount rate of 4 percent makes a euro or dollar after 30 years – a common period to include in CBAs – worth about only 30 percent of a euro or dollar now. A discount rate of 7 percent would reduce its value to about 13 percent and a discount rate of 10 percent to about 6 percent. After a period of 100 years even the moderate discount rate of 5 percent reduces the value of one unit of a currency to only 0.8 percent.

To put it the other way around, Table 5.4b is the inverse of Table 5.4a. It shows that assuming a discount rate of 10 percent, it takes 13 781 units of a currency in 100 years to be worth as much as one unit now.

Table 5.4b   *The importance of discounting: units of currency that are needed*
in a future year to have an equal value to one unit in the base year

Year	Discount rate (%)									
	1	2	3	4	5	6	7	8	9	10
1	1.01	1.02	1.03	1.04	1.05	1.06	1.07	1.08	1.09	1.10
2	1.02	1.04	1.06	1.08	1.10	1.12	1.14	1.17	1.19	1.21
3	1.03	1.06	1.09	1.12	1.16	1.19	1.23	1.26	1.30	1.33
4	1.04	1.08	1.13	1.17	1.22	1.26	1.31	1.36	1.41	1.46
5	1.05	1.10	1.16	1.22	1.28	1.34	1.40	1.47	1.54	1.61
6	1.06	1.13	1.19	1.27	1.34	1.42	1.50	1.59	1.68	1.77
7	1.07	1.15	1.23	1.32	1.41	1.50	1.61	1.71	1.83	1.95
8	1.08	1.17	1.27	1.37	1.48	1.59	1.72	1.85	1.99	2.14
9	1.09	1.20	1.30	1.42	1.55	1.69	1.84	2.00	2.17	2.36
10	1.10	1.22	1.34	1.48	1.63	1.79	1.97	2.16	2.37	2.59
15	1.16	1.35	1.56	1.80	2.08	2.40	2.76	3.17	3.64	4.18
20	1.22	1.49	1.81	2.19	2.65	3.21	3.87	4.66	5.60	6.73
25	1.28	1.64	2.09	2.67	3.39	4.29	5.43	6.85	8.62	10.83
30	1.35	1.81	2.43	3.24	4.32	5.74	7.61	10.06	13.27	17.45
40	1.49	2.21	3.26	4.80	7.04	10.29	14.97	21.72	31.41	45.26
50	1.64	2.69	4.38	7.11	11.47	18.42	29.46	46.90	74.36	117.39
60	1.82	3.28	5.89	10.52	18.68	32.99	57.95	101.26	176.03	304.48
70	2.01	4.00	7.92	15.57	30.43	59.08	113.99	218.61	416.73	789.75
80	2.22	4.88	10.64	23.05	49.56	105.80	224.23	471.95	986.55	2048.40
90	2.45	5.94	14.30	34.12	80.73	189.46	441.10	1018.92	2335.53	5313.02
100	2.70	7.24	19.22	50.50	131.50	339.30	867.72	2199.76	5529.04	13780.61

The main lessons to be learned from the discussion of discounting are, firstly, that even low to moderate discount rates reduce the value of long-term gains to very small proportions. Secondly, small differences in discount rates, for example 6 percent versus 4 percent makes huge differences in the very long term (e.g. 100 years). In the case of 6 percent versus 4 percent the difference is a factor of 7. These two lessons show the importance of discounting for valuing long-term effects (both costs and benefits). Discounting greatly reduces the value for future generations, even in the case of low discount rates. Doing so conflicts with multiple ethical theories, including utilitarianism and deontology (and therefore the Kantian tradition). In addition, there is a good argument for discounting benefits, but not in discounting harm (Birnbacher, 2006; Brown, n.d.). Note that the reason for discounting generally is a pragmatic one, not a moral one (Birnbacher, 2006).

This discussion is not a plea to stop discounting. I think certainly as far as discounting preferences from a consumers' perspective are concerned, there is a very strong case for it. But what to do with the resulting ignorance of the interests of future generations? One way to deal with it is to not discount in the case of, for example, climate change or the value of human lives. Another way is to assume an increase of the value, the price tag, to be put on, for example, GHG emissions, the value of a human life, or nature. Note that increasing such values using a higher interest rate than the discount rate increases future benefits to infinity, assuming an unlimited time horizon. In my opinion it is defendable to increase the values of at least some items relevant from an intergeneration perspective, for example by the same percentage as the discount rate, not discount them, or apply lower discount rates than usual. An economic reason for increasing[6] discount rates is that the environment is considered to be a 'luxury good': the more people earn, the more they are willing to pay for quality aspects, including a better environment (Baumol and Oates, 1988). In addition, as incomes increase, the quality of the environment often decreases, which could induce an additional price increase (Hoel and Sterner, 2007; Sterner and Persson, 2008). A very clear difference between current practice and using lower discount rates that would result, is that using lower discount rates would make GHG emissions count much more than nowadays is the case in CBAs. In addition, I think not discounting or increasing values is more relevant for GHG emissions and the depletion of fossil fuels and raw materials (as far as they can be considered as 'irreplaceable things') than for infrastructure. The value of infrastructure, to a large extent, is comparable with the value of many consumer goods and services, and could therefore be discounted, at least if the quality of infrastructure exceeds the certain minimum level that is needed from a sufficientarian point of view (see above).

5.7 CONCLUSIONS

The most important conclusions of this chapter are summarized below.

Transport is probably the sector with the highest environmental pressure. Not all of the impacts of transport on the environment are relevant from an intergenerational perspective.

The most important subjects for discussion from an intergenerational perspective are probably infrastructure, the use of fossil fuels and other non-renewable resources, and climate change.

Infrastructure (roads, railways, ports, airports) often lasts more than 100 years, and is extremely expensive to build, making intergenerational considerations very important. In addition, decision making and building infrastructure takes a long period of time, while infrastructure has a long-lasting impact on land use.

Ethical aspects of transport are at least: (1) that it is related to the large impact of the public sector; (2) that it is relevant for basic values, at least the freedom to move; (3) that adequate transport infrastructure is of crucial importance for societies, both from an economic perspective as well as from the wider societal perspective; (4) that transport infrastructure is very expensive; (5) that transport infrastructure lasts for a very long time; (6) that transport, more than any other dominant sector, relies heavily on fossil fuels, mainly oil; and (7) that building transport infrastructure often has long-term negative implications for communities and nature.

Energy use and CO_2 emissions are highly related, and are relevant from an intergenerational perspective. Climate change causes irreversible effects. The transport sector, probably more than any other large sector, relies heavily on fossil energy. Fossil fuels are non-renewable energy resources (at least not in the time frame of, say, 100 or 1000 years). Transport, probably more than any other category of consumption, allows us to consume energy and emit GHGs in large quantities over a short period of time – flying being the most extreme option.

Intergenerational justice does exist, though some philosophers argue otherwise.

Rawls thinks intergenerational justice exists when parties that make choices make them based on principles they would want earlier generations to have adopted. The perspective of Rawls on intergenerational justice is based on the contractarian tradition in political philosophy. The ideas of Rawls and Sen can lead to other conclusions than those of utilitarian philosophers.

Setting saving rates for non-renewable resources, including fossil fuels, is very difficult, for many reasons. Firstly it is questionable if it is reserves that matter, or opportunities for activities that result from the use of non-renewable resources, introducing the relevance of alternatives. Secondly, changes in population size could matter. Thirdly, savings rates probably do not apply to non-tradable resources such as the natural environment. Fourthly, distributional aspects matter. Fifthly, we do not know what future generations will need, appreciate, value, etc. Wolf (2003) provides an answer to the question of savings rates: institutions are humanly sustainable if, and only if, their operation does not leave future generations worse equipped to meet their needs than members of the present generation are to meet their own needs. Making the implications of the answer explicit is difficult.

The principle of cap and trade can lead to the optimal allocation of politically chosen maximum levels of GHG emissions from a utilitarian perspective. However, supply of GHG-emissions-intensive activities can be unfair from an egalitarian perspective, because allowing such activities makes the less advantaged worse off.

An important question is: how to deal with the estimation of the future value of infrastructure and discounting? A possible solution might be to do what-if analyses. Examples could include: what if future generations were to value the infrastructure that we decide upon today equally to the current generation (in absolute or relative [to income] terms, per person or in total)? What if the value were to increase according to the discount rate as assumed?

As a first point of departure, for the quality of infrastructure to be left for future generations is the 'constant level of maintenance' assumption. The quantity of infrastructure to be left for future generations is very difficult to assess; firstly because we are uncertain about future population size, and secondly, because we do not know what the transport needs of future generations might be. Thirdly, incomes of future generations matter, and fourthly, the availability of technology matters.

In the *ex ante* assessment of transport policy options, including infrastructure, the issue of non-renewable resources (including the use of fossil fuels) is poorly addressed. This concerns the attention that is paid to the subject in itself (as a problem to be reduced), the selection of alternatives for a policy problem or challenge, and the estimation of pros and cons of options. Nevertheless, long-term impacts can be very relevant from the perspective of intergenerational justice.

Even low or moderate discount rates reduce the value of long-term gains to very small proportions. Small differences in discount rates, for example 6 percent versus 4 percent, make huge differences in the very long term (e.g. 100 years). To better include intergenerational justice, an option could be to not discount some outcomes of interest, or to increase their value, for example as strongly as the discount rate.

6. Safety: indicators, pricing humans and democracy

6.1 INTRODUCTION

Questions related to safety and ethics include:

- Is it ethically OK to express the value of a human life in monetary terms?
- Is it relevant for the *ex ante* evaluation of policy options if people stay at home because they think the transport system is not safe enough?
- Is the distribution of safety risks over population groups relevant? If so, why, and how to deal with it?
- Is the life of a victim more valuable than that of the offender?
- What to value: the willingness to pay for risk reductions, or changes in Quality Adjusted Life Years?

Transport policy making largely relates to accessibility, the environment and safety. Nowadays, almost all countries have safety related policies. Common ingredients of such policies include speed limits that vary by road category, regulations for drinking (maximum alcohol content in the blood), wearing helmets on motorized two wheelers, and safety related design criteria (as often expressed in manuals) for road and rail infrastructure.

In the *ex ante* evaluation of transport policies safety effects are generally included. Because of the evaluative perspective of this book (see Chapter 1), this chapter also primarily deals with the ethics of safety from an evaluation perspective. However, the relationships between transport safety and ethics are more wide ranging. Fahlquist (2009) discusses the ethics of road safety using the concepts of criminalization, paternalism, privacy, justice and responsibility. For example, the use of vehicles (e.g. road vehicles, flying aircraft) also includes ethical aspects. Is speeding or drink driving a criminal act, and why (not)? The ethics of the use of vehicles is not included in this chapter. For a discussion of this subject, and contrary to most other subjects discussed in this chapter, virtue theory is very helpful.

According to the *Stanford Encyclopedia of Philosophy* (n.d.), 'virtue ethics is currently one of three major approaches in normative ethics. It may, initially, be identified as the one that emphasizes the virtues or moral character'. This means it is not the consequences that matter (as in case of consequentialism) or the duties or rules (as in case of deontology). In addition, design is not explicitly included in this chapter. To some extent, the ethics of design overlap with the ethics of evaluation; for example, the design of maximum speeds on different road classes is often based on evaluations of the pros and cons of different speed limits. However, some design aspects do not overlap explicitly with the evaluation perspective as discussed in this chapter, examples being the design of vehicles as far as safety aspects are included, the design of safety aspects of infrastructure, and the design of education programmes for children in schools.

In line with choices for demarcation made in Chapters 4 (social exclusion as the main focus in discussing the ethics of accessibility) and 5 (intergenerational justice of environmental impacts), this chapter also has a specific focus, and does not aim to discuss all ethics of transport safety from an evaluative perspective. This chapter discusses the (ethical aspects of) use of safety indicators for evaluation purposes, the question of whether or not a price tag should be used to value fatalities and injuries – and if so, which price tags and democracy of decision making with respect to safety.

This chapter mainly focuses on road traffic because world-wide road traffic accounts for by far the highest number of fatalities in absolute terms, and even more so on a per kilometre basis.

Section 6.2 first gives an overview of safety, followed by Section 6.3 which discusses safety indicators. Section 6.4 discusses the moral dimensions of pricing human lives and risks. Section 6.5 elaborates on democratic issues of safety. Section 6.6 applies the checklist of Section 3.6 to safety issues. Section 6.7 finally summarizes the main conclusions.

6.2   SAFETY: A BRIEF OVERVIEW[1]

The general awareness of the negative safety impacts of transport mainly originates from the US. In the 1950s, the rapidly increasing numbers of road fatalities raised serious concerns. Partly initiated by activists such as Ralph Nader, regulations for the crash-worthiness of road vehicles were introduced in the USA and other western countries. Mainly due to 'safer vehicles' (seat belts, energy-absorbing zones, airbags, etc.), 'safer infrastructure', the introduction of limits for alcohol levels in the blood while driving, and better education, the transport system got safer. In addition,

Table 6.1   Road fatalities for selected EU countries, 1970–2006

	Belgium	Germany	France	Italy
1970	2950	21332	16448	11004
1980	2396	15050	13672	9220
1990	1976	11046	11215	7137
2000	1470	7503	8079	6410
2006	1069	5091	4709	5669

Source: EU (2008).

the health care system improved, which also contributed to a decrease in fatalities. As a result, the number of fatalities in many western countries decreased from the 1970s on, despite the increase in vehicle and person kilometres travelled.

To express safety levels, indicators that are often used include numbers of fatalities in total, per distance travelled, or per capita. Comparable indicators for (seriously) injured people are also used.

Table 6.1 shows the trend of improved safety levels using the number of road fatalities in selected EU countries between 1970 and 2006. Note, however, that in many developing regions and countries the number of fatalities is because mobility increases at a much faster rate than is compensated for by the decrease in accident risks (as was the case in many western regions and countries until the late 1960s or early 1970s).

6.3   TRANSPORT SAFETY INDICATORS

In this section I first discuss safety indicators. Next, I discuss the relevance of these indicators from an ethical perspective. The aim of the section is to explain that the choice of safety indicators often made for *ex ante* evaluations of transport policy options, could lead to overlooking ethically relevant aspects of these policy options.

Common Safety Indicators

As explained above, the most often used indicator to express safety is the number of fatalities, either in total (e.g. for a country) or per capita or travel indicator, followed by comparable indicators for numbers of injuries. In the case of past developments, the numbers are generally based on registered accidents. Depending on the quality of the registration system, under-registration might occur. For *ex ante* evaluations, forecasts are made for future developments of such indicators. The most common way to forecast such indicators is by multiplying the kilometres travelled (by mode) and expected accident risks per road class. Accident risks are expressed as the risk of getting killed in a road accident per (billion) kilometres or mile(s) per travel mode per road class. Because in most countries the trend in these numbers is decreasing (travelling gets less risky), assumptions (in some cases based on extrapolations) about future changes in these risks are made.

For evaluation purposes, especially in the case of CBAs, it is common to express safety levels in monetary terms. Fatalities are especially valued, but in some cases also injuries. For an ethical discussion on pricing fatalities and injuries, see the next section.

One can debate if these indicators express safety well enough. At least two categories of indicators seem to be missing: perceived safety and its impacts, including the stress of perceived safety and avoidance costs.

Perceived Safety

Objective safety and perceived safety do not always match. Traffic situations can be unsafe, but people do not perceive them as such, or objective numbers show that risk levels are low, but people might feel unsafe. Research has shown that the correlation between objective and subjective safety is often poor, not only in the area of road safety (Vlakveld et al., 2008), but also elsewhere in society (Nilsen et al., 2004). Does this matter? From a CBA (utilitarian) perspective the answer could be that it matters if people have a willingness to pay (WTP) for an increase in perceived safety *even if objective safety does not change equally*. One can seriously debate this. People might be prepared to pay for increased safety, but only if objective safety increases. If they think a traffic situation gets safer, but then they know it does not, one can seriously doubt if they still have a WTP for an increase in perceived safety. In fact, one can doubt if perceived safety will increase at all if people know the real safety levels. A comparison can be made with medicine. People might buy drugs because they think they work, but if they were to be convinced they do not have any effect, the WTP probably is zero.

What is probably more relevant is the stress that is caused by perceived (low) safety levels. Even if no accidents happen, the stress and worries that people experience because of low perceived safety levels have a negative impact on human beings. To the best of my knowledge, these impacts (whether expressed in monetary terms or not) are not explicitly included in *ex ante* evaluations of traffic safety. At best, they are implicitly included in questionnaire based safety research. For example, if people are asked for their WTP for increased safety, the answer could also include issues of worries and stress.

Avoidance Costs

Another category of indicators that is generally ignored in *ex ante* evaluations is avoidance costs. Avoidance costs are costs made to improve safety, and can be split into several categories:

- Infrastructure related costs
- Vehicle related costs
- Costs related to the health system
- Costs related to changes in human behaviour.

Infrastructure related costs include costs to reduce the numbers or severity of accidents, crash barriers being an example. These costs are generally included in the costs of infrastructure, and so in *ex ante* evaluations.

Vehicle related costs are costs to reduce the chance of an accident ('active safety', such as the costs of better braking systems and lane warning departure systems) and costs to reduce the severity once an accident happens ('passive safety', such as the costs of crash zones and airbags). These costs are 'fixed costs' – they do not depend on distance driven.[2] If such costs come at the cost of decreased fuel efficiency (e.g. heavier cars use more fuel) or higher other variable costs (e.g. maintenance costs) these costs are included in the variable costs of vehicles.

Characteristics of the health system have an impact on numbers of fatalities and (seriously) injured; for example, if a trauma helicopter is at the scene shortly after a serious accident, a person may survive, while the quality of the medical treatment of injured persons also matters. Such costs are often allocated to the (insurance companies of) people responsible for accidents, and included in accident related costs.

The fourth category of avoidance costs is the costs of changes in human behaviour because of (perceived) safety. People can adapt their travel behaviour because of perceived low safety levels: they may change mode, route or destinations, and hence kilometres travelled and trip frequencies. For example, older persons may prefer to stay at home because they think travelling is too risky. Or a person may prefer to cycle, but travels by car because of a perceived low safety level of cycling. A specific change in behaviour, not related directly to the categories as presented above, is that parents may not allow their children to travel to school independently because of (perceived) risk, and so bring their children to school themselves. In that case, the change does not relate to the travel behaviour of the child but to that of the parent. Or parents may want their children to use the school bus instead of cycling to school.

Such adaptations come at a cost. A person that wishes to travel, but stays at home because of a low perceived safety level, is worse off than when in a (perceived) safer situation that does not stop her from travelling. In addition, parents that bring children to school may value negatively the loss of time, and maybe the adaptation in their own activity patterns, while the school bus and car are more expensive than the alternative of cycling. Furthermore, if adaptations result in a decrease in the use of slow modes, there are losses related to health – for example, the health benefits of cycling are substantial. In a Norwegian study on the costs and benefits of cycling infrastructure in cities, these benefits counted for more than half (55–75 percent) of all benefits of cycling (Saelensminde, 2004).

Note that behavioural changes can also result from perceived high levels of safety; for example, a person driving a car with ABS or Adaptive Cruise Control (ACC) could drive faster, because of a high level of perceived safety. Such 'negative avoidance costs' (benefits) are not further discussed in this book.

Avoidance costs, even behaviour related avoidance costs, can be estimated, at least theoretically. The idea is that safety related costs play a role in mode choice or route choice models, and may also affect the number of trips made and the destination of trips. An example of safety as a road attribute in a route choice model is given in De Blaeij (2003). However, the usual way of dealing with accident risks is to incorporate them in mode specific constants and route specific constants, which means that safety aspects remain implicit. Avoidance costs are particularly relevant from an ethical perspective because 'freedom of movement' can be at stake – see below.

The Links between Safety Indicators

Figure 6.1 conceptualizes how categories of safety indicators are related. This diagram shows that objective safety, subjective safety and non-behaviour related avoidance costs are directly influenced by the transport system. The transport system includes the hardware (infrastructure), vehicles, orgware (such as timetables of trains and buses), and the way people use the system. The way people use the system relates, for example, to the impact of choices of individual car drivers on congestion levels and, as a result, on travel times. Subjective safety has an impact on behaviour related avoidance costs: people adapt their behaviour based on *perceived* safety levels. Objective safety can have an impact on perceived safety,

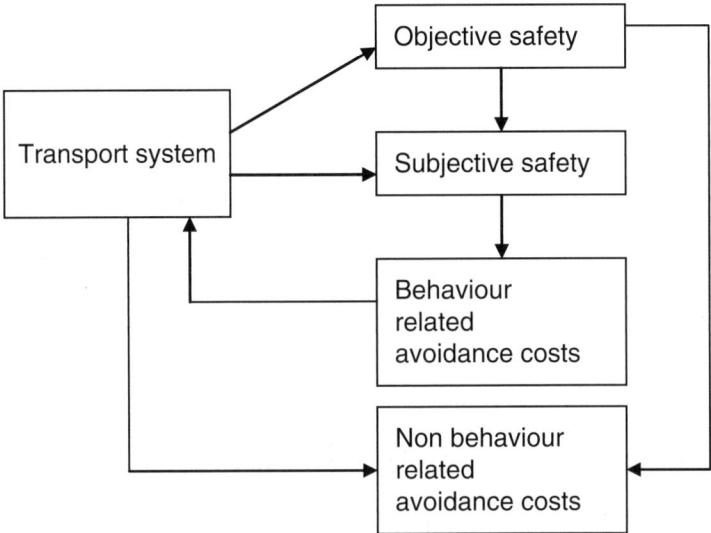

Figure 6.1   Relationships between safety indicators

but the correlation between them is not very strong, as explained above. Adaptations in behaviour resulting from perceived safety can have an impact on the transport system. If people travel less or change modes because of perceived safety, this can have an impact on the use of vehicles, infrastructure, congestion levels, etc. The avoidance costs that are non behaviour related result from characteristics of both the transport system, and objective safety levels; for example, the length of crash barriers relates to the length of the motorway network, and the total costs in a country of making road vehicles safer, relates to the number of road vehicles. Costs allowed for trauma helicopters (health system related avoidance costs) probably to some extent depend on objective safety levels. An important conclusion from Figure 6.1 is that ignoring avoidance costs not only leads to errors in CBA, but could also result in not fully understanding their relevance for travel behaviour, and their impact on travel behaviour on the transport system, and next on other safety indicators.

The Link with Ethics

An important question from the perspective of this book is: what is the relevance of this from an ethical perspective? Firstly, I would argue that if people adapt their travel behaviour, and in some cases even their activity behaviour (as in the example of the older person that stays at home because of a low perceived safety level), the freedom to move is at stake, as well as the freedom to participate in activities, as discussed in Chapter 4 on social exclusion. The indicators that are generally chosen to evaluate transport policy options do not include such changes in behaviour, and certainly not the 'freedom to move' impacts.

Secondly, it is very likely that the pros and cons of policy options related to the transport system are not equally distributed over groups of the population, and this distribution is relevant from an ethical perspective – see Chapter 3. Trade-offs can exist between car users and others (e.g. children and the elderly that do not drive). Such trade-offs exist in both directions. It is the non-car user who benefits from restrictions with respect to car use, at the cost of car users. In the case of giving priority to car users, they benefit, at the cost of non-car users. How distribution related impacts should be evaluated depends on the ethical perspective. CBA and a related utilitarian perspective would allow for a straightforward calculation of utilities. However, egalitarian theories would specifically be interested in distribution effects. A focus on, for example, the 20 percent of people who are 'worst off' in the transport system, probably would result in a shift to policies that favour the safety of the non-car user. The perspective of strong sufficientarianism (see Section 4.6) could even imply that absolute priority should be given to improve safety, if safety levels are below the minimum level. A problem then exists in that a sufficientarianism approach relates to persons, not to (segments of) infrastructure or vehicles, whereas safety policies often do not focus on individuals, exceptions being traffic education, driving lessons, and obligations like wearing helmets and not drinking. Safety policies often try to make infrastructure or vehicles safer. In such cases, impacts are very difficult to translate to individuals, and overall individual safety levels are very difficult to estimate. This is because they need travel data on an individual basis, including all trips (and all modes). The sufficientarianism approach implies 'personalizing' safety, and therefore bringing the approach into practice is not at all straightforward – needs to forge links between people and safety relevant policy options. To conclude, in *ex ante* evaluations of safety impacts of policy options, the indicator choice can easily lead to overlooking such ethically relevant impacts on distribution.

Conclusions on Indicators

To conclude: numbers of fatalities and injured persons (and their expression in monetary terms) are very important, but do not give a complete picture of safety indicators that are relevant for *ex ante* evaluations. In addition to these indicators, adaptations of travel and activity behaviour matter, and are linked to the value of the freedom to move and participate in activities.

In addition, ethical dimensions are relevant, firstly in the case of adaptations of behaviour, secondly because of distributions of the pros and cons of safety relevant policy options, and thirdly because of pricing safety levels – pricing is the subject of the next section.

6.4   PRICING HUMAN LIFE

Introduction

This section discusses the following questions:

1. Is it morally OK to express fatalities in monetary terms at all?
2. What are the pros and cons of doing so in the case of *ex ante* evaluations?
3. Which methods are available to express human lives in monetary terms, and what are their pros and cons?
4. How to include future changes in safety, and is discounting on moral grounds OK?

Is Pricing Human Lives OK?

In the community of persons being involved in *ex ante* evaluations of transport projects and policies, the subject of pricing human lives is one of the most controversial. I have been involved in many discussions about this subject. Some persons intuitively think it is immoral to price human beings, while others strongly support doing this. I have to disappoint beforehand those who expect a clear and undisputable answer to the question in the heading of this paragraph: there is no clear answer. The answer depends on the theory one uses (see Chapter 3). The two most extreme positions probably follow from the Kantian perspective and the utilitarian perspective. I will firstly discuss these two perspectives, followed by the perspective of contractarianism.

Deontology – the Kantian perspective (rule based ethics)
In the category of rule based ethics, here I only discuss the Kantian perspective, because of its 'extreme' position. A Kantian perspective could easily lead to the conclusion that pricing the value of a human life is immoral. People should never be considered as a means to something else. Less safety cannot be compensated by, for example, shorter travel

times or lower emission levels. From a Kantian perspective, safety then is prioritized over travel times or noise levels. Even the suggestion that such trade-offs can be made, thus pricing human lives, can be considered as immoral. A potential problem with the Kantian perspective is that there are no clearly defined people who will lose their lives – *ex ante* evaluations of transport projects and policies relate to *statistical* lives, it is all about probabilities, not individuals (see below).

The utilitarian perspective

This perspective holds that people may not necessarily price their own life or the lives of others, but they do evaluate risks; for example, a person buying a new car considers the safety level (at least the perceived level of passive safety, the crash worthiness of a car, as expressed in the Euro NCAP ratings) but also many other characteristics of a car, such as price, size, performance and emotional values. In addition, people know that driving at 120 km/h is less safe than driving at 100 km/h, but they trade-off travel time, and maybe the fun of driving against safety (and fuel costs). Thus maximizing any form of utility should include safety, and this can be done, based on the preferences of humans as consumers or – more generally – persons making choices. Some have even claimed that striving for *maximum* safety levels is unethical. An example is provided by the discussion on the Swedish 'Vision Zero' (for road traffic). One of the architects behind the vision, Claes Tingvall, stated that the requirements of the Vision are so strong that 'Whenever someone is killed or seriously injured, necessary steps must be taken to avoid a similar event' (Tingvall and Haworth, 1999; cited in Elvebakk and Steiro, 2009). This position is claimed to be naïve, overly ambitious, and even unethical (Fahlquist, 2006). Elvik (1999; cited in Fahlquist, 2006) asserts that the aim to eliminate road traffic deaths would demand such substantial resources that other areas where people's lives are at risk would suffer. Similar debate can also be found in the literature on intergenerational justice: risk reductions come at a cost. The price of risk reductions to zero can easily be too high (Davidson, 2009).

Deontology – the doctrine of double effect

Deontology recognizes the principle of the 'doctrine of double effect', according to which there is a moral difference between causing harm or evil as an unintended side-effect of an intended action or policy, and intending the harm or evil directly, either as an end or as a means to an end. From this perspective, it at least would make a difference if a fatality results from someone's immoral risky driving behaviour that deliberately endangers the life of others, or from 'normal' driving behaviour. In the case where people drive riskily, they do not intend to harm others (nor themselves) but they accept they are endangering others, examples being drunk driving and speeding. One could argue that a fatality resulting from immoral driving behaviour should not be priced, contrary to a fatality as a result of 'normal' accidents.

Contractarianism

A contractarianism perspective could hold that a person could be asked questions about which agreements she would like to make with others. Such agreements could include agreements on travel behaviour, including the use of vehicles and driving behaviour, and benefits for the traveller, but also risks to themselves and risks for other travellers. From this perspective, pricing is not really needed, but it is an option, because it could improve the process of making agreements.

The Value of a Statistical Life (VOSL)

After discussing these theories, this section now introduces a fundamental concept that is often used if safety is included in CBA: the Value of a Statistical Life (VOSL). Several people have recognized that moral objections against pricing human lives can be raised. In medicine and medical ethics, traditionally many people have objected to doing so (Elvik, 2002). In economics and in the transport and safety community this is done much more often, despite the critics. An often used 'solution' to (potential) moral critics is not to directly price lives, but to price what is called a 'statistical life'. The result is the indicator VOSL (also abbreviated in the literature as VSL). This indicator is an 'anonymous indicator' that is used to calculate 'statistically' how many people might lose their lives in traffic in a future year under certain given circumstances. In fact, a value is put on risk, and this risk is multiplied by traffic or travel volumes. Proponents argue that people may not be able to say how much their life is worth, but they are able to say how much they are prepared to pay for lower risks. Consequently, if we know the WTP for lower risks, we have an indication for the VOSL. Examples of choices that people make, that give an indication of the WTP for lower risks, are the examples of buying a new car or driving speed as introduced above. This implies that the term VOSL is actually somewhat misleading. Its essence is that it represents the valuation of people exposed to travel risks in terms of an amount of dollars (or other currency) per unit of risk reduction. Consider the case of a group of travellers who are prepared to pay $200 per year to drive in a safer car so that the risk of a fatal accident is reduced by 1/10 000 per year. This is equivalent to saying that 10 000 travellers would be prepared to pay $2 million and that this would reduce the risk for these 10 000 travellers by

1/10 000 each. The expected number of lives saved would then be equal to 1. A convenient way to represent the willingness to pay for this group is to say that its collective value of a statistical life is equal to $2 million. Hence the use of the VOSL concept is nothing more than a handy way to represent consumers' preferences on risk reductions. When the use of the term gives the impression that human lives are valued, this is a regrettable misunderstanding, which could easily be avoided by abolishing the concept of VOSL and replacing it with the willingness to pay for risk reductions. Consider for example the case that a safety enhancing investment is proposed for the roads used by these drivers, which would lead to an identical reduction in risks of 1/10 000 per year. Then what is done in CBA is simply to adopt the willingness to pay in the private domain to make cars marginally safer, and apply the same figure in the context of a public decision to make roads marginally safer. Hence, CBA of safety enhancing measures can be carried out in terms of willingness to pay for marginal risk reductions.

However, applying the concept is not completely straightforward. The three first reasons relate to the notion of risk.[3] The first is that the concept of the VOSL (and certainly how it is used in practice) assumes no relationship between the VOSL and risk levels. However, the level of risk can have an impact on the VOSL, because it has an impact on choices. Generally speaking, a higher risk leads to a higher monetary value of risk changes (Hammitt, 2007; Morton, 1991). The risk level therefore can cause variations in the outcomes of choices, leading to other VOSLs. In other words: the patterns of choice, and so the VOSLs, are *probability dependent*. As a result, VOSLs based on stated or revealed preferences of people may be probability dependent. Due to the increasing VOSL with risk levels, and maybe VOSL being about infinite in the case of risks nearing the value of 1, it can even be argued that the VOSL is not the same as the value of a person's life (Hammitt, 2007).

Secondly, if the VOSL is based on choices of people, it assumes 'right' perceptions of risk. One could criticize the usefulness of VOSL if it is based on misconceptions of risks of people. A problem occurs because research has shown that people are poorly able to deal with very small risks, and to translate a small risk reduction into a monetary benefit (De Blaeij, 2003; Kahneman and Knetsch, 1992; Kahneman and Tversky, 2000; Kahneman et al., 1982, 1999). VOSL based on WTP for lower risks may be primarily useful if risk levels in a particular *ex ante* evaluation match those of the cases of the stated or revealed preference research.

Thirdly, risks vary widely by nature, the distinction between voluntary and non-voluntary risks being an important one, but also one that is difficult to make. In addition, attitudes towards risk vary between individuals

(Cranor, 2009). One could debate if the expected number of fatalities (risk levels multiplied by a volume indicator, such as person miles travelled) of motorcycle drivers with a very risky driving style (speeding, overtaking at places where it is not allowed, braking late) should count equally compared to the same number of expected fatalities in the case of train travellers (see Cranor, 2009, for a discussion).

Fourthly, the VOSL generally includes the valuation of statistical lives of the people involved, but not their descendants, though there could be a good reason for doing so (see Broome, 2005). (The explanation is quite complicated and needs a lot of text to explain – doing so is beyond the scope of this book.)

Fifthly, in the case where one would argue that each person is equally important, and thus the VOSL (at least within one country) should not depend on income levels, an inconsistency can occur between the VOSL and VOT because the VOT is income dependent. This inconsistency can be solved using the 'equity value of time' (see Chapter 3).

What Are the Pros and Cons of Pricing Lives in the Case of *Ex Ante* Evaluations?

If one thinks pricing human lives is unethical, this is an extremely important reason not to do so, probably overruling all other arguments. One could even take the position that raising the question at the head of this paragraph is not OK, because it seems to suggest that the pros and cons can be compared or traded-off.

On the other hand, there may be good reasons to evaluate human lives. One reason is that people trade-off safety levels and other impacts of their choices anyway, so using prices for changes in risks (and multiplied with volume indicators resulting in fatalities) based on people's preferences, contributes to a balanced way of including peoples preferences in *ex ante* evaluations.

A second, and related, reason could be that if a CBA is carried out anyway, outcomes of interest that are not expressed in monetary terms probably have less impact on decision making. Many researchers and policy makers have the impression that decision makers, certainly in the case of a CBA, primarily look at financial indicators like benefits minus costs, the benefit-to-cost ratio, or the return on investment. If safety were not to be included, its impact on decision making could be less, compared to including safety, in monetary terms. On the other hand, if safety levels were hardly to differ between choice options, for example in alternatives for new roads, expressing them in monetary terms will hardly influence indicators, as just mentioned. In that case, a + or – to compare choice options may have more impact. But is 'more impact' necessarily 'better'? We would not like to rule out the possibility that in addition to underinvestment in traffic safety, there may also be overinvestment, which would imply that less resources are available for other welfare enhancing activities. As explained in Chapter 3, what is important in the case of *ex ante* evaluations is the quality of (research as input for) decision making. I argued that a practical rule of thumb could be that the quality of decision making is higher if the decision makers make the choice they would have made, (1) if they had had all potential choice options available, (2) if they had been fully informed and, (3) if they had been to evaluate different choice options. Unfortunately, to the best of my knowledge, no scientific research has been carried out to find out which way of including safety in *ex ante* evaluations in the area of transport leads to the highest quality of decision making. For the time being, my impression is that expressing safety in monetary terms more often increases the quality of decision making than it decreases this quality.

Which Methods are Available to Express Human Lives in Monetary Terms, and what are their Pros and Cons?

An overview of methods
The current state-of-the-art in valuing (statistical) lives is that both material and immaterial costs should be included (De Blaeij et al., 2003). Material costs include damage to vehicles, and in some cases also infrastructure, as well as the costs of medical treatment and the loss of worker's production capacity. Immaterial costs include loss of the quality of lives of the victims and the people they love (family, friends, others).

Several methods are available to express human lives in monetary terms. This is not a book on CBA or welfare economics, but on ethics. The discussion of methods, therefore, will be brief. A first distinction can be made between consumer based methods and others. In the CBA community, the impression is that consumer based preferences are generally to be preferred: who else is better able to value the importance for a consumer than the consumer herself? I will discuss related methods below. Nevertheless, is it good to realize that other methods exist. Such methods are labelled as 'costs per life saved methods' (De Blaeij, 2003). These methods mainly look at choices of policy makers in the past: one can look at the implicit VOSL that results from policy measures taken in the past. This could be done within or outside the transport system. Examples in the transport system could be safety regulations to reduce risks of car or rail accidents; examples outside the transport system could be regulations for safety standards in industry.

In the category of consumer based methods, a distinction can be made between willingness to pay (WTP) and willingness to accept (WTA) methods. For several reasons, WTP values are of more use that WTA values. One of the reasons is that WTA values that follow from questionnaires could be biased, because of strategic behaviour by respondents. In addition, WTA can more easily be non-realistic: people might (implicitly or explicitly) suggest that they have a much higher WTA than they really do when it comes to paying for risk reductions once they actually have the choice (see, e.g. Hanemann, 1991; Perman et al., 2003).

WTP methods include Revealed Choice and Revealed Preference (RC/RP) and Stated Choice and Stated Preference (SC/SP) methods. For reasons of simplicity, below I will refer to SP and RP methods. RP methods focus on what people in the real world have been shown to be willing to pay for decreased risk. One can, for example, look at the WTP for airbags that were optional in new cars. A complication is that choice options often do not only vary with respect to safety levels, but also with respect to other characteristics. A bigger car generally is not only safer, but also more comfortable. The toll roads in France are not only safer than the *Routes Nationals*, but also result in shorter travel times, and maybe a lower appreciation of scenery. SP research asks people what they would be willing to pay for a decrease in risk, for example for future additional airbags. RP methods have the advantage that it is real choices that are looked at, not choices in less reliable, hypothetical situations. On the other hand, people may have wrong perceptions on (changes in) risks when making choices, which could influence their choices. SP research has the advantage that the researcher can present (changes in) risk levels. Another advantage is that RP data often are not available. In SP research people can be asked about many hypothetical situations, even if they do not exist (yet). See for a discussion on SP and RP methods in the area of safety De Blaeij (2003) and De Blaaij et al. (2003). The VOSL measures as found in meta-analyses that review many studies are in the order of magnitude of US$3–6 million, often in prices of 1995–2000 (e.g. De Blaeij et al., 2003; Dionne and Lanoie, 2004).

A discussion of methods

Below I will discuss these methods using the theoretical contributions of Chapter 3.

A very important question with regard to value of safety is: does each fatality have an equal value, or not? If one answers this question with 'yes' the conclusion would be that it is as bad if a 90-year-old blind and deaf person dies two weeks prematurely due to high concentrations of ozone, as if a 15-year-old school child is killed in a road accident. A concept to deal with such questions is the concept of QALYs (Quality Adjusted Life Years) which has been developed to express the combination of quality and quantity of lost life years (e.g. Hammitt, 2002). It is widely used in medical economics and in environmental economics. Equation (1) presents how QALYs are calculated.

$$QALYs = \sum_{i=1}^{M} q_i T_i,$$ (1)

Equation (1) shows that total lifespan is divided into M periods that are indexed by i. The periods are defined so that only one health state is experienced in each period. The duration of period i is T_i and the 'health-related quality of life' (HRQL) associated with that period is characterized by a weight q_i (Hammitt, 2002).

The QALY concept firstly has the advantage that quantity and quality of lost life years do count. A second advantage is that it can also be used to include injuries causing permanent negative health impacts: even if the quantity of life years of an injured person remains the same, the loss of quality can be expressed.

The QALY concept is not sufficiently developed to be used over time and different countries. The indicator as such of course may be used for reasons of comparisons, but its use in decision making is generally assumed to be topic specific. Compare the USA versus the Indian health system: the QALY concept is not to be used for comparing the quality of both systems, nor for cross-country decision making (which probably does not occur anyway). Secondly, risk and risk distributions are related to QALYs: People employ no single set of assumptions to compare risk (distributions) consistently: they have no single way of comparing different distributions of quality of life over people and over times within a life.

The use of the concept of QALYs may have serious consequences if it is to be used for *ex ante* evaluations. A first consequence is that it is not without dispute to compare very young persons with others. To again (as in Chapter 3) quote Morton (1991: 112): 'For very few people would think that, for example, one should sacrifice more for the safety of a newborn baby than for that of a fifteen-year-old child'. A second consequence is that an inconsistency can occur between WTP and the concept of QALYs. A good overview of the discussion on WTP versus QALYs can be found in Hammitt (2002). He states that although both methods are based on individual preferences, the underlying assumptions differ. The different bases result in different conclusions about the relative value of reducing health and mortality risks to individuals that differ in factors such as age, health conditions and income. The choice between methods depends on

Table 6.2   Ethical preferences: comparisons of fatality categories

	SMRS
10-year-old pedestrian	4.646
30-year-old pedestrian	3.030
30-year-old driver	2.489
50-year-old pedestrian	2.394
50-year-old driver	2.159
70-year-old pedestrian	1.428
70-year-old driver (base case)	1

Source: Johansson-Stenman and Martinsson (2008).

judgements about constraints to be placed on individual preferences, and what factors should be considered in aggregating preferences across people. QALY estimates generally vary less across people and studies than WTP estimates because the QALY framework imposes greater constraints. QALYs impose constraints on individual preferences. Its basis is quite egalitarian. In contrast, WTP imposes few constraints on individual preferences (Hammitt, 2002).

The inconsistency between WTP based VOSL and the QALY concept is illustrated by researchers who have demonstrated the relationship between the WTP and a statistical life and age. For example, Shepard and Zeckhauser (1984) found that the VOSL peaks near the age of 40, and is less than half as large at ages of 20 and 65. The increasing VOSL between the age of 20 and 40 contradicts the QALY concept, which suggests a decreasing value of life or risk changes as age increases. An explanation may be that between the ages of 20 and 40 income increases. But probably even a person having an increased WTP between the ages of 20 and 40 might prefer to get killed in a road accident at the age of 40 compared with the age of 20. Consequently, at least the inconsistency is notable. Another example of such an inconsistency between the QALY approach and the VOSL approach is highlighted by De Blaeij (2003), who argues that the VOSL peaks between 50 and 65, and hence only starts to decline beyond 65 years. In this analysis, a correction has been applied for income levels, hence the age pattern has not been distorted by age–income interrelationships.

Johansson-Stenman and Martinsson (2008) did research on people's *ethical preferences* and the value of life, and found a decreasing value for older people. Table 6.2 presents their results. The values are 'relative value of life' figures (a 70-year-old driver = 1). These relative values are simply the ratios between probit coefficients of their model. The social marginal rate of substitution (SMRS) figures thus express how many saved 70-year-old drivers would be equivalent to one saved individual of a certain age and type of road user for each of the six samples. For example, the value of 4.646 in the first row should be interpreted as respondents equating saving 4.646 70-year-old car drivers to saving one 10-year-old pedestrian.

Table 6.2 shows the strongly decreasing 'ethical preference value' of a life with age. In addition, it shows that pedestrian fatalities are evaluated higher than otherwise equal drivers. Table 6.2 provides food for thought on age dependent valuations of fatalities. The obvious difference between the values of Table 6.2 and the willingness to pay values discussed above is that the first are based on ethical preferences that are not necessarily reflected by people's willingness to pay in particular choice situations. Note also that Table 6.2 is most probably the result of an aggregation across age levels. It may well be that a young person would propose a much steeper curve than an old age person. It is also important to note that, apart from ethical viewpoints that may change in the course of time, also consumptive preferences may well change over time, possibly leading to increasing VOSL levels during parts of the life cycle.

A second potential problem is raised with respect to categorizations other than those that are age based. One category is children. Children hardly have any money, so their WTP for reduced risks will be very low. One can seriously debate if even doing research into the WTP of children for risks is morally OK. One could argue that what then matters is the WTP of their parents (Leung and Guria, 2006). But suppose a 10 year-old-child lost her parents. Would that imply that the WTP is very low? Would it make the life of the child of less value than the life of her friend that still has both parents? On the other hand, if the parents still live, the WTP for reduced risks of children may very well depend on income, as well as on the number of children they have. Would this really matter? Probably egalitarian theories like those of Rawls and Sen (see Chapter 3) are of more use than utility based WTP studies to judge the ethical aspects of valuing the lives of children. Another categorization that could be made is between people who are not, versus those who are, responsible for their own bad health, such as smokers and users of illicit drugs. Researchers have found several differences (Johansson-Stenman and Martinsson, 2008). Many people think that persons responsible for their own bad health should be given lower priority (e.g. Anand and Wailoo, 2000; Cookson and Dolan, 2000).

A further distinction could be made between involuntary risks versus voluntary risks, with the first category valued more highly (e.g. Hansson,

2009; Mandeloff and Kaplan, 1989; Slovic et al., 1985), and, lastly, people think risks that are difficult to avoid should be valued more highly than those that are not (e.g. Subramanian and Cropper, 2000). Note that several of such differences do not match the utilitarian perspective (see Chapter 3); from a utilitarian perspective it would not matter if, for example, a person gets killed in an easy to avoid accident, versus a difficult to avoid accident.

It has to be added that the above discussion on the valuation of life risks of different people is somewhat theoretical, compared with real-world applications of the VOSL in cost–benefit analyses of transport policies. Real-world applications avoid the use of differentiation values for different types of people at risk, and just apply an average value. There are probably two reasons for this. Firstly, the overall quality of estimates of VOSL is probably not strong enough to allow specific values for various subgroups. Secondly, the researchers responsible for the cost–benefit calculations may fear debates on the 'unethical' assumptions on which the calculations are based, so that they prefer to stay on the safe side by using just the average VOSL. A similar reason would be that researchers doing CBA would anticipate that application of strongly differentiated VOSL levels might lead to conclusions that decision makers would not swallow, like a low priority for traffic safety themes that would in particular benefit children (because of their low willingness to pay). Thus, by using an average value for the VOSL, analysts responsible for CBA make sure that the potential gap between market-oriented economics based policy support on the one hand, and the domain of policy convictions and equity concerns on the other hand, can be kept to a manageable size.

A third subject for (methodological) discussion is discounting future safety effects. As show in Chapter 5, discounting strongly reduces long-term benefits. Applying discount rates to human lives would imply that one person now is of much more value that an equivalent person in the future. However, discounting future QALYs conflicts with the utility-theoretic justification: future persons and related QALYs are not less valuable than current people. Discounting probably also conflicts with egalitarian theories. What then to do in the case of investments that need to be made now, and have long-term impacts on safety, for example safer infrastructure? The 'solutions' as described in Chapter 5 (not discounting lives, increasing the value equally to the discount rate) may be useful in dealing with this. At least sensitivity analyses with different assumptions may show the importance of different assumptions for the outcomes of a CBA.

Not discounting can be problematic in some cases. Discounting QALYs can be justified in the case of cost-effectiveness calculations. Treating individuals equally implies that if the costs of an intervention are discounted, then the effects should be discounted as well. If the effects (added QALYs) are not evident, then postponing implementation is always to be preferred (e.g. Hammitt, 2002; Keeler and Cretin, 1983).

In cases where discounting is justified, the question is: which discount rate should be used? In the case of cost-effectiveness calculations, the same discount rate as for costs would lead to consistency within the method. If consumer preferences were to be the point of departure, an important question is how people discount the future utility of their lives. Ng (1992) suggests that individuals may discount their future utility at a rate smaller than the rate of return for financial assets, whereas Shepard and Zeckhauser (1984) assume these rates are equal (Hammitt, 2002).

A fourth subject for methodological discussion is the interaction between risk influencing factors. For road safety, risk levels result from (at least) speed of driving, characteristics of cars (active and passive safety levels), infrastructure characteristics, and the quality of the health care system. In addition, some of these determinants interact, and this interaction has an impact on final risk levels; for example, if cars become safer, drivers may drive faster. The combined impact on risk levels may be infrastructure dependent. Understanding such interactions, of course, is first of all a challenge for researchers. But an important ethical question is whether changes in determinants, and their interactions should have design consequences. Should, for example, safer cars lead to higher maximum speeds on motorways? Calculations based on the 'optimal' design of speed from a utilitarian perspective would argue so. On the other hand, higher speeds can have changes in the distributions of risks; for example, those on a low income may have smaller, less safe cars, and drive at lower speeds compared to people with a high income who have big, new, safer cars. Would that matter? Egalitarian theories would argue it does; consequentialism would probably conclude it does not.

Fifthly, a methodological question relates to the suitability of models to forecast accidents, fatalities and injuries. The traditional way of forecasting such indicators is by multiplying transport volume indicators and accident risks – see Section 6.3. In my opinion the improvement of the quality of forecasting risks is a challenge. Currently changes in risk factors are often based on assumptions, not on advanced models. In addition, in safety literature it is generally recognized that traffic volumes and risk factors interact. This interaction is often ignored; including the fact that this is a second model related challenge. These methodological improvements are of course important, regardless of the ethical aspects of future safety levels.

Sixthly, there is a methodological discussion on the impact of context on the VOSL. Should, within a country or region, the same VOSL for the same group of people be used across different risk categories? The WTP for the same risk might depend on the risk category at stake; for example, if a person runs a risk voluntarily, she may more easily accept a risk level in relation to a non-voluntary risk such as in the case of third party risks (see above). Should decisions to be made in the medical sector use equal VOSL for comparable groups of people (corrected for QALYs), as in the transport sector? See Hansson (2007) for a further discussion, who argues that the context would matter in the case of the values used. Hansson also states that in different policy areas divergent social traditions occur with respect to valuations of risks and (statistical) lives, as a result of which, CBAs for road projects and for clinical trials and dietary advice do differ. Espinoza (2009) also concludes that risks are often incommensurable, and that people in their preferences for risks and risk acceptability include other factors than those generally included in WTP methods. For example, people think the acceptability of certain risks partly depends on the question of whether alternatives for the cause of the risk exist: if they exist, a certain risk level is less acceptable. Similarly, Roeser (2009) concludes that for lay people the judgements of risk depend on several factors generally not included in economics methods, such as whether risks and benefits are fairly distributed, whether or not a risk is voluntarily taken, the availability of alternatives, and whether the risk might be catastrophic. She even concludes that 'affect or emotion is an invaluable source of wisdom, at least in so far as it comes to judgements about the moral acceptability of risk' (Roeser, 2009: 183).

Finally, a key question for a methodological discussion concerns the transferability of results over time and space. To start with transferability over space: it can be highly ethically problematic to transfer the outcomes of one country to another country; for example, the VOSL based on WTP in the USA will not be of value to evaluate lives of people in Bangladesh, or vice versa. See for a discussion of the impact of the world region under consideration on the ethics of fatalities Lorenzo et al. (2010). In addition, the transferability of VOSLs over time deserves attention. If people get richer, their WTP for risk reductions will very likely increase. But are the lives of rich people of more value than those of poor people? In other words, is the WTP the best method to value a statistical life? On the other hand, an ageing population would – ceteris paribus – lead to a decrease in the VOSL if it were based on the QALY concept.

6.5   DEMOCRATIC CONSIDERATIONS OF SAFETY

In this section I discuss democratic considerations of safety. A first question is: which concept of democracy is useful from the perspective of the

ex ante evaluation of safety? As explained in Chapter 3, at least two interpretations of democracy exist: (1) the traditional, more formal interpretation in terms of elections and ballots; and (2) democracy as 'government
by discussion', the latter interpretation being widely accepted in political
philosophy (Sen, 2009). The first interpretation raises the question of how
to include (risks of) people that cannot vote, in particular children? One
can argue that their parents will include implications for risks for their
children in their voting behaviour. But then the risk is that people without
children might overlook, at least to some extent, these implications – see
above. The interpretation of 'government by discussion' could lead to the
involvement of school children in debates on safety measures, at least near
schools or in their own neighbourhoods. We may of course not expect children to be able to evaluate risks and compare policy measures, but they
can contribute by expressing their perceived risks, listing (perceived) risky
situations, and coming up with ideas. Even if this were not to have any
impact on final decisions, it could contribute to better *ex ante* evaluations,
because the process of evaluation matters – see Chapter 3.

A second discussion from a democratic perspective is related to the question of whether it matters that people travel voluntarily or not voluntarily in
general, or with a specific mode. This question relates to the choice to travel
at all, versus not to travel, to the question of how much (time, kilometres)
to travel, and to mode choice. Before starting the discussion, it should be
stressed that it is very difficult to conclude which travel is voluntary or not. A
10-year-old living with her parents in a small rural town has to go to school
in one way or another because of compulsory education. Furthermore, the
nearest primary school may be at a distance of 5 km, in a neighbouring town.
The child has no choice but to travel to school. Another clear example: a
person may completely voluntarily decide to go to a concert. There is no
doubt about the choice being voluntary. But what if her daughter is singing
at the concert? She may feel it to be her parental duty to go to the concert,
even if she would not like the music. A few more 'grey' examples: a person
living in a rural area may think she has no choice but to commute by car due
to a lack of public transport (see also Chapter 4), but maybe she moved to
that area recently because she likes living in the countryside. Is she a forced
car commuter or not? The same discussion applies to accepting a job offer
far away from home. Even if a person were to argue that the other option
is to be unemployed, so there is not a real choice; but other options could
include moving to a house nearer the new working place, or accepting a job
that she may want less. Consequently, I would argue choices are not just
either voluntary or not, this is not a 0–1 variable. It is rather a continuous
variable. And even if mobility choices are seen as 0–1 variables, considering running a risk as voluntary is not that simple (Hansson, 2009). But for

reasons of clarity of discussion, let us assume the distinction between voluntary and non-voluntary travel. Then an important question is whether it matters that a person is at risk (or even killed), if it were a voluntary choice to travel or not. From a consequentialism perspective, this would not matter: only the impacts matter. A deontologist could argue that it is a matter of moral principle to not involuntarily expose people to certain risk levels, even if they would accept equivalent voluntary risk levels (in comparable or other situations). Many countries have safety regulations to protect people from being exposed to involuntary risks, say at workplaces or from third party risks (e.g. risks for residents that an airplane crashes on their house or a neighbouring factory explodes), that are way below the voluntary risks that people run while participating in the transport system. Thus, many policy makers would argue that it matters if people are exposed to voluntary versus involuntary risks. I was not able to find empirical evidence, but people have told me that in Europe if the regulations that many countries have for industry were to be applied to lorry drivers, it would be forbidden for companies to have their drivers driving lorries at all: the risks would be too high. From a utilitarian perspective, one could argue that even in the case of involuntary risks, one cannot force employers to introduce safety measures that are very expensive, and where the employees exposed to risks would prefer to get additional money to compensate for the higher risk levels.

A third discussion in the area of democracy is whether it matters which groups of population are at risk. Would it matter if transport safety risks were equally or unequally distributed over the population (at a per capita basis or per kilometre travelled)? What if the less advantaged in several other aspects (e.g. with respect to income, capabilities, welfare, well-being – see Chapter 3) are also those who are most at risk? Assume a new expensive car type could be introduced into the market. These cars are much safer for those using them, but less safe for other road users. At a national level, the increase of safety levels for those using them is larger than the decrease for other road users. What should we think of this market introduction? A consequentionalist could argue the car should be introduced. From a utilitarian perspective it would be good to do so if all persons counted equally. There is also probably an additional utility increase because the WTP for risk reductions of those buying these cars will be higher than the WTP of the other road users. This is first of all because the buyers of the cars, on average, have higher incomes, and secondly because of self-selection: those who value risk reduction strongly will very likely be more than averagely inclined to buy the safer cars. From a deontological perspective, one could argue that it is immoral to allow the safer cars to be offered on the market. On the other hand, from the perspective of egalitarian theories one could argue that what matters is the well-being of those who are already worst off (i.e. the 20% of the population who are most disadvantaged). Consequently, the introduction of the cars into the market would not be a good idea. To conclude: different ethical theories could draw different conclusions.

6.6   APPLYING THE CHECKLIST IN SECTION 3.6 TO TRANSPORT SAFETY

This section discusses the relevant items of the checklist in Section 3.6, as far as they are not discussed in the sections above. Sometimes multiple items of the checklist are combined for reasons of textual efficiency.

What is the Problem or the Challenge?

Most western countries have explicit safety policies, and safety is an important subject in policy plans. In addition, safety implications are often included in the *ex ante* evaluation of policies and projects. From this perspective, not much seems to be missing. Nevertheless, one can question the current safety targets of many countries. If western countries have visions or targets, these generally include reductions in the numbers of fatalities for the coming one or two decades of a few dozen percentage points, Sweden with its 'Vision Zero' being the main exception. But let us assume that we were now to have a transport system that is not based on individual motorized transport, and has hardly any fatalities. What then if it was proposed to change that transport system in a particular country to a system largely based on individual motorized transport (as western countries nowadays have), offering huge benefits in travel time gains, accessibility and travel flexibility, but at the cost of the number of fatalities rising by 20 percent compared to the numbers that country currently has? I would not be surprised if many people would consider that even proposing the change was unethical. One can discuss therefore the current targets of western countries from an ethical perspective: they are probably more related to the general wish to reduce the number of fatalities, than on ethical principles.

What Are the Choice Options?

In line with the discussion above about the ambitions of safety policies, one could debate if 'very safe choice options' should be included more often in *ex ante* evaluations. If the targets were to allow the transport system to be less safe, than the standards set by an ethical point of view, for example, additional choice options to those currently being debated could be considered. One can think of increasing the age at which persons are allowed to drive motorized vehicles (mopeds, motor bikes, cars, vans, lorries), forced dynamic Intelligent Speed Adaptations,[4] regulations to forbid selling (new) cars and other road vehicles that can drive faster than allowed on motorways, etc.

What Are All the Important Pros and Cons of the Choice Options?

Safety is generally included in *ex ante* evaluations. One can debate if the 'right' indicators are used – see above. The most important category of missing indicators could be adaptations in travel and activity behaviour as a result of perceived low safety levels.

Who Are the Winners and Losers?

In line with the preceding sections in this chapter, I would argue that there is a general lack of attention paid to who the (statistical) victims are. Depending on choices with respect to the valuation of victims and the basis for valuation (e.g. WTP, QALYs), choices could be made on how to value distinct categories of victims (e.g. by age class), between 'victims' (such as pedestrians and cyclists that stick to the traffic rules), and people who get killed because of their own risky behaviour (e.g. those who speed or drive drunk). In addition, attention could be paid to those who adapt their travel or activity behaviour because of changes in (perceived) safety levels. Note that many people travel using multiple transport modes. Many cyclists, for example, are also car drivers. In this case, the labels of 'winners' and 'losers' do not relate to people in general, but are context-dependent.

Can Losers be Compensated, and Will They be Compensated?

Many western countries give people who have (permanent) loss of capabilities as a result of traffic accidents legal rights for compensation. But it is questionable if the resulting payments fully compensate for the loss in quality of life – probably because immaterial losses are often poorly compensated. Theoretically, such compensation is possible. But what if an injured person caused the accident she suffers from? One could argue she could insure herself.

In the case of fatalities, the persons who lose their lives certainly cannot be compensated. At best, and only theoretically, some of their surviving relatives can, to some extent, be compensated.

Are there Particular Trade-offs?

Many measures to increase safety levels come at a cost, so trade-offs do exist. Costs can be direct monetary costs (e.g. of infrastructure), but also other costs, such as longer travel times due to a reduction of maximum speeds or the fun of driving.

Do Irreplaceable Things Exist or Not?

This is a difficult to answer question. On the one hand, one could argue that each individual is irreplaceable – a Kantian perspective suggests so. On the other hand, one can argue that anybody can be replaced, at least in some of her roles.

Maximization or Not?

Theoretically, policy makers could go for maximum safety levels. But these would come at serious costs, costs that are probably politically, from a benefits-to-cost perspective, and from the perspective of society, unacceptable – see the discussion on trade-offs.

Does Closed Partiality Occur?

Closed partiality could occur, at least to some extent, if those whose risks increase are not fully included in both defining the problem or challenge, in selection of policy options, or in the evaluation and decision making process. One can consider here the case of children.

Are Additional Values Affected, and If So: Which, for Whom and in Which Way?

Specific values, such as the freedom to move and to participate in activities, are briefly discussed above.

Are Commitments or Duties at Stake?

Special commitments, for example made by politicians, can be at stake. Politicians could have promised to implement measures to improve safety, for example as part of a package of measures, and to compensate for other measures that increase risk.

A Final Comment

I must say that it is much easier to list the implications of applying the checklist of Section 3.6 to the subject of safety, than it is to translate such ideas to practical applications – there is a long way to go, and the additional effort needs to be compared to the additional gains, at least in terms of the quality of decision making (see above and Chapter 3).

6.7 CONCLUSIONS

The most important conclusions of this chapter are summarized below.

In most western countries, the safety implications of possible policies and projects are generally included in *ex ante* evaluations. Many countries even have explicit safety policies. Partly as a result of safety policies over the past decades, both absolute numbers of fatalities, and even more so accident risks, have strongly decreased, despite the growth of volumes of road transport.

Numbers of fatalities and injured persons (and their expression in monetary terms) are very important, but do not give a complete overview of safety indicators that are relevant for *ex ante* evaluations. In addition to these indicators, adaptations of travel and activity behaviour matter, and are linked to the value of the freedom to move and participate in activities.

Pricing or not pricing (statistical) human lives in the case of *ex ante* evaluations is a controversial subject, which raises several questions:

1. Is it morally OK to express fatalities in monetary terms at all?
2. What are the pros and cons of doing so in the case of *ex ante* evaluations?
3. What methods are available to express human lives in monetary terms, and what are their pros and cons?
4. How to include future changes in safety, and is discounting on moral grounds OK?

The answer to the first question highly depends on the ethical theory that is used. The answer to the second question is that probably pricing safety improves the quality of decision making, but to the best of my knowledge there is no research to underpin this expectation. Thirdly, several methods exist to estimate the Value of a Statistical Life (VOSL), willingness to pay (WTP) methods being the most common category of methods. Results based on WTP methods could conflict with the concept of Quality

Adjusted Life Years (QALY). Fourthly, it is questionable if, and how, future victims of transport should be discounted.

From an ethical perspective it could matter whether people travel voluntarily or involuntarily. Different theories conclude differently.

From an ethical perspective it could matter which groups of the population are the victims of the transport system or are at risk. Again, different theories conclude differently. In *ex ante* evaluations, not much attention is paid to the question of who the losers (victims) of accidents are, whereas it could really matter from an ethical and evaluative perspective.

Despite the decrease in road fatalities, in the past decades the current level of fatalities could be considered unethical. Much more ambitious policies than most western countries nowadays have are possible, and could lead to putting other choice options on the agenda.

Increased safety levels often come at a (monetary or non-monetary) price. Trading-off, therefore, is inevitable.

It is much easier to list the implications of applying the checklist from Section 3.6 to the subject of safety, than it is to translate such ideas into practical applications – there is a long way to go, and the additional effort needs to be compared to the additional gains, at least in terms of the quality of decision making.

7. The ethics of doing transport research

7.1 INTRODUCTION

Questions related to the ethics of doing research include:

- What do codes of conduct tell us about the ethics of doing research?
- How independent should a researcher be?
- How impartial should a researcher be?
- What to do if the client's interest strongly conflicts with those of the wider society?
- To what extent should research be verifiable?
- Where does political responsibility end, and lying or manipulation start?
- Should a researcher disseminate non-confidential research if the findings are relevant for society, but the client does not appreciate this?
- Should ethical standards for universities differ from those for consultancies?
- What is the quality of cost estimates and demand forecasts for large infrastructure projects?
- Which options are available to reduce the immoral behaviour, that results in poor quality cost estimates and demand forecasts?

Doing research in general can easily result in ethical dilemmas. What to do with the client's wishes if accepting them would result in less objective research? How 'good' should research be, to be able to draw conclusions? How to trade-off clear communication of findings and scientific nuances? Transport research is no exception to this rule. This chapter discusses the ethical aspects of doing research in transport. The ambition is to make transport researchers, especially those doing research in the area of *ex ante* evaluations of transport projects and policies, aware of the ethical dimensions of their research. Although researchers in other areas can also benefit from this chapter, the ambition is not to cover all areas of research.

Because of the focus of this book, this chapter does not cover all aspects of doing transport research, but is limited to research that is directly relevant for *ex ante* evaluations. A broader scope could include, for example, the ethics of specific research methods, including the ethics of interviewing persons, and of dealing with statistics; such aspects are not included – see Beach (1996) and Resnik (1998, 2007).

The most important ethical theory that is helpful to discuss the ethics of doing research is virtue theory (see Chapter 6). The discussions and dilemmas presented in this chapter strongly relate to what a virtuous person (or research group) would or should do.

This chapter is organized along three lines. The first is a theoretical line. Section 7.2 discusses codes of conduct for research. Many countries have codes of conduct for categories of researcher (and others, such as engineers). These codes give some guidance about what a virtuous person or group of researchers should (not) do. The second line is to give an overview of literature in the area of cost overruns and demand shortfalls (Section 7.3). A major reason for cost overruns and demand shortfalls is 'strategic behaviour' which makes it highly relevant from an ethical perspective, and even more because of the huge potential impacts on the quality (and as a result, usefulness) of CBAs. The third line is an empirical one. Section 7.4 presents an interview-based study with researchers in the area of transport, focusing on real-world dilemmas of doing research in the area of *ex ante* evaluations of transport projects and policies. Section 7.5 reflects on the ethics of doing research. Section 7.6 finally summarizes the main conclusions of this chapter.

Chapter 8 goes into more detail in the area of the ethics of transport modelling, since modelling plays a very important role in transport research related to *ex ante* evaluations.

7.2   THEORY: CODES OF CONDUCT

The transport research community is not at all the only community that faces ethical dilemmas; all areas of research face these. Ethical dilemmas, of course, also appear in many other areas, such as design, engineering, the medical sector and business. Every conscientious researcher realizes that ethical issues are important. For example, no reasonable person would think it is OK to manipulate results, to fake interviews, or to send strictly confidential information given in an interview to the media. Consequently, there are general principles that most researchers will recognize. Principles could relate to, for example, independence, impartiality, confidentiality, treating the client respectfully, or the verifiability of findings. An explicit way to deal with the ethics of doing research is to formulate so-called codes of conduct.

Note that even if a researcher does not agree with the way codes of conduct are formulated, she might sympathize with the underlying principles.

Many countries, professionals' organizations and others have developed codes of conduct. Multinational firms even often have their own codes (Kaptein, 2004). Some (categories of) companies have codes of practice, an example being a code of practice for alcohol advertising (e.g. Jones and Lynch, 2007). This section discusses codes of conduct for researchers, and is largely based on four references giving an overview of codes of conduct (Bullock and Panicker, 2003; Resnik, 1998, 2007; Van de Poel and Royakkers, 2010).

Such codes are also necessary for researchers, because the underlying principles, as well as the codes themselves, might easily be violated, such as in the case of research carried out at universities (see Resnik, 2007). Resnik, for example, discusses the significant impact funders of academic research can have on the results. Money has an impact on problem selection, experimental design[1], subject recruitment, collecting and recording data, analysing and interpreting data, authorship of publication, publication and data sharing, and peer review and replication. One of Resnik's conclusions is that a strong correlation exists between the source of funding and the results of research.

In the literature, the terms 'ethics codes' and 'codes of conduct' can be found. Here, I will use them interchangeably. If I refer to references, I will use the terminology of the authors.

In very general terms, codes of conduct are codes in which organizations lay down guidelines for the responsible behaviour of their members. Codes of conduct are formulated for a variety of reasons, such as increasing moral awareness, the identification and interpretation of the moral norms and values of a profession or a company, the stimulation of ethical discussion, as a way of increasing accountability to the outside world, and to improve the image of a profession or company (Van de Poel and Royakkers, 2010).

Ethics codes vary widely in many dimensions – see below. Bullock and Panicker (2003) give a nice introduction in this area:

> Ethical conduct in professional activities is an issue that occupies legislatures, regulatory agencies, educators, and professional societies across every discipline, whether focused on research, academia, industry or service. Most professional activities are covered under multiple levels of control. For example, there are principles and regulations specifying research/professional activities at the international level . . ., the national level . . . at the institutional level . . . as well as from disciplinary societies. . . . Ethics codes and policies . . . come in many shapes and sizes, ranging from simple, one-page statements of principles, to long, detailed, manuals of conduct covering the many details of professional

life. Which kind of code a discipline adopts, if it adopts a code at all, is a function of the different professional roles adopted by members of the association, the discipline's perceived obligations and responsibilities, and the discipline's own history. (2003: 159–160)

Bullock and Panicker also give an overview of possible categorizations of ethics codes:

- *Breadth:* the breadth of an association's ethics code refers to the array of activities it attempts to cover. In general, the more diverse the discipline the broader, and perhaps more general, the code.
- *Depth:* the depth of a code refers to its detail – whether it simply suggests ethical principles to follow in very general terms, or also complements these principles with detailed behaviour and actions. Some codes include norms and rules that contain guidelines on how to act in specific situations, such as the acceptance of gifts, fraud, conflicts of interest, confidentiality, corruption or bribery (Van de Poel and Royakkers, 2010).
- *Purpose:* the general aim of ethics codes is to set out the standards of conduct that apply within a domain or discipline. Bullock and Panicker (2003; see also Van de Poel and Royakkers, 2010) present three categories of more specific purposes: (1) the codes can be aspirational: they can provide ideal goals, behaviours and perspectives that all members of the discipline should strive to attain; (2) the codes can spell out common practice; and (3) codes can serve a regulatory and punitive function. Bullock and Panicker conclude that only a very small number of associations supplement their ethics codes with detailed reporting or grievance procedures, provide information about procedures for handling allegations of misconduct or unethical behaviour, or specify sanctions against those who violate the code. This, according to Bullock and Panicker, is not surprising because much of the behaviour covered in ethics codes is regulated in other venues.

Professional codes generally relate to three domains (Van de Poel and Royakkers, 2010): (1) conducting a profession with integrity and honesty, and in a competent way; (2) obligations towards employers and clients; and (3) responsibility towards the public and society.

Common issues in ethics codes include (Bullock and Panicker, 2003):

- Honesty in conducting and reporting research (refrain from falsification, fabrication)
- Fairness and integrity in intellectual ownership and authorship

- Respect and humane treatment for the research material, be it animate or inanimate
- Responsibilities to use public funds appropriately and to share publicly funded materials and data
- Open dissemination of research results
- Responsibilities to preserve research records and artefacts
- An obligation to avoid discrimination and harassment in all activities
- An obligation as publisher to uphold integrity in reviewing and publishing research (generally included when an association has a strong publishing function)
- An obligation to review the works of others.

A specific category of ethics codes relates to scientific research.[2] Resnik (1998, 2007) discusses what he calls the principles of ethics in science:

- Honesty (being objective, unbiased, truthful)
- Carefulness (avoid errors, bias, conflict of interest[3])
- Objectivity
- Openness (share data and results, methods, ideas, techniques and tools; allow others to review work, be open to criticism)
- Freedom (scientists should be free to study any problem or hypothesis)
- Credit (credit should be given where it is due, but not where it is not due)
- Respect for intellectual property
- Respect for colleagues and students
- Competence ('maintain and enhance your competence and expertise through lifetime education. Promote competence in your profession and report incompetence' [Resnik, 2007: 47])
- Confidentiality
- Education
- Social responsibility (avoid causing harm to society, attempt to produce social benefits)
- Legality (obey laws)
- Stewardship of resources ('make fair and effective use of scientific resources' [Resnik, 2007: 48])
- Opportunity ('scientists should not be unfairly denied the opportunity to use scientific resources or advance in the scientific profession' [Resnik, 1998: 65])
- Mutual respect (treat colleagues with respect)
- Efficiency (use resources efficiently)
- Respect for subjects (do not violate human rights or dignity).

Resnik (1998: 69) emphasizes that 'different standards could be justified in different social circumstances'. In addition, he states that some of these principles apply to individuals, and others to social institutions, and that the principles can conflict. Resnik (2007) considers objectivity as the most important principle.

> Science ought to be objective because democratic societies need objective beliefs and methods to help resolve controversial moral, political, economic, cultural and social debates. To help with the resolution of these debates, scientists should attempt to give unbiased testimony in public forums and should try to develop theories, hypotheses, methods and concepts that are free from personal, cultural, social, moral or political bias. (Resnik, 2007: 75)

In addition, many codes also address the issue of credentials: one must not overstate, exaggerate or lie about one's expertise or competence. In addition to these more or less universal codes, Bullock and Panicker (2003) also give an overview of not-universal but area specific issues – these will not be discussed here.

Researchers can face dilemmas related to all codes as summarized above. In addition, dilemmas can occur because codes of conduct can conflict (Beach, 1996; Van de Poel and Royakkers, 2010). For example, on the one hand a researcher has obligations towards the client, on the other hand she should be honest. But what if the client wants to have some influence on a research report or article? Completely ignoring the client's wishes, and acting as if the report was written on the researcher's own initiative, could result in ignoring the client's interest, but how far can one go? Under which conditions should confidentiality (as asked for by the client) be prioritized over societal interests? An example illustrating such a dilemma: suppose an alderman of a local municipality wants to know if concentrations of Particulate Matter (PM) do or do not exceed WHO standards. The researcher finds out that the concentrations do not exceed the standards, but NO_2 concentrations do exceed the standards. Let us assume the alderman is fair and honest, but could get into serious political trouble if the research study reported exceeding the NO_2 standard. How then to trade-off obligations towards the client and professional integrity? This is a serious dilemma. The 'solution' to such dilemmas could even be country and culture specific.

The fact that ethics are strongly interwoven with law, politics and religion illustrates the importance of culture and thus place and time (Resnik, 1998). Van de Poel and Royakkers (2010) give the example of stakeholder principles that guide the relationship between a company and stakeholders. The most mentioned stakeholder principles are transparency,

Table 7.1   Codes of conduct of the Dutch Association of Universities in the Netherlands

Part of the code	Principle
Scrupulousness	Scientific activities are performed scrupulously, unaffected by mounting pressure to achieve.
Reliability	Science's reputation for reliability is confirmed and enhanced through the conduct of every scientific practitioner. A scientific practitioner is reliable in the performance of his research and in its reporting, and equally in the transfer of knowledge through teaching and publication.
Verifiability	Presented information is verifiable. Whenever research results are publicized, it is made clear what the data and the conclusions are based on, where they were derived from, and how they can be verified.
Impartiality	In his scientific activities, the scientific practitioner heeds no other interest than the scientific interest. In this respect, he is always prepared to account for his actions.
Independence	Scientific practitioners operate in a context of academic liberty and independence. In so far as restrictions of that liberty are inevitable, these are clearly stated.

Source: VSNU (2004).

honesty and fairness. In American codes, honesty is more often included than transparency, whereas in European and Asian codes the relation is reversed. Van de Poel also gives the example of Japanese companies: these relatively more often cite trust as a stakeholder principle, compared to American and European companies.

For academic research, many codes of conduct also exist, and can be found on the internet. Table 7.1 gives an overview of codes of conduct for scientific practices, as formulated by the Association of Universities in the Netherlands (VSNU, 2004). I have selected this code because of its use in the empirical part of this chapter (see Section 7.4). The code is organized along five so-called Parts, each having a dominant principle.

For a further discussion on the ethics of doing academic research, see for example, Gass (1994), Beach (1996) and Resnik (1998).

How important are codes of conduct? Firstly, as expressed by Van de Poel and Royakkers (2010), it is important to realize that the formulation of codes of conduct is not the only activity that professional associations and companies can undertake to stimulate responsible behaviour by their members. Other activities include the appointment of a confidante or committee with whom moral problems can be discussed, or the organization of training sessions for dealing with moral dilemmas. Secondly, Van de Poel and Royakkers (2010) argue that codes of conduct do not give strict prescription. Ethics are not about uniformly prescriptive behaviour, but require individual moral judgement, and are situation dependent. Van de Poel and Royakkers argue that the non-prescriptive nature of codes of conduct is not at all a problem, because codes of conduct often are advisory and aspirational (see above) – I agree. This nature of codes of conduct is nicely illustrated by the code of the Association of Dutch Universities: after presenting the principles and elaborating on them, the document ends with a list of 13 example dilemmas without giving solutions. Thirdly, the utility of codes of conduct is not self-evident. Schuurbiers et al. (2009) evaluated how the Netherlands code of conduct for scientific practices, as formulated by the Association of Universities in the Netherlands, was used at the university Department of Biotechnology at Delft University of Technology, the Netherlands. This advisory code of conduct not only aims to hold scientific practitioners to properly exercise their duties, but also to maintain public trust in science. They conclude that respondents 'did not consider the code of conduct as such to be a useful instrument'. The code 'leaves a number of important questions unanswered in relation to visibility, enforcement, integration with daily practice, and the distribution of responsibility' (Schuurbiers et al., 2009: 213). Fourthly, much research is based on teamwork. In such cases, it is unrealistic to assign full responsibility to individual researchers (Swierstra and Jelsma, 2006, cited in Schuurbiers et al., 2009).

Despite these qualifications, I think codes of conduct at least 'do no harm', and in several cases could provide ethical guidance for researchers, both individually, as well as in their roles as members of a research team. In addition, as Mulvey (1994) explains, it is important to realize that researchers often face the prisoner's dilemma[4], for example because they compete. At the same time, clients might benefit from researchers that do their research 'not completely independently' – see next section. 'Researchers may be unlikely to cooperate when there is no binding contract to act for the common good – most people are myopic maximizers.' Related to this: 'improved professional conduct is unlikely to come from within, especially when the incentives are so strong in the opposing direction' (Mulvey, 1994: 72).

7.3 AN OVERVIEW OF LITERATURE ON RESEARCH IN THE AREA OF LARGE INFRASTRUCTURE PROJECTS

Introduction[5]

Decision making with respect to large infrastructure projects[6] is often partly based on *ex ante* evaluations of costs and impacts. Impacts include economic, environmental and social impacts, sometimes aggregated in a cost–benefit analysis. For such *ex ante* evaluations, the quality of the demand and costs forecasts is very important. Good quality cost forecasts are important both for the question of whether the project is worth its costs, as well as for budgetary consequences, and possibly for changes in project specifications. Good quality demand forecasts are important for both the benefits of a potential new transport infrastructure project, because most benefits result from the actual use of the project, and for the environmental impacts of the project. Because the quality of costs and demand forecasts is often poor, a major reason being the 'strategic behaviour' of those having an interest in a positive decision to build new infrastructure (see below), this topic is very relevant from an ethical point of view, and can be seen as a special case in the area of the ethics of doing research.

This section aims to answer four questions: (1) what is the quality of demand forecasts of large infrastructure projects; (2) what is the quality of cost forecasts of these projects; (3) how can current practices with respect to assessing the demand and cost forecasts be improved; and (4) which recommendations can be made to improve the quality of costs and demand forecasts from an ethical perspective? Questions 1–3 will be answered using a literature review focusing on large infrastructure projects, often referred to as megaprojects, question 4 will be answered by using the findings of the literature review and Section 7.2 (codes of conduct).

How Accurate are Travel Demand Forecasts?

The quality of demand forecasts
Before giving an overview of literature, it is important to notice that I found only a few references in which a systematic comparison between forecasts and actual demand is made. This in itself is striking, considering the huge costs and impacts involved, and the substantial differences observed.

One of the most important pieces of research into the quality of forecasts in demand and costs and actual demand, as well as costs after finishing projects, is the study of Flyvbjerg et al. (2003a). Their analysis is based on a large database containing data on many projects. Some of the characteristics of the database are:

1. The database contains 258 projects.
2. Projects were carried out in 20 countries, including 181 projects in Europe, 61 in North America and 16 in other countries.
3. The value of the projects[7] is some US$90 billion (1995 prices).
4. The projects include railways (58), roads (167) and so-called 'fixed links' (bridges, tunnels).
5. Projects were finished between 1927 and 1998.
6. Projects were selected on data availability.
7. The researchers compare costs at the time of decision making with the actual costs.
8. The study only includes construction costs (and not, for example, costs of maintenance or providing the train services).
9. Construction costs range from US$1.5 million to US$8.5 billion (1995 prices).

In relation to the 6th item, the authors conclude that this might cause some bias, for various reasons. Projects with good data availability might be better managed than average, resulting in lower than average cost escalations. Secondly, data availability itself increases the likelihood of good management; it is possible that people responsible for projects with large cost escalations might be less willing to provide the researchers with the information requested. Finally, the authors argue that even if cost figures are provided, these might be relatively favourable figures (from the point of view of the provider).

Considering the 7th item, the authors argue that the real decision to construct the project might have been made before the formal decision, and that the early informal cost estimates are often much lower compared to the estimates at the time of the formal decision making. Comparing estimates at the 'real' time of the decision, therefore, might have resulted in much larger cost escalations than those presented in their work.

Pickrell (1992) also focused on the differences between forecasts and actual demand. His research includes rail infrastructure (light and heavy rail) in the US. In seven out of eight cases the actual demand was less than half of the forecasted demand, in one case the difference was 'only' 28 percent. He states that differences may result from the input of exogenous data, the model structure and the use of models in the forecasting process. The most important cause of differences between forecasts and actual demand is that connecting bus services were poorer than assumed.

In general, the causes they include in their study (demography, employment, Level of Service characteristics and costs of car use, including parking costs) explain less than half of the differences between forecasts and actual demand. As only eight projects were considered in this study, the conclusions should be regarded with some reservation.

Trujillo et al. (2002) conclude that overestimations of demand for road projects caused by strategic behaviour are in the range of 25 to 60 percent. Based on projects in OECD countries, Skamris and Flyvbjerg (1997) conclude that the difference between demand and forecasts is in the range of 20–60 percent.

It can be concluded that only a few authors pay attention to the quality of demand forecasts for infrastructure projects. Considering the huge costs and impact on exploitation, this seems strange. In general, overestimation of demand is more common than underestimation, especially for rail projects.

Causes for discrepancies between demand forecasts and actual demand

In this part, I distinguish between two categories of causes for discrepancies between demand forecasts and actual demand. Firstly, shortcomings in the forecasting methodology occur, and secondly, there is the manipulation (or, formulated in a less negative way, strategic behaviour) of interest groups. Because of the ethics perspective of this book, I will not discuss methodological aspects, but refer to Van Wee (2007a) for a discussion on this literature.

Trujillo et al. (2002) carried out research in Third World countries, which does not match the scope of this book. But because their analysis is highly relevant also for western countries, their research will be summarized below. They looked at the games played in privatization in the transport sector, in particular with respect to demand forecasts. For example, if a project is not a full public project, this will result in the fragmentation of the process among actors, leading to asymmetry in information, which might lead to strategic behaviour in the interaction between actors. In these countries the governments tend to be over-optimistic with respect to demand forecasts, because in the case of auctions the results are more favourable for them. This behaviour is further encouraged because, in general, the persons involved do not have the same job and responsibilities when negotiations restart, and forecasts turn out to be over-optimistic. They conclude that three factors are very important for strategic behaviour: the (often hidden) preferences of actors; the information structure; and, in particular, information asymmetry and possibilities for acting. 'Possibilities for acting' refers to the opportunities offered by the formal and informal structures for strategic behaviour. Trujillo et al. (2002)

mainly focused on information asymmetry. Overestimations in demand for road capacity are in the range of 25 to 60 percent. Strategic reasons may not only be an incentive for overestimations, but also for underestimations. For example, a company offering transport services may have an interest in low demand forecasts, especially if there are only a few competitors. Trujillo et al. further conclude that politicians have an incentive to positively decide upon the construction of a large infrastructure project because – at least according to Trujillo et al. – they have more to gain by announcing a new infrastructure project than they have to lose by having to raise taxes later. Finally, they state that, in the USA, there are companies that are willing to 'sell' their forecasts, combined with insurance against a difference greater than a specified limit. This seems an interesting concept, both from the perspective of the quality of decision making (see Chapter 3) as well as from an ethical perspective: it could increase the chance that researchers act according to codes of conduct (see Section 7.2).

Flyvbjerg et al. (2005) also conclude that, for rail projects, strategic behaviour is the main reason for overestimations of demand. Such overestimations, combined with cost underestimations, increase the chance of agreement to construct the infrastructure.

Wachs (1989) also reflects on the manipulation of forecasts and elaborates on the ethical aspects of forecasting. He focuses on the pressure of consultants to manipulate forecasts. It should be noted that his conclusions are not based on research but on reflections partly based on his own experience. Wachs (1990, found in Skamris and Flyvbjerg, 1997) concludes that manipulation of demand forecasts occurs. He demonstrated this for several projects by interviewing officials and politicians involved in the projects.

It can be concluded that strategic behaviour is in general more important for differences between forecasts and actual demand than shortcomings in travel demand models including the data used.

How Accurate are Cost Estimates?

A comparison of forecasted and actual costs

Probably the most interesting study of all that I found on comparisons between forecasted costs and actual costs is the one carried out by Flyvbjerg et al. (2003a). Related to this study several articles were published, one of them being 'How common and how large are cost overruns in transport infrastructure projects?' (Flyvbjerg et al., 2003b).

All cost figures are expressed in US dollars as at 1995, using historical sector (construction manufacturing) and geographical indices. The most important conclusions are:

1. Cost escalations occurred in 86 percent of all projects; 14 percent of the projects had costs equal to or lower than the forecasted costs.
2. The average cost escalation was 28 percent.
3. The conclusion that underestimations of cost occur much more often than overestimations is significant ($p < 0.001$).
4. The conclusion that the size of the underestimations is bigger than that of overestimations is also significant ($p < 0.001$).
5. The largest cost overruns occur for rail projects (average: 45%), followed by fixed links (34%) and roads (20%).
6. Cost overruns for tunnels are larger (48%) than for bridges (30%), the difference not being significant, possibly due to low numbers.
7. For high speed rail links costs overruns are larger (average: 52%) compared to urban rail links (45%), whereas conventional rail links have the lowest cost overruns (30%). Again, the difference is not significant, possibly due to low numbers.
8. On average cost overruns are smaller in Europe (26%) and North America (24%) compared to other countries (65%).
9. For bridges and tunnels the average cost escalation is 43 percent in Europe and 26 percent in North America, the difference not being significant, possibly due to the low numbers.
10. Cost overruns for rail projects are smaller in Europe (34%) compared to North America (41%), the difference not being significant.
11. Cost overruns for roads are larger in Europe (22.4%) compared to North America (8.4%), the difference not being significant.
12. There is no relationship between the year of finishing the project and the size of cost overruns. Obviously a learning effect does not exist. This is despite the increased participation of civilians in decision making in more recent projects.

Another study with a relatively large sample is the study of Odeck (2004) who carried out research into cost escalations for roads built in Norway between 1992 and 1995. His database contains 620 projects carried out by the Norwegian Public Roads Administration (NPRA), which has a share of 40 percent in the budgets for road construction in Norway. The most important conclusions Odeck makes are that average cost escalation is 8 percent (7.88%), ranging from −58 to +183 percent, and that cost overruns occur slightly more often than underruns (52% versus 35%). Note that the average cost overruns are much smaller compared to those found by Flyvbjerg et al. (2003a) for European roads (22%). The difference might be explained by the Norwegian three-step procedure to increase the quality of cost estimates (see Odeck, 2004), resulting in lower cost overruns. This example shows the risk of *ecological fallacy*: conclusions that are valid for, for example, Europe as a whole do not necessarily hold for one specific European country.

Pickrell (1990, 1992) carried out a study into eight urban rail projects in the US. Four projects were *light rail* projects, the other four *heavy rail* projects. The average cost overrun was 61 percent, ranging from −10 to + 106 percent.

A study of the Auditor General of Sweden (1994) (found in Odeck, 2004) into 15 road and rail projects gives an average cost overrun of 86 percent for roads (−2 to +182%) and 17 percent for rail projects (−14 to +74%). Of all projects, two-thirds were still under construction at the time of research, making it likely that final cost overruns might be considerably larger.

Nijkamp and Ubbels (1999) carried out research into cost overruns of infrastructure projects in the Netherlands and Finland, including five motorways, two tunnels and one bridge. After correction for inflation, costs were underestimated in six cases and overestimated in two cases. Underestimations were in the range of 0–20 percent.

To summarize, all the studies show that cost overruns are common for infrastructure projects. However, the magnitude differs significantly within and also between studies. Probably the most representative study is the one carried out by Flyvbjerg et al., (2003a), firstly because of the size of the database and secondly because of the wide geographical coverage.

Causes for cost escalations

Based on the database as described above, Flyvbjerg et al. (2004) ana-lysed the causes of cost escalations, and distinguished between technical, economic, psychological and political causes. Here, I will only focus on causes that are relevant from an ethics perspective, and exclude technical or methodological explanations – see Flyvbjerg et al. (2004) for an over-view of all explanations. The ethically relevant causes are most important: based on research into megaprojects, Bruzelius et al. (2002) concluded that differences between forecasted costs and actual costs are not so much the result of the unpredictability of real costs due to the uncertainties of future developments, but more of the behaviour of those supporting the project in pushing the decision in the direction of constructing the infrastructure project by presenting flattering forecasts. Generally speaking, the cause of inaccurate forecasts is not inadequate models and data, but inadequate institutional approaches and regimes. Bruzelius et al., therefore, focus their research on improvements in current practices of these institutional aspects.

To summarize: the conclusion of Bruzelius et al. (2002) that the most important cause of cost escalations is strategic behaviour seems plausible, and is at the same time shocking.

Possibilities for Increasing the Quality of Demand and Costs Forecasts

This section will focus on the possibilities for increasing the quality of demand and costs forecasts, and is largely based on Bruzelius et al. (2002), Flyvbjerg et al. (2005) and Trujillo et al. (2002). I will focus on only those factors that are related to strategic behaviour.

Bruzelius et al. (2002) conclude that good decision making is not only a matter of better information and methods, but also of institutional arrangements to improve accountability. Concerning current practices, they list two important characteristics:

1. The decision-making cycle does not include a pre-feasibility stage before the decision to carry out decent research is taken. Over-commitment of resources and political prestige therefore may occur at an early stage. The authors conclude that this may lead to a polarization at an early stage of the project.
2. Parties for whom the project is disadvantageous, and interest groups, are included in the process only at a relatively late stage, and only to a limited extent.

They conclude that the most important shortcomings of current practice are, (1) a lack of clear targets and instruments, to measure how the targets can be realized, and (2) a system to reward good performance and punish bad performance.

They further conclude that four basic instruments could ensure an adequate process:

- Transparency
- Specification of performance
- Explicit formulation of the regulating regime and defining (or, if possible, eliminating) the policy risks before the decision making
- The inclusion of risk capital.

Flyvbjerg et al. (2004) conclude that often planners do not have an interest in improving the quality of forecasts: they like to see the project constructed and financed. Hence producing an optimistic forecast is very attractive. In this situation, they recommend two types of accountability: (1) public sector accountability by transparency and public control; and (2) private sector accountability through competition and market control. Their suggestions for increasing transparency and public control of public sector accountability include:

- An independent peer review of the demand forecasts
- A benchmark for comparable forecasts
- Forecasts, peer review, and benchmarks available for the public, including related documentation
- Public meetings at which stakeholders and the public can express criticism and support. The results should be integrated into planning and decision making
- Scientific and professional conferences
- Professional and legal sanctions applied where manipulation is found.

Their suggestions for private sector accountability through competition and market control include:

- Private money should be included in the project, as it should not be wholly financed by public parties
- People and organizations making the forecasts should be held financially responsible for misinterpretation or manipulated forecasts.

In conclusion, this section presents several ideas to improve the quality of demand forecasts in cases where strategic behaviour is at stake:

- The introduction of 'better' institutional arrangements
- The introduction of clear targets and instruments to measure how targets can be realized, and to reward good performance and punish bad performance
- Improve transparency, for example by making information generally available
- The inclusion of an independent peer review
- The introduction of measures to reduce or avoid strategic behaviour, including manipulation; these measures can be clustered into: (1) measures to improve public sector accountability by transparency and public control; and (2) measures to improve private sector accountability by competition and market control.

A Reflection from the Perspective of Ethics

This section further discusses options to improve the quality of demand and costs forecasts, but – contrary to the section above it – is not based on a literature review but is rather a general reflection, inspired by the literature review and Section 7.2 (codes of conduct). Because strategic behaviour is probably the most important reason for too low cost estimates and too high demand forecasts, a very important question is: how to deal with the ethics of forecasting? As long as some consultants are prepared to write 'any' reports if they get paid for it (see above and the work of Wachs, 1989, 1990), a moral problem exists. The question is how to improve the related ethics. In this section, I will discuss some solutions.

Firstly, one answer might be to include ethics in BA, MA, PhD and other training and education programmes. It is possible that research into the area of ethics might contribute to a better quality of forecasts. To the best of my knowledge, most BA, MA, and PhD education programmes generally do not at all, or only briefly, pay attention to the ethics of doing research (and design).

Secondly, I like the (US) concept of companies that are willing to 'sell' their forecasts, combined with insurance against a difference larger than a specified limit, as presented above. In my opinion, this idea deserves consideration for countries outside the USA too. A 'guaranteed' quality of forecasts, including penalties for deficiencies, might be a criterion on which to select consultants, or even a *conditio sine qua non*.

The concept of companies selling their forecasts with a guarantee is output oriented: it only relates to the quality of the results (not the research itself). In addition, input related concepts (the quality of the research itself) could be improved. First of all, and inspired by the ISO quality system, a system for establishing codes of conduct, and how to deal with them, probably even including codes of conduct with a regulatory and punitive function (see Section 7.2), could be designed and implemented. Secondly, for CBA and related research (such as travel demand), guidelines could reduce the chances for manipulations. Several countries currently have such guidelines, such as the UK (NATA), Scotland (STAG), and the Netherlands (OEI). Thirdly, independent researchers or research institutes could play an official role in checking the quality of demand forecasts and cost estimates, or even of a full CBA. Here, two options (separately or combined) are available. On the one hand, such a check can be made after the (draft) CBA, and can reduce the chances of manipulation because of this final check. On the other hand, such researchers or institutes could be involved during the research process. In that case, they might improve the quality of the research by giving advice, ideas and warnings in the case of potential 'errors'.

These three options focus on the researchers. In addition, a fourth option is to focus on the demand (client) side of research. If researchers manipulate results, this often is because the client asks them to do so. Codes of conduct or guidelines could also be formulated for those asking for the research. Again, these could even be regulative and punitive.

Finally, I think that codes of conduct and guidelines can be very useful, but the best solution probably is that researchers and clients are intrinsically motivated to do the research 'right'. We can compare this with a tax system. Several rules, checks, software programs, and databases (e.g. with bank accounts) could be linked in order to reduce the chances of manipulation (tax evasion), but probably nothing works better than having taxpayers who honestly want to fill in their forms. There is of course not an easy recipe for *how* to increase the intrinsic motivation of researchers and clients. Probably their attitude is a reflection of the general morality of society. It is beyond the scope of this book to discuss this subject.

Conclusions and Discussion

The most important conclusions for Section 7.3 are, firstly, that only a few authors pay attention to the quality of demand and costs forecasts of infrastructure projects. Considering the huge costs, and the impact of exploitation, this seems strange. Secondly, in general, overestimation of demand is more common than underestimation, especially for rail projects. Thirdly, strategic behaviour seems to be more important for the explanation of differences between forecasts and actual demand, than shortcomings in demand models. Fourthly, cost overruns are common in infrastructure projects. Fifthly, cost overruns are partly the result of strategic behaviour, resulting in a too low cost estimate being available at the time of decision. Sixthly, the introduction of measures to reduce, or avoid, strategic behaviour and manipulation, could result in improving the quality of demand forecasts and cost overruns, and example measures include CBA or other *ex ante* evaluation frameworks, codes of conduct, and guidelines for CBAs and related research.

   Although this section is about large infrastructure projects only (because of the focus of the literature review and – more generally – the attention paid to this subject in academic literature), much of its findings and conclusions could also apply to other infrastructure projects, and maybe even non-infrastructure related policy options.

7.4   DILEMMAS: AN INTERVIEW-BASED STUDY

Introduction

As promised in the introduction to this chapter, the third line of this chapter is an empirical one. Eight researchers were interviewed, with the aim of finding out:

1. What experiences they have had with respect to ethics and ethics related dilemmas
2. To what extent they are aware of ethics, and the ethical dilemmas of other researchers
3. To what extent researchers in the area of *ex ante* evaluations of transport policies and plans are familiar with codes of conduct
4. The opinion of these researchers about these codes of conducts.

I used a method highly inspired by the Grounded Theory method. This is a social sciences method (not a theory) that is highly inductive, and based on qualitative data (often based on multiple data collection methods), and is generally used if no *a priori* hypotheses or expectations exist. Results from interviews lead to a kind of overall picture of the subject. Interviews are held until a certain level of saturation is reached – the researcher has the impression that adding more interviews will not, or only to a very limited extent, result in new insights. According to the Grounded Theory method, results are coded, and codes are grouped into concepts. For more information on Grounded Theory, see Glaser and Strauss (1967).

The way I applied elements of the Grounded Theory method is as follows. Based on, (1) the questionnaire study as presented in Chapter 2, (2) literature on codes of conduct as presented in Section 7.2, (3) other literature (including some of the literature reviewed in Section 7.3), and (4) own experiences and discussions with others over the past 25 years, I derived a list of questions for semi-structured interviews:

1. What experiences do you have with ethics, in your role as a researcher?
2. Which ethical dilemmas have you faced as a researcher? How did you deal with them?
3. Are you aware of the ethical dilemmas of other researchers or ethically relevant practices, either in general or in the area of transport? What are these? Please elaborate.
4. Have you ever heard of codes of conduct for research or engineering, or other areas?
5. If yes: which? What do you know about them?
6. Have you heard of the codes of conduct of the Association of Universities in the Netherlands?
7. To what extent do you agree with the codes of conduct of the Association of Universities in the Netherlands? [The codes were shown on hard copy.]
8. Can you reflect on the practical applicability of these codes?
9. Do you have any other ideas about ethics and research in general, or in the area of transport in particular?

Before the interviews, it was made explicit that I did not aim to evaluate the morals of the interviewees, but only to find out about their experiences and dilemmas. It was emphasized that I did not intend to judge or determine what is 'right' or 'wrong', but only to get an impression of dilemmas and how people have dealt with them. I explained that I preferred to hear about real dilemmas and related behaviour, I did not want socially desirable answers. In addition, I explained that impartiality and independence are not 0–1 variables (independence or not), but a continuous concept (level of independence). Reported interview results were sent to interviewees for corrections.

I did not use the full Grounded Theory: I did not code results in concepts, but only presented the results of interviews (the other four sources as presented above were used to inform to the questionnaire). I did use the inductive nature of the method and the ideas of interviewing up to a level of saturation and using the interviews that had already been held in interviews that followed. I did not tell interviewees prior to an interview who else I had already interviewed, or was going to interview. This was firstly for reasons of privacy, and secondly to avoid any influences on answers.

Grounded Theory is a methodology which aims to develop new theory based on data. I did not intend to arrive at a theory, but only at an overview of ethical dilemmas of researchers.

I interviewed eight people who have done research in the area under consideration. At the time of the interviews, three interviewees worked for consultancies, three worked for consultancies but had worked for universities in the past (one of them only for a few months), one worked for both a consultancy and a university, and one worked for a university. They all were involved in research in the areas of CBA, MCA, Environmental Impact Assessment (EIA), or other policy analysis, either because they did such research themselves, or because they did research that was used as input for such *ex ante* evaluations. Research could relate to projects and policies at spatial scales ranging from the local to the (inter)national level.

Seven of the people I interviewed were persons that I had known for many years, and that I expected to be open and honest in their answers, while one person was recommended by someone I know well. The reason for selecting people I know well, is that interviewees must feel comfortable and trust the interviewer. I could very well imagine that interviewees would not be as open in the case of an unknown interviewer.

The results should be treated with some care, firstly because of the relatively low numbers of interviews. Secondly, interviews were held with Dutch people only, which potentially could cause bias (see also Chapter 2).

The minutes of the interviews were sent to the interviewees for corrections – all responded and suggested some minor changes.

After eight interviews, the results tended to saturate. To avoid generalizations based on only a few interviewees, the main findings of the first three questions were converted into 54 propositions, which were then sent to the interviewees, with the request to score them on a scale from -3 (completely disagree) to $+3$ (fully agree) (or 9: not applicable). In social sciences, for methodological reasons, propositions are formulated both positively as well as negatively, to avoid influencing the respondents in a certain direction. In this case, the propositions were formulated in the wording of the interviewees. If they were 'negatively' (critically with respect to ethical issues) formulated, I did the same. The advantage is that I could maintain the formulations of the respondents as much as possible. In addition, formulating propositions positively (and opposite to the formulations of the interviewees) would in all likelihood immediately have been recognized by the respondents. I think they would have been very well capable of avoiding bias, due to the way the propositions were formulated.

Because the questions related to codes of conduct were more specific, these were not included again in the propositions.

Results: Ethical Dilemmas

Ethical dilemmas

Tables 7.2–7.6 give the scores on the propositions related to the first three questions, ordered in categories.

Table 7.2 shows the scores on statements related to the relationship between the researcher and the client. I discuss the propositions not strictly in the order given in Table 7.2, but in another order to get a more fluent storyline. The first subject relates to regional CBAs and related research. Before being able to understand some of the propositions and their responses, it is important to realize that many transport infrastructure projects are regional projects. The majority (6 out of 8) of the respondents agree that regional authorities have the tendency to prescribe too positive scenarios in the case of the *ex ante* evaluation of infrastructure projects (proposition 2). For example, if a high increase in road traffic allows a new road to perform better in CBA terms, they prefer to select scenarios with a relatively high level of economic growth (or other assumptions that result in more road traffic, such as an increase in regional employment). Then the results are influenced in the desired way, generally to increase the chances of a positive decision (to build the project). Five out of eight respondents agree with proposition 3 that researchers sometimes act according to the prescriptions of regions to use too positive scenarios, in the case of the

Table 7.2　Scores on statements related to the relationship between the researcher and the client

		−3	−2	−1	0	1	2	3	9	average	SD
1.	A higher level of independence results in fewer assignments.	3		3		1	1			−1.12	1.885
2.	Regions have the tendency to prescribe too positive scenarios in the case of the *ex ante* evaluation of infrastructure projects.		1	1		2	3	1		1.00	1.690
3.	Researchers sometimes act according to the prescriptions of regions to use too positive scenarios in the case of the *ex ante* evaluation of infrastructure projects.		1	1		4	1		1	0.43	1.397
4.	The stronger the relation between research and policy, the more difficult it is to stay neutral.	1			2	2	2	1		0.75	1.832
5.	Sometimes research results are adapted to outcomes favourable for policy.	1	1	2		3			1	−0.57	1.618
6.	In the Netherlands researchers hardly ever adapt calculations to support the results the client wishes to see.		2	3	1	1		1		−0.38	1.685
7.	Clients often want the seal of independence of the research institute, but nevertheless try to influence the results to their advantage.					2	4	2		2.00	0.756
8.	In the case of *ex ante* evaluations (such as CBAs) governmental bodies want to influence results via the prescription of scenarios.			1		3	3	1		1.38	1.188
9.	Civil servants try to influence analyses of a problem or challenge in a too early stage by mixing up this analysis and policy, governance or financial issues.		2	1		2	3			0.38	1.768

Table 7.2 (continued)

		−3	−2	−1	0	1	2	3	9	average	SD
10.	In the case of the *ex ante* evaluation of policy options the client may select any option.			1		3	1	2	1	1.43	1.397
11.	In the case of infrastructure projects the client often wants the project to be realized.					2	6			1.75	0.463
12.	In the case of infrastructure projects the client often wants to influence results.			1		5	2			1.00	0.926
13.	Some CBAs are kept 'low profile' because the clients have no interest in the dissemination of the results.				2	3	2	1		1.25	1.035
14.	The interests of the client are more important than those of society (e.g. presenting results to the media). Researchers should respect these interests, even if from the perspective of society they would prefer to act differently.	2		1	1	2		2	0	0.12	2.357
15.	If a researcher does non-confidential research for a governmental body and the media ask for results, the researcher **is allowed** to present them.	1	1	2	1		1	2		0.13	2.295
16.	If a researcher does non-confidential research for a governmental body and the media ask for results, the researcher **should** present them.	3	3		1		1			−1.63	1.768
17.	A researcher can accept the points of departure of the client, even if he would prefer to make other choices, as long as he makes this explicit.			1	1	1	2	3		1.63	1.506
18.	If research includes making an inventory of potential solutions, and one of the solutions is a solution the client does not want to be included, it is unacceptable to delete it.					2	4	2		2.00	0.756

ex ante evaluation of infrastructure projects; two disagree (and one does not know). In the Netherlands at the national level, CBAs are supervised by independent researchers, but not at the regional level. A solution to reduce ethical dilemmas and to increase the quality of CBA could be to institutionalize such supervision also at the regional level.

The second subject I discuss is the relation between research and policy in general. Seven of the eight respondents agree with proposition 4: the stronger the relation between research and policy, the more difficult it is to stay neutral. Results with respect to the related proposition 5, 'Sometimes research results are adapted to outcomes favourable for policy', are mixed: three agree and four disagree (and one does not know). Five of the eight respondents think that in the Netherlands researchers adapt calculations to support the results the client wishes to see (proposition 6). All respondents agree with proposition 7: 'Clients often want the seal of independence of the research institute, but nevertheless try to influence the results to their advantage'. This proposition shows why ethical dilemmas can easily occur: the clients want 'the best of both worlds': the seal of independence, but also impact on the results. The wish to influence results in the desired way is also expressed by the scores on proposition 8 (which is strongly related to proposition 2, but now more general): seven of the eight respondents agree that in the case of ex ante evaluations (such as CBAs), governmental bodies want to influence results via the prescription of scenarios. One of the respondents explicitly mentioned in the interview the experience that civil servants try to influence analyses of a problem or challenge in a too early stage by mixing up this analysis and policy, governance, or financial issues (proposition 9). Five of the eight respondents agree, while three disagree.

A third subject of discussion is the impact the client may have on the research questions asked, and points of departure taken. All but one respondent agree with proposition 10: in the case of the ex ante evaluation of policy options, the client may select any option. The results fairly well match those of proposition 17 (a researcher can accept the points of departure of the client, even if he would prefer to make other choices, as long as he makes this explicit) and 18 (if research includes making an inventory of potential solutions, and one of the solutions is a solution the client does not want to be included, it is unacceptable to delete it). Only one respondent disagrees (slightly: score is -1) with proposition 17, none with proposition 18.

Combining interview results and the scores on propositions 8, 10, 17, and 18, the general picture is that respondents generally think the client can decide on the 'what' question (what should be analysed) but not on the 'how' questions. Nevertheless, clients try to influence the research results.

This is probably caused by the fact that in the Netherlands the governmental body that has the task to (try to) realize a project, is also the client of the research. In other words, the client wants the project to be realized (proposition 11, confirmed by all respondents). At least in the case of infrastructure projects, governmental bodies try to influence results: seven of the eight respondents agree that in the case of infrastructure projects the client often wants to influence results (proposition 12). This mixing-up of the client trying to influence the decision making via the research process is also confirmed by proposition 13: 'some CBAs are kept "low profile" because they have no interest in dissemination of the results'. This particularly applies to CBAs, if it shows that the (by the client) preferred option is outperformed by other options, or if for all options, costs (strongly) exceed benefits.

The dilemma of the interests of the client, versus those related to independence, is not the only dilemma related to Table 7.2. Another dilemma is balancing the interests of the client versus those of society. Proposition 14 relates to this dilemma, that is, the interests of the client are more important than those of society (e.g. presenting results to the media). Researchers should respect these interests, even if from the perspective of society they would prefer to act differently. Three respondents disagree, and think the interests of society are of more importance than those of the client, four think the interests of the client are more important. Three of the eight respondents think that if a researcher does non-confidential research for a governmental body and the media ask for results, the researcher is allowed to present them, four disagree (and one is neutral) (proposition 15). Only one respondent thinks that if a researcher does non-confidential research for a governmental body and the media ask for results, the researcher *should* present them (proposition 16).

Despite the attempts of clients to influence results, six of the eight interviewees do not think that a higher level of independence results in less assignments (proposition 1).

Table 7.3 shows the scores on propositions related to transport research in the Netherlands.

Before discussing Table 7.3 it is important to realize that the Netherlands has a standard approach for CBA, the so-called OEI guidelines of 2000 (Eijgenraam et al., 2000) (and some amendments that followed the guidelines a few years later). The guidelines were introduced as a result of manipulated research supporting positive infrastructure decisions in the 1990s (see Chapter 3). As explained above, for national projects independent researchers supervise CBA. In addition, most nationals CBAs and some of the regional CBAs use results of the Dutch National Model System (NMS), or the standardized Regional Model System (RMS), that

Table 7.3   Scores on propositions related to transport research in the Netherlands

	−3	−2	−1	0	1	2	3	9	average	SD
19. The Dutch transport research community is quite professional, as a result of which few ethical dilemmas occur.			2	1	3			2	0.17	0.983
20. The OEI guidelines (and amendments) improved the ethical quality of CBA based on these guidelines.	1				4	2	1		1.00	1.773
21. There is less discussion on items included in the OEI guidelines than for others.		1		1	2	2	2		1.25	1.669
22. If a second opinion is asked for, this leads to a higher quality of CBAs.					2	2	4		2.25	0.886
23. The quality of traffic forecasts is higher if the NMS or RMS is used compared to other transport models.	2		1	1	1		1	2	−0.50	2.345

is familiar to the NMS. At the regional level often other models are used (not RMS), for example a model of a consultant.

In a few interviews respondents explicitly stated that the Dutch transport community is quite professional, leading to few ethical dilemmas (proposition 19). Five of the eight respondents confirm this proposition, one is neutral, and two slightly disagree (score: −1). It seems that according to the respondents, the OEI guidelines have a positive impact on the ethical quality of CBAs: seven of the respondents agree with proposition 20: 'The OEI guidelines (and amendments) improved the ethical quality of CBA based on these guidelines'. The positive impacts of the guidelines on CBAs are also expressed by the scores on proposition 21 (there is less discussion on items included in the OEI guidelines than for others): six of the eight respondents agree. All respondents confirm proposition 22: if a second opinion is asked for, this leads to a higher quality of CBAs. Note that these second opinions are often carried out by two of the respondents (and by me). Results on the positive impacts of the use of NMS and RMS are mixed: three respondents disagree with proposition 23 (the quality of traffic forecasts is higher if the NMS or RMS are used,

Table 7.4   Scores on propositions related to the importance of the role of the researcher

	−3	−2	−1	0	1	2	3	9	average	SD
24. What is an ethical dilemma depends on the role of a researcher.	1				1	3	2	1	0.88	1.808
25. Research at consultancies is carried out always within constraints of time, money, or time of delivering results.					1		7		2.75	0.707
26. Research at universities is carried out always within constraints of time, money or time of delivering results.		1	3	1			3		0.50	2.138
27. It is worse if a university turns out to be not independent compared to a consultancy.	2	1		2	1	2			−0.38	2.066
28. Universities should only accept assignments if they can publish the results.			1	1	1	2	3		1.63	1.506
29. The publication culture at universities makes staff members claim co-authorship, even in cases where they do not deserve it.			1		1	3	2	1	1.71	1.380
30. The pressure to achieve causes university researchers to work towards significance of results.			1	2	2	1	1	1	0.86	1.345

compared to other transport models), two agree, and three are neutral or don't know.

The overall picture is that the respondents think that the OEI guidelines increased the quality of CBAs for national projects in the Netherlands, and reduced ethical dilemmas for researchers. There is no consensus on the impacts of the NMS and RMS.

Table 7.4 presents the scores on propositions related to the importance of the role of the researcher.

Table 7.4 discusses the role of the researcher. In particular, it pays attention to the potential difference between researchers employed at universities versus those working for consultants. Firstly, a very general role-related proposition (24) was formulated: 'What is an ethical dilemma depends on the role of a researcher'. Six researchers agree with this proposition, one is neutral, and one strongly disagrees (score: -3). Consequently, a majority thinks that the role of the researcher is of importance for the question of what an ethical dilemma is. Proposition 25, 'Research at consultancies is carried out always within constraints of time, money or time of delivering results' receives very strong support: seven respondents score $+3$ (strongly agree) and one scores $+1$. At universities, pressure of constraints seems to be much less. Proposition 26, 'Research at universities is carried out always within constraints of time, money, or time of delivering results' is (strongly: $+3$) supported by three respondents. However, four disagree (and one is neutral). Proposition 27 is based on the idea of some respondents that people often think that universities are more independent than consultancies. As a result, it may be worse if a university were to turn out not to be independent compared to a consultancy. Results are mixed: three respondents disagree, three agree, and two are neutral.

Another role-related subject focuses on the domain of the research a university should do. Among academic researchers in the Netherlands, there is often claimed to be a wide belief that universities should not do consultancy, unless there are specific reasons for doing so. A specific reason could be to study the practice of consultancy (applying the method of participating observation) or to do an analysis over several consultancy projects. The exceptions both answer academic questions. In order to be able to draw a line between consultancy and academic research, a guide-line could be that universities should only accept assignments if they can publish the results (proposition 28). Six of the respondents agree with the proposition, one is neutral, and one slightly disagrees (maybe having the exceptions in mind as discussed above).

In most countries, university staff are expected to publish in academic journals. For the position of full professor and associate professor, and in several countries also for assistant professors and postdoctoral scholars, having a nice list of publications is of high importance. This could easily lead to ethical dilemmas, or even unethical practices with respect to (co-) authorship. Proposition 29 relates to the related culture: 'the publication culture at universities makes staff members claim co-authorship, even in cases where they do not deserve it'. Six respondents confirm this proposition, one is neutral, and one does not know. Another dilemma at universities is related to a phenomenon called 'publication bias': reviewers and editors-in-chief of journals are believed to prefer empirical research that presents significant results. As a result, researchers are often believed to select data and methods of analyses so that results are significant. Proposition 30 relates to this phenomenon: 'The pressure to achieve causes university researchers to work towards significance of results'. Four respondents think this is true, two are neutral, one thinks it is not, and one does not know (scores -1).

To summarize, Table 7.4 shows that role-related ethical dilemmas can easily occur. A first dilemma relates to the trade-off between the quality of research and constraints (time, money, time of delivering results), a second dilemma relates to what research a university should or should not do, a third dilemma follows from the publication culture at universities.

So far, propositions were not related to the respondents themselves. Table 7.5 presents the scores on propositions related to personal viewpoints and choices of interviewees.

Propositions 25 and 26 (see above) have shown that time and money related constraints do occur in general. Proposition 31 shows that six of the eight respondents agree with the proposition 'If a research budget turns out to be lower than agreed upon, I adapt quality to time available'. Proposition 32, 'In a majority of my research ethical dilemmas do not play a clear role', has scores relatively close to zero (-1 to $+2$, average is 0.5, four respondents agree, three are neutral, one disagrees). Consequently, the conclusion is that ethical dilemmas do occur regularly. If they were to occur seldom higher scores would result. Six of the respondents have refused assignments because of ethical reasons (proposition 33). These results are in line with those of proposition 34 ('I prefer to have fewer assignments over giving up independence'): seven of the respondents agree with this proposition. In other words, they are willing to pay a price for independence.

In the interviews, one of the respondents expressed the ethical dilemma of independence versus moral obligations to personnel. Based on this dilemma, proposition 35 is formulated: 'I sometimes experience a tension between acquiring work for my personnel on the one hand, and independence on the other hand'. Results are mixed: five disagree, two agree and one does not know. For those who disagree, the reason could be that they do not see this as a dilemma – the choice could be easy (regardless the choice itself), but it could also be that they have not been in the position of this dilemma. Proposition 36 ('If I were to have to fire personnel because of a lack of work, I would accept an assignment resulting in giving up some of my independence') further deals with this dilemma by presenting the hypothetical situation of the (potential) dilemma. Five of the eight respondents scored 0 or 9 (do not know). This could indicate that the proposition is difficult to score, and could indicate that this is a real dilemma.

The next subject covered by Table 7.5 relates to the results of research. Five respondents agree with proposition 37 ('I look more closely at unexpected results of research or models than expected results. As a result,

Table 7.5　Scores on propositions related to the personal viewpoints and choices of the interviewees

	−3	−2	−1	0	1	2	3	9	average	SD
31. If a research budget turns out to be lower than agreed upon, I adapt quality to time available.	1	1			2	2	2		1.13	1.808
32. In a majority of my research ethical dilemmas do not play a clear role.			1	3	3	1			0.50	0.926
33. I have refused assignments because of ethical reasons.	1	1				3	3		1.25	2.375
34. I prefer to have fewer assignments over giving up independence.				1	1	3	3		1.88	1.356
35. I sometimes experience a tension between acquiring work for my personnel on the one hand, and independence on the other hand.	2	1	2		1	1		1	−1.00	1.915
36. If I were to have to fire personnel because of a lack of work I would accept an assignment resulting in giving up some of my independence.	1			3	2			2	−1.17	1.472
37. I look more closely at unexpected results of research or models than expected results. As a result, there is a tendency towards expected results.		1		1	4	1	1		1.29	1.704
38. I pay more attention to outcomes that my client would not like to see.			1		3	3	1		1.38	1.188
39. I sometimes adapt formulations to the clients' wishes.		2			3	1	2		0.87	1.959
40. If I obtain interesting results that the client does not want to see, I exclude them.	2	1	1	2		1		1	0.00	1.826
41. I did stop a running assignment because of ethical reasons.	5	1		1	1				−2.00	1.604
42. I did threaten the client to stop a running assignment for ethical reasons, after which the client adapted his position.	3	1		0		1	3		0.00	2.976

Table 7.5 (continued)

		−3	−2	−1	0	1	2	3	9	average	SD
43.	If I need to review work of others outside my own organization I pay attention to whom it concerns.	3	3			1	1			−1.13	1.885
44.	My research results (that are context-dependent) are misused by others in their research.					1	2	3	1	1	0.88	1.246
45.	If governmental bodies prescribe scenarios, and this may influence results, I accept this.	1	1			1	2	1	2		0.63	2.200
46.	If a colleague in my opinion makes wrong decisions in his research, I sometimes tell this to others.	1		2	1		2	1	1		0.29	2.138
47.	Under pressure of time I sometimes publish research results that in my opinion are not thorough enough, or that are not underpinned well enough.	2	1	1	1	1	1		1		−0.86	1.925

there is a tendency to expected results'). This does not necessarily mean there is an ethical dilemma involved: researchers might simply have good reasons to look more closely at unexpected results because they might be the result of an error – this is confirmed by two interviews. On the other hand, this practice indeed can lead to a tendency to expected results, and maybe therefore to some bias. Proposition 38 ('I pay more attention to outcomes that my client would not like to see') relates more directly to ethical dilemmas. Seven of the eight respondents agree with the proposition. This practice is a relatively strong indication that a bias towards results the client wishes could easily result. In line with proposition 38, proposition 39 ('I sometimes adapt formulations to the clients' wishes') is confirmed by six respondents. The classic example of formulations (also mentioned by three respondents in the interviews) is the choice between 'the glass is half empty' and 'the glass is half full'. Both express the same content, but the client prefers the latter formulation. Proposition 40 is an even stronger expression of adapting to the client: 'If I obtain interesting results that the client does not want to see, I exclude them'. Three respondents agree, three do not and two score 0 or 9. Only one respondent did stop a running assignment because of ethical reasons (proposition 41). However, four respondents scored positively on proposition 42: 'I did threaten the client to stop a running assignment for ethical reasons, after which the client adapted his position'. This is an indication that clients do try to influence researchers in a way they think is ethically unacceptable.

Proposition 43 ('If I need to review work of others outside my own organization, I pay attention to whom it concerns') is inspired by an interviewee who said this plays a role when (s)he reviewed papers for journals. Scores indicate that two respondents confirm the proposition, six do not. Five of the respondents scored positively on proposition 44: 'My research results (that are context-dependent) are misused by others in their research'. This typically relates to (mis)using the results in another context for the benefit of the user.

Propositions 2 and 3 (see above) discussed the prescription of scenarios to influence results by clients *in general*. Proposition 45 ('If governmental bodies prescribe scenarios, and this may influence results, I accept this') focuses on the individual respondents. Five respondents scored positively, two negatively. This could be an indication of a relatively high pressure to accept the assumptions of the client, even if the researcher knows the results are influenced by the choices in the direction the client wishes.

Another ethical dilemma can occur if other researchers make wrong decisions. In the Netherlands, it is quite common to tell people when you think there are errors in the research of others. But would one also do this if a colleague makes a 'wrong' decision? Proposition 46 ('If a colleague in my opinion makes wrong decisions in his research, I sometimes tell this to others') expresses this dilemma. Three respondents would not do so, three would, and two scored 0 or 9. Probably this is an indication of a realistic dilemma, as made explicit in the interview by one of the interviewees.

The general (potential) dilemma of dealing with constraints related to time and money is discussed above (propositions 25 and 26). What would be the impact of such constraints on the respondents? Proposition 47 ('Under pressure of time I sometimes publish research results that in my opinion are not thorough enough, or that are not underpinned well enough') deals with the constraint that showed up in the interviews most often: the time constraint. Four respondents scored negatively, two positively. It seems that the recognition of constraints is widely accepted to exist for consultancies (proposition 25) and to a lesser extent to universities (proposition 26), but only two respondents themselves admit to publishing results that are not thorough enough, or are not underpinned well enough. The results may seem to contradict the scores on proposition 31 (see above) showing that six of the eight respondents agree with the

Table 7.6   Scores on other propositions

		−3	−2	−1	0	1	2	3	9	average	SD
51.	Some policy relevant subjects would benefit from some support from science. In such cases it is undesirable to stay completely neutral.	5	1	1			1			−2.00	1.773
52.	Personal positions of researchers, e.g. with respect to the economy or the environment, influence research results.			1		1	3	3		1.88	1.356
53.	Researchers generally do not discuss ethical dilemmas with colleagues in their own organization.	4	1			1	2			−1.13	2.357
54.	Researchers generally do not discuss ethical dilemmas with colleagues outside their own organization.	2		3		1	1	1		−0.38	2.200

proposition 'If a research budget turns out to be lower than agreed upon, I adapt quality to time available'. But the results do not necessarily contradict: it is possible that researchers adapt the quality without presenting results that are not underpinned well.

To summarize, Table 7.5 shows that ethical issues are quite common and sometimes result in dilemmas. The majority of the respondents have refused assignments because of ethical reasons. It seems to be difficult to choose between independence and having to fire personnel. Results (at least: formulations) are adapted to some extent to the clients' wishes. Four respondents have threatened to stop a running assignment for ethical reasons, after which the client adapted his position. Five respondents accept the clients' prescription of scenarios that tend towards (for the client) favourable results.

Table 7.6 presents the scores on other propositions.

Proposition 51 is based on one interviewee who expressed a potential dilemma because some policy relevant subjects would benefit from some scientific support. In such cases it is undesirable to stay completely neutral. Results show that (s)he is the only respondent with a positive score. The other seven disagree. Obviously most respondents think a researcher should always be neutral, even if not being neutral would support a policy that from a scientific point of view probably results in benefits for society.

Proposition 52 ('Personal positions of researchers, e.g. with respect to the economy or the environment, influence research results') results from a few remarks of respondents expressing the view that the area of research of a researcher could reflect to her own interest; for example, an economist doing economic policy analyses might prioritize the economy more than the average researcher or citizen. The same could apply to a researcher in the area of road safety or the environment. According to the respondents, such personal interests could easily lead to bias: seven of the eight respondents agree with the proposition.

Proposition 53 ('Researchers generally do not discuss ethical dilemmas with colleagues in their own organization') and 54 ('Researchers generally do not discuss ethical dilemmas with colleagues outside their own organization') are based on remarks of interviewees saying something about this openness. Results are strongly mixed: five disagree, three agree or are neutral (both propositions). Obviously there is quite some heterogeneity amongst the respondents with respect to this subject.

Finally, a Principal Component Analysis (PCA) was carried out,[8] aiming to find out to what extent the propositions in the categories as presented in Tables 7.2–7.6 measure different issues. Results reveal that the propositions do measure different issues: clear patterns could be distinguished in each category of propositions as presented in Tables 7.2–7.6. The results of the PCA will not be discussed here because the added value compared to the results as presented above is (from the perspective of this book) limited.

Differences between consultancy and universities

It is possible that opinions and experiences with respect to ethics differ between respondents, based on their backgrounds. The eight respondents were split into two equally sized groups: those who (partly) work for a university or have worked for a university for multiple years, versus consultants. Below I discuss some remarkable differences. Note that differences are only indications, the low numbers of interviewees do not allow for statistical testing at the level of responses to individual propositions. The text below discusses only propositions with a difference in average scores between both groups of at least 2.00.

A first remarkable difference relates to the score on proposition 2: 'Regions have the tendency to prescribe too positive scenarios in the case of the *ex ante* evaluation of infrastructure projects'. Interviewees with a university background score on average 2.00, consultants score 0.00. The difference could relate to the perception on what is acceptable: consultants might not label the tendency to prescribe 'favourable' scenarios as *too* favourable – they might be more tolerant with respect to the clients' wishes.

A second remarkable difference is the score on proposition 5: 'Sometimes research results are adapted to outcomes favourable for policy'. Whereas persons with a university background have an average score of −1.75, consultants have an average score of 1.00. This matches the general belief that consultants may a bit more easily adapt to the clients' wishes. The difference might first of all be explained by the difference in market position of consultants versus universities: consultants are expected to be more oriented in the direction of the clients' wishes. In addition, the difference might be explained by the clients' selection of researchers. I here cite one of the interviewees: 'Clients tend to self-select: they do not usually ask a researcher with an independent reputation if their aim is to influence results'.

A third remarkable difference relates to propositions 15 and 16: 'If a researcher does non-confidential research for a governmental body and the media ask for results, the researcher **is allowed** to present them' (proposition 15) and 'If a researcher does non-confidential research for a governmental body and the media ask for results, the researcher **should** present them' (proposition 16). The average scores for interviewees with a university background on proposition 15 is 1.75, versus −1.50 for consultants; values for proposition 16 are −0.75 versus −2.50. The results show that interviewees with a university background tend to value the interests of society more highly compared to consultants, who value the client's interests more highly.

A fourth difference relates to the average score on proposition 17: 'A researcher can accept the points of departure of the client, even if he would prefer to make other choices, as long as he makes this explicit' – consultants score on average 2.75, interviewees with a university background 0.50.

Finally, scores on proposition 27 'It is worse if a university turns out to be not independent compared to a consultancy' differ: interviewees with a university background score 0.75 on average, consultants −1.50. In other words, interviewees with a university background slightly agree with the proposition – they may think they should have more strict standards with respect to consultancies, whereas consultants tend to disagree: they should have about the same standards with respect to independence.

As explained above, the differences are only indications because the numbers are too low to allow for statistical testing at the level of separate propositions. Nevertheless, a very elementary form of statistical testing is possible at the level of scores on the total number of propositions as discussed above. I excluded scores on proposition 2 because the interpretation of scores is less straightforward. For scores on propositions 5, 15, 16, 17 and 27 a cross table was derived distinguishing on the one axis consultants versus

Table 7.7   Scores on propositions 5, 15, 16, 17 and 27 by background of the respondent and priority for independence versus the client

	Priority for independence	Priority for the clients' interests
Consultants	4	17
University background	15	5

Note: Chi² = 16.47, significance < 0.01.

researchers with a university background, and on the other axis scores at each side of the average score per proposition, distinguishing priority for independence versus the interests of the client. The score of 9 on proposition 5 is excluded, resulting in 39 scores. Table 7.7 presents the results.

The difference is significant at the 1 percent level. The conclusion is that for scores on propositions 5, 15, 16, 17 and 27 there are significant differences between consultants and respondents with a university background: the first category prioritizes the client's interests over those of independence, the latter category has opposite priorities.

In addition, a correlation matrix was made to find out to what extent scores of individual respondents match. The most striking result is that only one (small: −0.13) negative value occurred between a consultant and a person with a university background, all other correlations are positive. As a result, although differences in scores on some propositions between the two categories of respondents are remarkable, the overall pattern is that both groups have more in common with respect to their scores, than that they differ.

Citations

In addition to these results below, I will give some example citations of individual interview results, partly related to propositions. Some citations are adapted for reasons of readability, or because of making them readable for the non-Dutch reader. Interesting citations that could endanger the anonymity of the interviewees were excluded.

I always respect clients. This does not result in ethical dilemmas for me.

The Dutch transport research community is quite professional, and as a result ethical dilemmas do not occur frequently.

An angry client is not a problem. I stay independent and accept a loss of turnover.

A consultant sometimes gets part of the tunnel vision of the client, resulting in lock-in and bias in estimates of costs or benefits.

I hardly face ethical dilemmas. Already in a meeting preceding a tender I will have explained my position: I work for a university, and therefore I am independent. Take it or leave it.

Clients tend to self-select: they do not usually ask a researcher with an independent reputation if their aim is to influence results.

Sometimes a conflict or trade-off exists between being 100% neutral versus having an impact on the decision making related to your research. Being not 100% neutral, and interpreting your results, could be the better decision.

Policy makers sometimes want to avoid sensitive subjects by excluding them via demarcations. I then always accept this.

Thanks to the OEI guidelines[9] there hardly is any discussion with respect to how to calculate effects. But if no price tags exist, there is discussion on the price tags to be used.

For calculating air pollution, standardized calculation methods exist, but for data no standardization exists. I have the impression that not standardizing datasets is done on purpose, to give the authorities some degrees of freedom.

Universities often think that other research institutes and consultants do their work too quick-and-dirty.

What is ethically acceptable depends to a large extent on the role you have and agree upon, and this role and the researchers' position should be made very clear and explicit from the start.

You can help a client by providing arguments that support his interests, but not in the role of an independent researcher or institute.

A lot of choices related to ethical issues are pure personal choices.

A major dilemma is: what to do if the research budget turns out to be not sufficient to do the research with the quality you think is needed?

For some companies a dilemma exists if they potentially can do a job in a country with a completely different culture with respect to corruption or bribing.

After writing the research report I consider my job as finished. And I have no problem with this. I know of others who then sometimes face a dilemma: should they inform others?

Everybody plays a game, nobody is completely independent.

Results: Codes of Conduct

Below the answers to the questions on codes of conduct are summarized.

Have you ever heard of codes of conduct for research or engineering or other areas? If yes: which? What do you know about them?
Four of the interviewees had heard about codes of conduct, in three cases because their organization has one. The fourth interviewee could easily mention a few. One interviewee recognized the label 'codes of conduct' and was aware they existed, but only vaguely. The three others had never heard of codes of conduct. Those who work for organizations that have a code of conduct have paid some attention to them, but in two cases they were not really a live issue in the organization.

Have you heard of the codes of conduct of the Association of Universities in the Netherlands?
Only one interviewee had heard about the VSNU codes of conduct, and even that interviewee did not know anything about them.

To what extent do you agree with the codes of conduct of the Association of Universities in the Netherlands? (The codes were shown on hard copy.) Can you reflect on the practical applicability of these codes?

Scrupulousness
Only one respondent supported the importance of scrupulousness in general and considered this to be applicable. Five of them sympathized to some extent with it, but considered it to be not always applicable, constraints with respect to time and money being the most important reasons for limited applicability. One of them explicitly emphasized that also in the case of PhD research (where there is relatively more research time), time constraints matter: the candidate has to finish the PhD research within a limited time frame (in the Netherlands: often four years). The two other interviewees thought this code of scrupulousness ridiculous: it does not work that way.

Reliability
Seven respondents supported the reliability code, although some remarks were made related to practical implications. For example, reliability is set within the constraints of the assumptions of the research, or time constraints do not allow the researcher to be 100 percent reliable (because it costs time). One respondent was critical about all codes of conduct, so

Table 7.8   Scores on propositions related to codes of conduct

	−3	−2	−1	0	1	2	3	9	average	SD
48. Codes of conduct are not really alive in practice.		2			1	1	3	1	0.75	1.909
49. Research should be reproducible.						3	5		2.63	0.518
50. Own integrity conflicts with helping the client.	3	1	1	1	1	1			−1.13	1.959

also about reliability: it is a utopia to think researchers can always work according to the codes of conduct of the VSNU.

Verifiability
Five respondents supported the importance and practical applicability of the verifiability code of conduct. Two gave support but with constraints. These constraints relate to: (1) time limits: being 100 percent verifiable would cost too much time; and (2) the idea of being *fully* verifiable. One respondent thought the code is a utopia.

Impartiality
Three interviewees supported the impartiality code of conduct and think it is applicable. Three interviewees supported the idea but emphasized that in practice this is not always possible. Two respondents did not support this code. One explicitly considered this not to be a problem, as long as one does not claim to be impartial, and makes clear for each specific case that one is not. Again, one respondent thought that this represents utopia.

Independence
Three respondents supported the independence code. Three others considered this to be only partially possible. The same respondent again explicitly considered this not to be a problem, as long as one does not claim to be independent and makes clear for each specific case that one is not. Again, one thought this is a utopia.

In addition to the propositions related to the first three questions asked of the interviewees, three propositions were included related to codes of conduct. Table 7.8 presents the results.

Table 7.8 shows that codes of conduct are not really live issues amongst the respondents (proposition 48): only two respondents disagree with the proposition expressing this. There is unanimous support for the proposition (49) that results should be reproducible. Five of the respondents disagree with proposition 50 that their own integrity conflicts with helping the client.[10]

Again a difference between consultants and interviewees with a university background is remarkable. The difference relates to proposition 50: 'Own integrity conflicts with helping the client'. Interviewees with a university background score on average 0.00, consultants −2.25. It seems that consultants do not at all see this conflict, whereas people with a university background are neutral. Maybe consultants accept the clients' wishes more easily without feeling uncomfortable with respect to their own integrity.

The overall result is that most support exists for verifiability and reliability. Most interviewees sympathize with the codes on impartiality and independence, but emphasize that in practice it is not possible to be 100 percent impartial and independent. The least support relates to the code on scrupulousness: constraints with respect to time and money make this a utopia. As explained above, one respondent thinks that, in general, the codes of conduct are a utopia. This researcher notes that, in practice, there are always reasons why acting according to the codes is not 100 percent possible.

My general impression is that codes of conduct in general are not really an issue, and certainly those of the VSNU are hardly known. There is some sympathy for codes of conduct, even if they are not at the forefront of the mind of the researcher. The overall picture is that practice often conflicts with acting at a level of 100 percent according to the codes of conduct of the VSNU. It is important to realize that the codes of conduct are codes for universities, not necessarily for all researchers.

Conclusions

Before summarizing the findings of Section 7.4 it is important to realize (as emphasized in Section 7.1) that I do not at all want to suggest a moral judgement of the opinions or decisions of the respondents. The results of Section 7.4 are presented in order to give an impression of ethics and ethical dilemmas related to the transport research community in the Netherlands, in particular focusing on researchers involved in the *ex ante* evaluation of transport policies. Secondly, it is important to realize that the results are based on eight interviews, and therefore cannot be regarded as more than indicative.

One important conclusion is that several dilemmas relate to clients who want to influence results. They might prescribe scenarios they prefer, formulate assumptions that are favourable for them, and try to persuade researchers to formulate results in a (for the client) more favourable way. The result that six of the eight respondents had threatened to stop their ongoing research for ethical reasons illustrates this.

A second conclusion is that respondents generally think the client can decide on the 'what' question (what should be analysed) but not on the 'how' questions (how should the research be carried out).

A third conclusion is that dilemmas occur related to balancing the interests of the client versus those of society.

Fourthly, the respondents think that the OEI guidelines (guidelines that explain that a CBA should be carried out for large national infrastructure projects, including how these CBAs should be carried out) increased the quality of CBAs for national projects in the Netherlands, and reduced ethical dilemmas for researchers. There is no consensus on the impacts of the standardized models NMS and RMS.

Fifthly, role related dilemmas can easily occur. A first dilemma in this category relates to the trade-off between the quality of research and constraints (time, money, time of delivering results); a second dilemma relates to what research a university should or should not do; and a third dilemma follows from the publication culture at universities.

Sixthly, most respondents think a researcher should always be neutral, even if not being neutral were to support a policy that from a scientific point of view probably results in benefits for society.

7.5   REFLECTION AND DISCUSSION

This section discusses some issues in the area of ethics and doing research. Although I did not find literature on the subjects discussed in this section, I do not claim originality for my ideas.

Personal Interpretation

As explained above, codes of conduct are often not so specific that in each situation one knows exactly what to do. A lot of personal interpretation is possible. Even the same situation can be interpreted completely differently by different persons. To illustrate this, I will give a personal example. In 2009/2010, together with two other researchers, I was asked to fulfil an arbiter role in a conflict between the Port of Rotterdam and Friends of the Earth Netherlands. The conflict was about future harbour extensions and environmental impacts. Both parties decided to stop their legal procedures and develop a policy package that should lead to certain environmental goals. The three arbiters had to check the scientific quality of the related research reports, and to advise on a possible policy package leading to the environmental goals. When the project was about 80 percent finished, the arbiters received an invitation from the Port of Rotterdam to attend a football match at the football club Feyenoord, in the private box of the Port of Rotterdam, together with representatives of Friends of the Earth (and others). I decided to go, one of the others deliberately decided not to go. I discussed this with him a few weeks after the football match. He had ethical considerations as a factor in not accepting the invitation: he wanted to avoid any suggestion of bribe or influence. On the other hand, I (not at all being a fan of football – I was not even able to give the names of any of the football players of either team) thought I was more or less obliged to go, for reasons of networking and informal contact, and to increase the acceptance of our report. This meant that we both had ethical considerations, but our conclusions were completely different.

Does the Role in which Research is Done Matter?

In the codes of conduct, I have not found evidence of the importance of the role in which people do research. I would argue that this role matters because the expectations of potential readers could very well be role-dependent. To illustrate this, I will give an example. Let us assume a report evaluating the pros and cons of the option to build a new rail line. On the one hand, this report could have been written as part of a PhD research project carried out at a well respected university, under the supervision of a well respected professor who did a lot of high quality research in the area, with an indisputable reputation, and financed by the National Science Foundation. On the other hand, the report could be a memorandum of oral pleading written by a consultant who is generally known to report any wishes of the client, with the research financed by the interest group supporting the new project. I would argue that the reader expects the report to be neutral and of high quality in the first case, but not at all so in the latter case. Consequently, from the point of view of expectations, and the related role the report could play in the decision-making process, I would argue that it matters who writes the report. For example, I would consider it morally much worse if the university report turned out to be manipulated, than in the case of the consultant's.

What to Do in the Case of Multiple Roles?

Some researchers have multiple roles, for example as a university professor and as a consultant. Can there be a difference between codes of conduct that is role-dependent? If so, would it make a difference whether or not the researcher in her role as consultant makes it explicit in the report that she is also a university professor?

The Role of Research: Why is It Carried Out?

In line with the discussion on the roles of researchers, I would argue that the (expected) use of the results matter, and that the methodology should probably be adapted to this use. Again, I will give an example. Let us suppose the *ex ante* evaluation of a policy to reduce the number of kilometres driven by older cars without modern technologies to reduce emissions (e.g. a scrappage scheme). How 'good' should the quality of the research be? In option 1 I suppose a Ministry of the Environment that wants to propose a package of policy options to reduce NO_2 concentrations, including prescribing technologies in specific categories of manufacturing industry, technologies for several categories of road and non-road transport, and technologies for power plants. The policy package will be primarily based on cost-effectiveness, expressed as costs for society per kg of reduction in NO_2 emissions. In option 2 the client is the same Ministry, but now the research is carried out to find out if WHO standards for NO_2 concentrations will be met. I would argue in the first case the quality could be much lower compared to the second case. At my previous job, at the Dutch National Institute of Public Health and the Environment (RIVM), we produced many calculations of cost-effectiveness of potential future policies and technologies. Cross-sector comparisons have shown many times that cost-effectiveness of distinguishable options could easily vary by a factor of 10 or 100 (and sometimes even more). For such purposes, a simple methodology most of the time will 'do the job': if a method that would take three months of study instead of half a day would probably change the cost-effectiveness of an option by not more than 10 percent, spending three months is probably a waste of time, since for the purpose such small differences are not at all relevant. But let us now turn to option 2. I assume it is very important to find out if, and to what extent, the policy could lead to no longer exceeding the WHO standards. In that case, the results could make a huge difference with respect to whether or not a new residential area would be built. Then probably the high quality research taking three months would be the best choice, especially if it is uncertain if the air quality standards will be met or not.[11] To summarize, I think the methodology should be 'fit for purpose'. If a 'quick and dirty' method were to be chosen because spending more time and money is not worth the effort, I would argue that the researcher has to make this explicit, and link it to the aims of the study, to avoid misuse of the results.

Can One Hide Behind 'Demarcations' or 'Methodology'?

In the case of contract research clients often have a limited scope. For example, a local municipality might be interested in the effects of infrastructure policies for its own territory. What then to do if a researcher finds out there are non-negligible effects just outside this territory, and knows that reporting these effects could significantly influence the decision-making process? Let us suppose the client definitely does not want these effects to be reported. Can the researcher simply make a remark in the 'demarcations section' about which effects are (not) included?

Another example: what if the client asks for effects up until a certain future year, whereas the researcher knows that after that year impacts are expected that certainly could be relevant for decision making?

A third example: what to do if two methods are available to calculate noise levels of a new road, resulting in different noise levels? Method A is proven to be better than method B, but the client prefers method B because of his interests. Can the researcher simply make explicit that method B is used, or should she use method A despite the client's wishes? In addition, what to do if, in the tendering phase, the client makes explicit that method B should be used? Challenging this wish probably results in not getting the project. To make this example even more complicated: suppose the competitor is known for being even more 'flexible' with respect to the client's wishes. In all likelihood the competitor will decide to use method B, and probably will even use biased inputs. In this case, declining to tender because of the obligation to use method B could result in an even more biased research.

A final example: what to do if a before-and-after study needs to show the effects of policy changes, whereas the conclusions would certainly be influenced by the choice of the years? This is not just a hypothetical example: research has shown that this choice can have huge impacts on outcomes and conclusions (Olsson et al., 2010). The client may have preferences for the choice of years, to influence the conclusions. Can one hide behind 'points of departure'?

To conclude: one can debate from an ethical perspective to what extent a researcher can hide behind the client's wishes by making the implications explicit in the demarcations section of the research report.

The Formulation of the Research Aim

Another dilemma is the formulation of the research questions and aims. What to do if these are not the 'best' formulations, considering the (likely) use of the research? Let us again take the example of the policy to scrap older cars because of air pollution. What to do if the research question, formulated by the association of car importers, is: '*Will NO$_2$ standards be exceeded if the policy were to be implemented?*' The researcher might simply calculate concentrations for a scenario including the scrappage policy. But what to do if the researcher finds out that the NO$_2$ standards will be met anyway, even without the policy, but the association does not want this to be reported because it wants to use the report in its own interest? Can one hide behind a methodology section that describes that concentrations for (only) one scenario (including the policy) are calculated?

Value-free Versus Objective Research

As explained above, the empirical research as described was not carried out with the intention to put any moral value on the respondents. This does not mean that I think any position with respect to the ethics of doing research is OK – the existence of codes of conduct are an indication for the relevance of moral issues related to research. It is not the aim of this book to discuss the literature on the ethics of doing research. However, I want to briefly reflect on the difference between 'value free' research and 'objective' research. Doing science is certainly value related. The choice to become a researcher might be value laden, as is the choice to become an academic researcher or a consultant doing research. The choice of research topics is often value laden, both from the perspective of the client, as well as from the perspective of the researcher. Even the choice of methods and data can be value laden. Douglas (2009) labels such values as 'the indirect role of values'. In addition, a direct role exists. She states that

> the direct role must be constrained to those choices in the early stages of science, where one is not yet deciding what to believe from one's research or what empirical claims to make. Once a scientist has embarked on the course of research, the indirect role of values should be the only role of values, whether social, ethical, or cognitive. . . . In the case of politicized science, the norm against a direct role for values in the decision about empirical claims is violated. When scientists suppress, or are asked to suppress, research findings because the results are unpalatable or unwelcome, values are playing a direct role in the wrong place in science. When scientists alter, or are forced to alter, the interpretations of their results because they are unwelcome by their funders or their overseers, values again are playing an unacceptable, direct role. (Douglas, 2009: 112–113)

For a further discussion on values and doing research I refer the reader to her book.

7.6   CONCLUSIONS

The most important conclusions of this chapter are summarized below.

Codes of conduct/ethical codes are codes in which organizations lay down guidelines for responsible behaviour of their members.

Codes of conduct are formulated for a variety of reasons, like increasing moral awareness, the identification and interpretation of the moral norms and values of a profession or a company, the stimulation of ethical discussion, as a way to increase accountability to the outside world, and to improve the image of a profession or company.

These codes can be categorized by depth, breadth, and purpose.

Professional codes generally are related to three domains: (1) conducting a profession with integrity and honesty, and in a competent way; (2) obligations towards employers and clients; and (3) responsibility towards the public and society.

Codes of conduct can conflict; for example, obligations to clients can conflict with professional integrity and honesty.

(Interpretations of) codes of conduct can be discipline, country, and case specific.

Codes of conduct do not give strict prescriptions; personal interpretations are important for using them in practice.

In the case of large infrastructure projects, cost overruns and demand shortfalls are very common. Strategic behaviour of those who benefit from a positive decision to build is probably the most important reason for cost overruns and demand shortfalls.

Strategic behaviour leading to cost overruns or demand shortfalls may be reduced by codes of conduct that can be punitive. In addition, guarantees by consultants (or other research institutes) for the quality of cost and demand forecasts could increase their quality. In addition, explicitly including ethics more in education programmes could contribute to 'better' research.

The empirical study presented in Section 7.4 shows that researchers face several ethical dilemmas, the most dominant dilemmas being related to the client's interests versus those of independence or society. In addition, Section 7.4 shows that the respondents think that the OEI guidelines (guidelines that explain that a CBA should be carried out for large national infrastructure projects, and include guidance on how these CBAs should be carried out) increased the quality of CBAs for national projects in the Netherlands, and reduced ethical dilemmas for researchers.

The roles of researchers could matter for the question of what is morally good or not; for example, it could be morally much worse if a report of a well respected university group turned out to be manipulated, than if a manipulated report were to be written by a consultant well known for writing memoranda of oral pleading.

The quality of research should probably depend on its use. The selection of methods in relationship to the aims of the research, including its value for other purposes, should probably be reported explicitly.

There probably are limits with respect to the options for a researcher to 'hide' behind formulations of research aims or questions, demarcations, or methodological choices.

8. The use of models

8.1 INTRODUCTION

Questions related to modelling include:

- How reliable are models in the case of large changes in independent variables? Is their use in the case of large changes OK?
- To what extent do models make policy makers aware of problems?
- To what extent do current transport models reproduce current thinking?
- Do current transport models present the indicators that are needed for *ex ante* evaluations of ethically relevant issues?
- Who should be allowed to use transport models?
- What to do if multiple models for the same problem exist, that result in different outcomes?
- Should the researcher (only) present model outcomes, or correct these outcomes based on expert judgement?

In addition to the previous chapter, this chapter aims to further elaborate on the ethical dimensions of research by discussing the ethical dimensions of the use of models. The aim is to increase awareness of the ethical dimensions of model use in the clients asking for a study in which models are used, modellers themselves, those researchers that apply models, and those that use model results (formal clients and other actors such as interest groups). In this chapter, I only discuss models used for the *ex ante* evaluation of policy options.[1] As a result, other model types such as decision models are excluded. In fact, only transport and impact models are discussed. Within those categories, this chapter does not discuss all transport and impact models, but concentrates on those models generally used for *ex ante* evaluation of transport policies and plans.

The term 'model' is often defined broadly; for example, Allison et al. (1994: 13) define models as 'any system of relations used to represent another system of relations'. This definition is one of the broadest I know. For example, it also includes 'models of models' such as meta models. Other definitions are a bit more restrictive, and define models as schematic representations of a part of reality. But even such definitions are broad, and include both mathematical as well as conceptual models. In this chapter, I use the word model in a more limited way: the word is used for mathematical models only. Transport models refer to mathematical models that represent a part of the transport system. Another limitation is that I use the word models in this chapter not for 'models for science' but for 'models for problem-solving' (Little, 1994) or more particularly, for 'quantitative models used for the *ex ante* evaluation of transport policies and plans'.

Below, the term 'outcome of interest' is used for a specific area of interest in the case of (in this case, *ex ante*) evaluations, for example, safety, noise, accessibility. An indicator expressing the value of an outcome of interest is labelled an 'output indicator'. The terms 'model output' (general) or 'model output indicator' or 'output variable' (specific) are used to label the output of models, which are either directly or indirectly used to calculate output indicators.

Section 8.2 firstly gives an introduction to transport models and their use, and describes why the use of models is so popular in the transport research arena. Secondly, Section 8.3 gives an overview of model categories. Section 8.4 then discusses the ethical dimensions of the use of models, based on the checklist in Section 3.6. Section 8.5 discusses the ethical dimensions of the use of models from other perspectives, including the model categories as presented in Section 8.3. Section 8.6 summarizes the main conclusions.

8.2 AN INTRODUCTION TO TRANSPORT MODELS AND THEIR USE

What Do Transport Models Do?

Modelling plays an important role in *ex ante* evaluations of transport policy choice options, for instance in reviewing alternatives for infrastructure plans. Such models typically generate values of output indicators that are either directly of interest for policy alternatives, or provide the basis to calculate the value of the (final) indicators that are of relevance. They do so for one or multiple future years. In the case of infrastructure plans, the future years are generally a few decades in the future. Policy options include, for example, options for changes in infrastructure (new roads or railway lines, adding capacity to existing roads, harbour and airport extensions), options for public transport services, options for pricing and land-use alternatives, and their transport implications at multiple spatial scales (national, regional, local level). Note that this last policy option is more a spatial planning option than a transport option. But if the transport implications of land-use alternatives are important, the same models are generally used as those for the transport policy related options. Land-use options are therefore also mentioned.

The values of the output indicators not only depend on the policy assumptions, but also on several other factors, often called 'external forces'. In the case of passenger transport, these include factors such as demographic variables (mainly population size, the distribution over age classes and household classes), economic variables (incomes, size of the labour force per sector), prices of fuels or crude oil, and technological changes expressed in vehicle characteristics. For goods transport, factors that are often included in models are economic variables such as overall economic growth, or growth per sector, and their implications for tonnes to be lifted and transported for specific goods categories, trade patterns (resulting in the origins and destinations of goods), and factors related to changes in logistics. External forces generally are input variables for models. It is usual to combine values for variables of such external forces in scenarios.

Note that models are not only used to estimate the values of output indicators for given policy choice options, but also to explore the future in general, regardless of policy options. This exploration can result in awareness of problems that may occur, or challenges to be faced. In a next step (reducing or solving problems, meeting challenges), policy options of course become relevant.

The Popularity of Transport Models for *Ex Ante* Evaluations

Why is the use of models to explore the future in the area of transport so popular? The main reason is that there is no good alternative for obtaining an impression of what might be the effects of policy options, or which trends in relevant output indicators can be expected. This results from the fact that many of the factors interact in a complex way. Taking passenger transport as an example, travellers make multiple choices related to trip frequency, mode choice, destination choice, the time of day at which they travel, and route choice. In addition, they make choices with respect to their means of transport; for example will they buy a car, or even more than one, and which car type (fuel type choice, size, age, etc.)? Will they buy (and use) a bicycle? All such choices are influenced by many factors, related to the travellers themselves (e.g., age, income, personal preferences), characteristics of their households, employment status, locations of potential destinations, characteristics of travel options (costs, travel time, convenience, perceived safety, etc.), and social and cultural values. In addition, determinants for travel choices to some extent interact; for example, improvements in transport infrastructure could induce land-use changes. In turn, due to land-use changes infrastructure can change; for example, because policy makers decide to build additional infrastructure to connect new residential areas to the current infrastructure system, and so to the rest of society. Over time, due to land use and transport changes, the wants and needs of people change. Due to changes in infrastructure people might choose other destinations for activities such as working, visiting family and friends, recreation, sports and education, even if land-use patterns were not to change. Next to the many determinants for travel and activity decisions and their interactions, impacts on the environment and safety result from not only these, but, in addition, from more determinants, related to the use of vehicles and technology, and even more interactions. Figure 8.1 conceptualizes all such interactions.

Without models, it is almost impossible to get a useful score on outcomes of interest and their related indicator values, in order to compare policy options. Note that even advanced transport models (see Section 8.3) do not include all these determinants and their mutual and dynamic interactions.

A second reason why models are quite popular in the area of the *ex ante* evaluation of transport policy options is that they provide quantitative information that is needed for *ex ante* evaluations – see Chapter 3. Travel time changes, not only because of new or changed (e.g. upgraded) infrastructure, but also on an origin–destination basis, can be easily estimated using models. Similarly, the volumes of people and vehicles travelling between specific origins and destinations, as well as the levels of use (vehicle intensities) of infrastructure can be estimated using models. Because most benefits from improvements in the transport system result from reduced Generalized Transport Costs (GTC – see also previous chapters) and increased transport volumes (see Chapter 3), models are very useful to make possible quantitative estimations of dominant benefit categories. The quantitative estimation of other relevant indicators, such as noise levels, emission levels, concentrations of pollutants, and safety levels, is generally also based on models. These models use output of interest from transport models, in particular traffic forecasts, as input. They also estimate the impacts under consideration using additional (impact) models.

A third reason for the popularity of models is their (perceived) neutrality. These models are almost without exception calibrated, in some cases validated, and many of them are used very frequently, and as a result well tested. As a result, the use of models could reduce the options for manipulation, or at least the chance of introducing subjective elements.

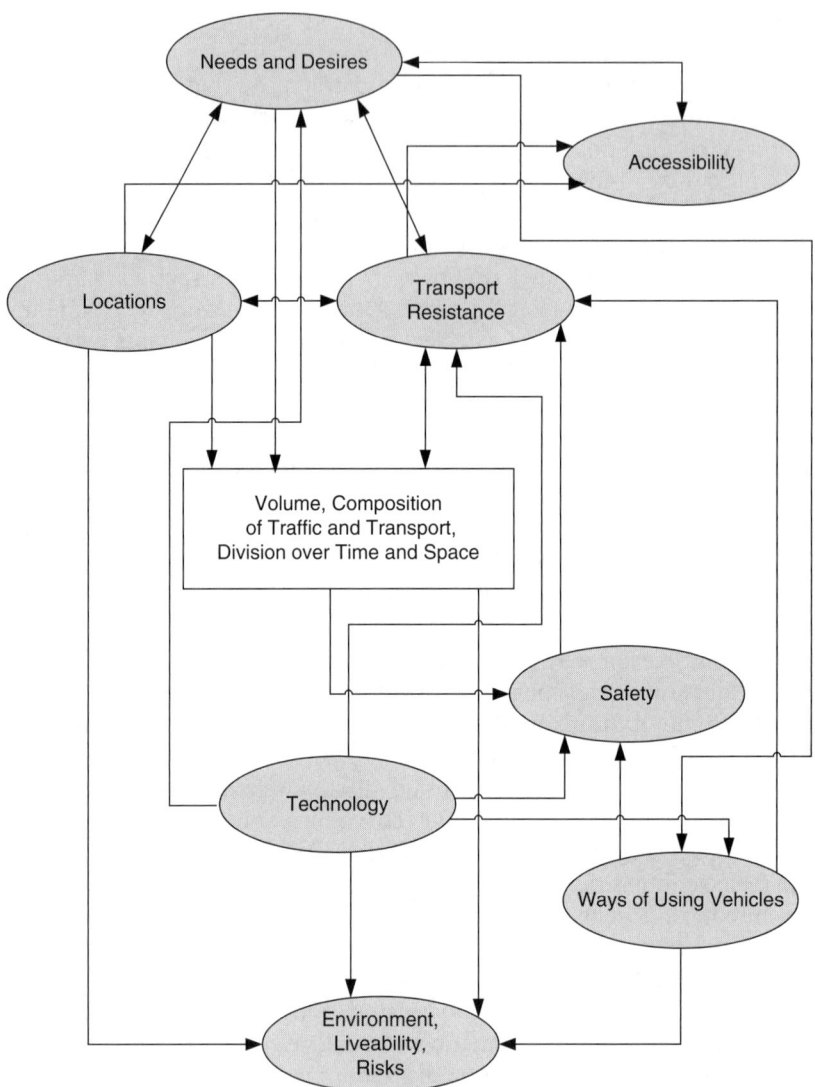

*Figure 8.1   A conceptual framework for factors having an impact
on transport volumes and the impact of transport volumes
on the environment, accessibility and safety (Van Wee,
2009).*

8.3   A BRIEF OVERVIEW OF CATEGORIES OF MODELS

Models can be categorized in several ways. This section discusses the most important distinctions.

Scope of Models

One distinction with respect to the scope of models is transport models, versus impact models. Within transport models, a distinction can be made between models for passenger transport and those for goods transport. Within passenger transport models, a distinction can be made between trip or tour based models and activity based models. In the category of impact models, a distinction can be made between categories of impact, such as noise levels, emission levels, safety levels, etc. Conceptually, activity based models are in my opinion a more elegant way to model transport, because they model transport as derived from activities. However, in the practice of *ex ante* evaluations, tour or trips based models nowadays are still much more popular, when compared to activity based models. Trip or tour based models directly model trips or tours and do not start with modelling activities first. Their popularity partly results from the much longer tradition in developing and applying such models, compared to activity based models. A major advantage of trips based models in the case of the use of their outcomes for CBA, is the fact that they generate numbers of trips between locations, and their generalized transport costs – these results can be directly used to calculate transport benefits (changes in travel times, induced demand). As a result, as far as transport models are concerned, this chapter will focus mainly on tour or trip based models.

Modelling Techniques

Distinctions can also be made based on modelling techniques. One distinction is between aggregate models and disaggregate models. Aggregate models estimate values of output variables based on aggregate characteristics of zones. Disaggregate models, nowadays the most common model type, model the choices and behaviour of individuals, not zones, although individuals still travel between origins and destinations clustered in zones. A second distinction is between static and dynamic models. Static models estimate values of output indicators for a given future year as if dynamics are not relevant: they calculate an equilibrium situation. Dynamic models can also estimate values of output variables for a given future year, but the core of what is modelled is *changes*. Such models typically model the *change* in a variable (e.g. car use) as a result of a change in one or more of the other variables (e.g. fuel price, travel time), and model such changes over a sequence of years (a period in time), not for only one year. A next distinction relates to the modelling technique used for choices to be made (e.g. mode choice, destination choice). Revealed preference models are based on real-world choices people make; stated preference models ask people what they would do in hypothetical situations. The latter models are needed if no real-world data are available. An example could be what people would do if a new maglev line were to be built to connect two cities. Modellers cannot measure revealed preferences, as the technology is not yet in use (the exception being China).

Other Distinctions

Models can be categorized based on several additional distinctions. Two of them are firstly that models, regardless of their scope and several aspects of modelling techniques, can be distinguished as descriptive or explaining models. In descriptive models, relationships are described regardless of causality. Explaining models include causality. Secondly, models can be spatial or non-spatial. Spatial models include locations of activities and transport facilities, non-spatial models do not include such locations. Transport models generally are spatial models. Vehicle fleet models, such as car ownership models and models estimating national emissions of vehicle fleets, generally are non-spatial.

Relevance of Models Overview

A lot more can be said about modelling – for example about calibration and validation, the shape of the functions describing relationships between variables (e.g. linear, exponential, s-shaped), techniques for the estimation of parameters, model structure types, etc. It is beyond the scope of this section to discuss models in depth. Several handbooks exist that can be used for further reading (e.g. De Dios Ortúzar and Willumsen, 2001; Hensher and Button, 2000). For the purposes of this book (and the rest of this chapter in particular), it is important to realize that a wide range of models exist, and are used to *ex ante* evaluate transport policy options. In addition, it is important to realize that the choice of the model type itself can have impact on value of output indicators, and as a result have ethical dimensions. Both issues are addressed below.

8.4   ETHICAL ASPECTS OF MODELLING – THE CHECKLIST IN SECTION 3.6

This section discusses ethical aspects related to the choices to be made in the area of transport and modelling. The section is partly based on the guidelines as presented in Section 3.6. Not all questions and items of the checklist are discussed, but only those with (potentially) strong ethical implications.

What is the Problem or the Challenge?

The first ethical question is whether or not a problem or challenge is addressed at all. For example, one may think that climate change due to human activities does not occur, or at least ignore it, and not ask related questions, which is a choice in itself. Or one might only focus on climate change or the emission of greenhouse gases in the next decade or so, ignoring long-term changes or problems. To take another example: one might even not ask questions about the social exclusion effects of reducing subsidies on rural public transport. Such choices include ethical aspects in themselves.

This chapter is on modelling, not the general process of *ex ante* evaluation. As a result, this step does not seem to be relevant for a discussion on modelling and ethics. But there still are some relationships. Firstly, the choice to model a part of the transport system, and the use of such a model to explore possible futures of that part of the transport system, can make persons, organizations, and institutions (including governmental bodies and interest groups) aware of problems that may occur in the future or the challenges to be faced. Secondly, modelling may frame the mindset about problems and their causes – see the following subsection.

What Are the Choice Options?

The selection of choice options is the next step, and this can include ethical aspects. Again this is a general issue, not one specifically related to transport. But as explained above, the choice to model a specific part of the transport system may not increase awareness only of possible future problems or challenges, but also of causes for problems and the framing of policy options to reduce them. In other words: the choice for the inclusion of explanatory variables in models might have an impact on the mindset with respect to possible policy options; for example, if a modeller developing a model for car ownership were to distinguish between cultural minorities, extremists could interpret results in such a way that immigration policies could be proposed to reduce the growth of car use.

Linked to both the definition of the problem or challenge, as well as to the choice options, Martens and Hurvitz (2011) conclude that current four-step transport models have some ethical weaknesses. The first weakness is that they use current travel patterns for forecasting, and therefore in a way reproduce current differences in accessibility and mobility. The second weakness is the use of the level-of-service criterion: links that do not provide the aimed for level-of-service will be 'shortlisted' for capacity extension or other ways of improvement. Current travel patterns therefore play an important role in the provision of new infrastructure. According to Martens and Hurvitz (2011: 182), the result of both weaknesses might be that the application of the four-step model 'will exacerbate the existing gaps between high-mobile and low-mobile groups, in terms of available transport facilities and accessibility'. Martens (2006) takes a normative position to solve this problem, by replacing current demand-based approaches with modelling that is based on the principle of needs of different population groups. Activities to be included are basic needs like health, education, work and social contacts.

What Are All the Important Pros and Cons of the Choice Options?

The selection of output indicators (pros and cons) to be modelled can also potentially be ethically relevant. This firstly relates to the choice if an indicator type is evaluated at all, using a model based *ex ante* study. Secondly, the choice of the particular indicator is relevant. If, for example, safety is relevant for the *ex ante* evaluation of policy options, the choice of safety indicators becomes relevant. Probably the (yearly) number of fatalities is the most important indicator in many countries. But what if a policy were to reduce this number, but increase the number of severely injured? Probably it is worth knowing this. To take a more extreme example: suppose two proposed locations for future schools for a new residential area – one location is at the other side of a busy and, for children, dangerous to cross, road, the other is a very safe location in the middle of the neighbourhood, so that all children older than seven years can safely walk or cycle to school independently. Suppose for option one the (by parents) perceived safety level of a trip to school for the children is so poor that they are not allowed to travel to school independently. As a result, the number of children involved in accidents might be about zero. Because the location of option 2 is inherently safe, the number of children involved in accidents is also about zero, although they travel independently. But is the safety level of both location options then evaluated equally? For a further discussion on safety indicators, see Chapter 6.

Another example could be noise levels, or concentrations of pollutants.

An indicator could be the percentage or number of dwellings that face noise exposure levels higher than a politically defined maximum (e.g. 60 dB(A)), or the percentage of dwellings at which concentrations of PM10 are above 40 micrograms per M^3 (the EU standard). Such a norm-based indicator could be of value. But such indicators would ignore, for example, an increase of noise levels from 50 to 59 dB(A), or a decrease in PM10 concentrations from 39 to 30 micrograms per M^3. The increase in noise levels will certainly result in more noise nuisance and lower monetary values of affected houses. In addition, because no no-effect level for PM10 exists, the decrease in concentrations from 39 to 30 can have very important health benefits. To summarize: both with respect to the choice of the selection of output variable types, as well as their specific indicators, ethical aspects are important because the perception of the ethically relevant pros and cons of policy options could be influenced.

Who Are the Winners and Losers?

Often model based *ex ante* evaluations do not report at all who are the winners and losers, whereas from an ethical perspective this can be very relevant – see Chapter 3. In addition, it can be relevant from the perspective of possibilities for future implementation of policy options – opposition often comes from those who lose. Thus if winners and losers are reported, the question is: which categories are distinguished? Is a distinction made between income classes, and if so, which? Or is a distinction made between, for example, location categories (e.g. regions, neighbourhoods, rural versus urban areas)? Or specifically between households that face lower or higher noise levels? Choices to model such distinctions are ethical choices, and have an impact on the potentially relevant output of models in the case of *ex ante* evaluations. It could be an option to involve relevant actors in the selection of categories of winners and losers to be distinguished.

Does Closed Partiality Occur?

In modelling terms this relates to the system boundaries. The general belief among transport modellers is that, in the case of changes in the transport system (policy induced or not), the geographical area to be included should be large enough to include all infrastructure, and all areas that might face significant changes. But this rule can easily be violated; for example local municipalities often have models for their territory. The neighbouring areas are modelled in less detail. Changes in the transport system within their territory might result in changes outside the local municipality under consideration, which can then easily be overlooked. The same applies to regions. Changes in one region can have impacts in other regions, impacts that could not even be visible in a model. This even applies to countries, if changes in countries were to result in changes in neighbouring countries.

In addition to such transport, and in some cases land-use related changes, effects like CO_2 emissions, or the depletion of fossil fuels, could be relevant worldwide.

Are Additional Values Affected, And If So: Which, for Whom, and in Which Way?

Additional values that could potentially be relevant in the case of the evaluation of transport policy choice options include 'freedom', in particular freedom of choice, and, as a result, the set of choice options (destinations, mode choice options) a person has. Indicators with respect to such choice options are generally not included in models, even though they could be calculated relatively easily in trip or tour and activity based models. This again (in addition to the subject of social exclusion – see Chapter 4) is a plea to explicitly estimate the value of accessibility indicators.

8.5 ETHICAL ASPECTS OF MODELLING – OTHER CONSIDERATIONS

This section discusses ethical aspects not particularly related to the checklist in Section 3.6.

The General Notion of the Ethics of Modelling

Very generally speaking, the ethics of modelling deals with the notion of harm (Mulvey, 1994). Due to the unethical use of models, harm can be done to (groups of) people, organizations, or firms; for example, if a model underestimates noise levels due to manipulation or the 'wrong' use of models, and as a result people living behind a (too low) noise screen face too high noise exposure, those people are caused harm. Or, a bit more indirectly, if a road is built after manipulation of demand forecasts, and the road is not (economically) feasible, the tax payer loses because more accurate forecasts would have resulted in decision makers deciding against building the road.

The Area of Application of Models

An important question is whether a model that was developed in the past is useful for a particular model study. It is very likely that a model is not suitable for the specific model study, for example because of discrepancies in the level of detail needed: the study could require much more detail than the model can deliver. In addition, the model could be useful for a limited range of scenario assumptions or policy measures, whereas the study is about more extreme scenarios or policy options; for example, a model can be useful to estimate impacts of fuel price changes within a range for +/− 20 percent. In that case, the model is not useful if effects of increases by a factor of five need to be estimated. To take another example: a model could be developed to estimate the effects of income increases on car ownership levels. It could be estimated using a small increase in income, assuming a linear relationship between income and car ownership levels. But this relationship is not linear over its full range, but S-shaped. For small changes, the assumption of linearity is OK, but not for large changes. Using a model for exceptional situations, or even wrong situations, are two major hazards of model use (Wallace, 1994b).

Who Should be Able to Use Models?

Some models are owned by companies, which need them for their position in the market. For commercial reasons, they will probably not allow others, such as competitors or (potential) clients, to use the model. But let us assume such commercial aspects were not relevant. A difficult to answer, and ethically relevant, question is: who should be allowed to use the model? On the one side of the spectrum one could argue that only the model builder, and others that are fully aware of the strong and weak points of models and their legitimate areas of application, should be allowed to use the model. This is to avoid wrong interpretations of output, or applying the model in research or policy questions for which it is not developed, or, at least, where its use it is not appropriate (see also Wallace, 1994b). On the other hand, a lot of scientific research theory is available for laypersons. Even the formulae for some models are published in journal articles, and the (at least theoretical) option for 'others' to use a model could increase the acceptability of output generated by a model. Consequently, which criteria should be applied in order to decide who can or cannot use the model, and who should set and apply them? This is very difficult. An intermediate position could be that a potential user should have 'a certain' level of knowledge. But is this sufficient? What to do if a person or institute certainly has the knowledge needed to use the model, but is not at all neutral, and will use the model for their own interests? Should they then not be allowed to use it? But then proponents may have other biased information. Let us assume a new toll road is going to be built by a private company that wants to save money on noise screens, and an interest group of residents is aware of this, and fears high noise levels. In addition, let us assume the interest group does not have the money to let a 'neutral' consultancy do the acoustic research. Should they not be allowed to use a model because they have a specific interest? Such questions are very difficult to answer, but highly ethical. At least some of the answers could be conditional; for example, transparency with respect to the input of models, version of the models used, output indicators, and corrections and interpretations of these to calculate outcome variables, could be of relevance for the answers on such ethical questions. I think that level of expertise and neutrality of potential users could, at least in some cases, be of relevance for answers on questions of model use. Note that both variables are continuous variables.

Scenarios

A first important choice to be made is the choice of scenarios for future developments in population growth, the economy, technology, etc. The choice for such scenarios can easily have an impact on outcomes of interest and related indicators; for example, other factors remaining constant (*ceteris paribus*), assuming a high level of future economic and demographic growth increases congestion levels, and as a result increases the benefits of potential new roads. A scenario assuming very high crude oil prices could suggest a possible new rail line to be more competitive compared to the car. Choices with respect to scenarios are not directly relevant for models, but indirectly: model studies need scenarios.

Related Policies

Assumptions with respect to policies related to those under study could potentially also have a strong impact on the values of output variables of models, and so on the evaluation of potential future policy options; for example, the benefits of new road infrastructure are lower if road pricing policies are assumed: pricing will decrease the additional benefits of new roads. To take a second example: negative impacts of future new roads on noise levels and emissions of pollutants and CO_2 are influenced by assumptions with respect to future regulations for emissions (noise, pollutants, CO_2) of new road vehicles, and other policies that could have an impact on these emissions (e.g. pricing policies to stimulate the buying of specific vehicles). Another example might be: the benefits of new rail infrastructure partly depend on related policies with respect to buses. To give an illustration: Pickrell (1992) studied differences between forecasts and actual demand of rail infrastructure (light and heavy rail) in the US. In seven

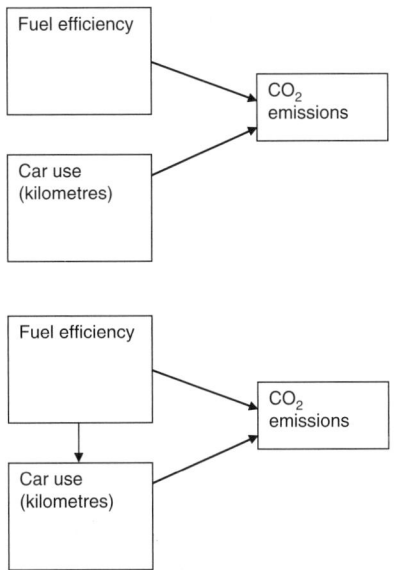

Figure 8.2   *Two model structures for the impact of energy efficiency on CO₂ emissions: (a) without – top – and (b) with – bottom – the impact of fuel efficiency on car use*

out of eight cases the actual demand was less than half of the forecasted demand, in one case the difference was 'only' 28 percent. He states that differences may result from the input of exogenous data, the model structure (see also next item), and the use of models in the forecasting process. The most important cause of differences between forecasts and actual demand in the study of Pickrell is that connecting bus services were poorer than assumed. In other words: demand for rail infrastructure was highly overestimated, mainly due to over-optimistic assumptions about policies related to connecting bus services.

Model Structure

The structure of a model to be used can potentially have important impacts on values of output indicators. The model structure is the structure that links all variables in the model, both output variables as well as input and intermediate variables. To explain this let us assume the example of a study on the impact of policies to increase the fuel efficiency of cars on CO_2 emissions. Figure 8.2 gives two potential model structures at a very aggregate level.

Both models express the fact that CO_2 emissions depend on car use and fuel efficiency. The bottom model structure, contrary to the top, includes the impact of fuel efficiency on car use. Let us now assume a policy that results in a reduction of energy use per kilometre of 50 percent (at the car fleet level). The top model structure would result in a reduction of CO_2 emissions of 50 percent, because CO_2 emissions directly relate to the use of energy (only). The bottom model structure would result in a lower reduction of CO_2 emissions: because of the lower energy use per kilometre driving a car becomes cheaper. As a result, car use will increase because fuel costs have an impact on car use levels (e.g. Graham and Glaister, 2004). This simple example shows that the choice for the model structure has an impact on the calculated effects of a certain policy. The choice for the top model structure would result in misleading results, in particular in an overestimation of the reduction of CO_2 emissions.

This example is relatively simple. In practice, modelling transport and its impacts often is much more complicated, as are the (potential) model structures – see Figure 8.1. And it is an illusion to suggest that it is easy to include all potentially relevant relationships between variables. But as a result, the choices for the model structure can be relevant for the calculated effects of policies. In my opinion modellers as well as users of models should be aware of the importance of the model structure for values of output indicators of models. At least the user of models should consider the option of changing model output in the case of estimating the effects of policies, if she has good reasons to do so – see below. In addition, for specific policy related questions it is often not possible to develop a new model, because this is too costly and might take too much time. Instead, often models that already exist and were developed for other reasons are used. In such cases I think an explicit check on the usefulness of the existing model should be made. This relates to the model structure, but also to all other modelling aspects, such as the selection of output indicators and the datasets used to calibrate the model.

The Choice between Competing Models

In some cases researchers doing a study in which models are used have the luxury of the choice between multiple, already existing, models. Then the question becomes: which model to use? There could certainly be multiple ethical dimensions related to this choice, mainly because different models might result in different values of output indicators. To illustrate this: Nijland and Van Wee (2005) looked at calculation methods, noise indices, and noise standards for road and railroad traffic in Europe, and found that equal assumptions in input could result in differences of more than 10 dB(A) noise levels, depending on the noise model used. Within one country, sometimes multiple noise models exist, that result in different noise levels. If the researcher prefers the calculated noise levels to be relatively low, she could choose a model resulting in relatively low noise levels. This example shows the ethical dimensions involved. This ethical dimension could be influenced by preferences of the client. As discussed in Section 7.5: what to do if the client prefers the researcher to choose a model showing relatively low noise levels, whereas the researcher knows that this is not the best model to use?

Specific Choices in the Case of Using a Model

Once a model is chosen, still many choices have to be made, that potentially can have an influence on the output, and as such could be ethically relevant. An example is that in the case of zones' base models, the choice for the zones to be used could be relevant. In the case of models that include the road network, assumptions with respect to average (or maximum) speeds have to be made. What to do in the case of a study on noise levels resulting from a new road, if the design of the road is such that speeding is very likely to occur? Should one use the official maximum speed level, or the higher speeds one expects to be the actual speed? In the latter case, the client could have serious problems, because the study would explicitly show that it is likely that people will speed.

Corrections of Model Output

In many cases, a researcher applying a model will be aware of the shortcomings of models. Transport models are a simplification of reality, and as a result will never produce exactly the 'right' output – if they do so this is a coincidence. An ethical question that arises is: what to do if the modeller is aware of the limitations of models and the impacts of these limitations on output? There are two ways to look at this. One way is that correcting models is often problematic, and should be avoided as much a possible, partly because there is a strong element of subjectivity in corrections to be made. To come back to the example of Figure 8.2: which elasticity for the impact of fuel costs on car use should one use? The literature gives a range for such elasticities. Should one use a value about in the middle of the range? This could make sense. But such elasticities are often estimated in empirical studies of one, or even more, decades ago. Moreover, higher income people are less fuel costs sensitive with respect to their car use. What if the study is about policy options to be introduced in, for example, ten years? Then it will take another decade or so before the majority of the car fleet is replaced under the regime of the new policies. If the scenario(s) used assume(s) increases in incomes, the middle value based on empirical studies of more than a decade ago might result in a too strong correction. Thus the correction of model outputs is not at all straightforward. The other way to look at the problem is that models are no more than a helpful tool to estimate effects. If the modeller is aware of important shortcomings, she should correct the model output, and transparently report the corrections, including the reasons for the corrections made. From this perspective, corrections should certainly be made if the modeller has good reasons to do so. In the case of the example above, using a low value in the range of elasticities (expressing the impact of changes in fuel costs on car use) would be the best option. I personally support the second way to look at this: models are no more than a useful tool. In my opinion, output should transparently be corrected if there are good reasons to do so – I have done this very often in policy related *ex ante* evaluations.

The Interpretation of Model Output and the Communication of Model Based Outcomes of Interest and Related Indicators

The interpretation of model output partly relates to corrections of this output as discussed above. Other interpretations relate to the selection of the often many indicators to be used for interpretation, and their aggregations. In addition, the presentation could be very important for decision making. Coming back to the example of indicators for noise and air pollutions: a map showing a green colour if noise levels of concentrations of PM10 are below a certain level, and a red colour if these exceed this level, is one way to report indicators. If a study is done only to check if legal problems will occur (i.e. if concentrations exceed legal standards) this might be OK. But if all the pros and cons of a policy need to be expressed, this may be a too sketchy way of presenting the results. Tables with dwellings per noise or concentration class would then be more helpful. If such outcomes of interest are included in a CBA, the first way of presenting the output is even misleading, because then only a value can be put on changes between the two classes, ignoring all changes below or above the threshold variable, and ignoring the difference between, for example, a change from 39 to 41 micrograms PM10 per M^3, and from 30 to 50 micrograms per M^3. The lesson is that, in the interpretation and communication of model output, several choices can be made that have a potentially great impact on the perception of effects of policies.

Another issue related to communication is the necessity to make explicit both the strengths and limitations of a model (Wallace, 1994a). In my opinion, this does not only apply to model developers, but also to those who apply models in evaluations.

A third issue related to communication is the presentation of uncertainty, often in terms of margins of outcomes of interest. Generally speaking, the advice could be to communicate the margins of outcomes. But then in some cases dilemmas can occur. Barabba (1994) gives the example of a researcher knowing that presenting the range (and not a point estimate) would be misused by the customer of outcomes: only those data from the extreme range of output would be used. The dilemma then is: what to do? Is this misuse a responsibility of the modeller anyway? And if so, is that a reason to not present the range of expected outcomes?

A final issue is that researchers should not hide behind model outputs. In the words of Barabba (1994): 'Never say the model says'.

Design Related Questions

Although this book takes evaluations as the perspective, I briefly elaborate here on the use of models in the case of design. In that case, a very important question is: what is the design task? Take the example of a new road or rail line near a particular neighbourhood. A design question could be: how high should a noise screen be to avoid noise levels above 50 dB(A)? Using an acoustical model, the researcher can calculate the 'right' value. But just answering such a design question could result in missing potentially policy relevant information. It could be that a small increase in the height of the noise screen would cost not much more money, but would significantly reduce noise levels in the residential area, and increase the values of houses much more than the increase in costs of the noise screen. This example shows that the way design questions are formulated also includes choices that could be of interest from an ethical point of view.

Codes of Conduct

Chapter 7 discusses codes of conduct in general, and of course the importance of such codes also applies to modellers. Barabba (1994) discusses this subject:

> in an effort to get access to scarce resources, some . . . model builders were overpromising, either by commission or omission, what the model could actually accomplish. Too often I was hearing, in response to some of the most complex and difficult questions, 'Of course, the model could answer that question. And at the push of a button!' (Barabba, 1994: 145)

Barabba goes on to say: 'there are just too many opportunities for opportunists' (Barabba, 1994: 159). In addition, Barabba explains that modellers are not at all a homogeneous group of professionals, but with many different backgrounds, and that as a result it is very difficult to agree codes of conduct. This notion relates to modellers in general. But even in the area of transport modelling, it is important to realize that researchers with many different backgrounds are involved, such as economists, civil engineers, planners, geographers, psychologists and policy analysts. To 'solve' this problem, Barabba produces a list of questions that a model user would want to ask a model builder:

1. How well does the model perform?
2. Has the model been analysed by someone other than the model authors?
3. Is documentation adequate for the users' needs?
4. What assumptions and data were used in producing model output?
5. Why is the selected model appropriate to use in a given application?
6. Will the model be run directly and specifically for the present purpose?
7. What is the accuracy of the model output?
8. Does the structure of the model resemble the system being modelled?
9. Is the model appropriately sensitive to the inputs being varied?

In addition, Barabba gives a list of questions that the model builder could internally ask when preparing the model:

1. Do I understand the problem?
2. Are the assumptions reasonable?
3. Is the method I have selected the best? Are there other possible ways to do it?
4. Can I get this done within the time frame available?
5. Are the data I am using to build and run the model correct?

These questions give some guidance for good conduct for modellers. There is one question that I want to emphasize: question 4 of the second list: Can I get this done within the time frame available? What I have read about codes of conduct implicitly seems to suggest that time and money are unlimitedly available. Of course this is not true. A modeller, as any other researcher, needs to respect the time and money available (though within limits), and the client also needs to trade-off the pros and cons of additional quality.

Client's Interest Versus other Interests

If a model builder builds a model for the client, she should respect the client's values and interests (e.g. Mason, 1994), but to what extent? What to do if the client wants the model builder to build a model that produces 'favourable' (from the client's perspective) outcomes? Again, the border between 'right' and 'wrong' is not always easy to draw, it is rather a grey area. Nevertheless, codes of conduct (see Chapter 7) suggest that the modeller cannot simply do what the client asks: at least some level of independence should be maintained; for example, a modeller should not build a model for a rail company that overestimates the expected use of a new rail line. If the model outcomes were to be used in a policy debate, doing so could easily lead to over-investments in rail, at the cost of the tax payer. But it is difficult to draw a sharp line. What to do if a car company wants a model builder to estimate the market of a car that can be legally built and sold, for example a huge SUV that can drive 300 km/h and that is extremely fuel inefficient? If the model itself is built 'correctly', should the modeller be blamed for her role in the development and sales of a car type that is highly undesirable from a societal perspective? Or should she do the job, arguing that if such cars should not be developed and sold, it is the government that should set regulations making such cars illegal?

8.6 CONCLUSIONS

Models are very popular in order to explore the future in the area of transport for at least three reasons. A first reason is that there is no good alternative for getting an impression of what might be the effects of policy options. This results from the fact that many of the factors interact in a complex way. The second reason is that they provide quantitative information that is needed for *ex ante* evaluations. The third reason is their (perceived) neutrality.

The main conclusion of this chapter is that modelling in its several aspects has many ethically relevant dimensions. Ethics are important for at least those clients asking for a study in which models are used, modellers themselves, those researchers that apply models, and those that use model results (formal clients, and other actors such as interest groups).

Modelling related ethical choices include at least the following aspects:

- The choice to model a part of the transport system, and the use of such a model to explore possible futures of that part of the transport system, can make persons, organizations and institutions (including governmental bodies and interest groups) aware of problems that may occur in the future, or the challenges to be faced.

- The choice in terms of the inclusion of explanatory variables in models might have an impact on the mindset with respect to possible policy options.

- The selection of output indicators (pros and cons) to be modelled can potentially be ethically relevant. This firstly relates to the choice of whether an indicator type is evaluated at all, using a model based *ex ante* study, and secondly to the choice of the particular indicator.

- Models could explicitly provide information on who could be the winners and losers of specific policy options. The selection of which categories of winners and losers to select could be made, together with relevant actors.

- The use of models for *ex ante* evaluations of policy options can easily lead to closed partiality: the interests of those not included in the models can easily be overlooked.

- The value 'Freedom' is poorly addressed in many model based studies. The inclusion of freedom to choose between choice options could be ethically relevant. Accessibility indicators expressing travel options per mode could be used as this freedom related aspect, and models can be very helpful in calculating accessibility indicators.

- The choice with respect to who has access to a model is ethically relevant.

- The use of scenarios for exogenous variables can have a significant impact on the values of output indicators, and as a result on the results of an *ex ante* evaluation of policy options.

- Assumptions with respect to policies related to those under study could potentially have a strong impact on the values of output variables of models, and as a result on the evaluation of potential future policy options.

- The model structure can have a strong impact on the values of output variables of models, and as a result on the evaluation of potential future policy options.

- If researchers can choose between multiple, already existing, models, an important question becomes: which model to use? There could certainly be multiple ethical dimensions related to this choice.

- Model output corrections could lead to 'better' results of *ex ante* evaluations of policy options. Ethical questions relate to whether the model output will be corrected, and if so, how?

- The interpretation of model output, and the communication of model based outcomes of interest and related indicators, can be ethically relevant in several ways.
- In addition to the use of models for the purpose of *ex ante* evaluations, the use of models for design questions can be ethically relevant.

9. Epilogue and discussion

This book has shown that, although the literature that explicitly discusses ethical aspects of transport is limited, there certainly are many ethical dimensions related to transport, at least in the *ex ante* evaluation of transport projects and policies. The importance of such issues is recognized by the respondents to the questionnaire study, as described in Chapter 2.

Chapter 3 discusses the use and ethical aspects of Cost–Benefit Analysis (CBA) in transport. It shows that, although CBA is a very attractive tool for the *ex ante* evaluation of transport projects and policies, its use is not indisputable. Criticisms include – among others – the limitations of utilitarianism, the use of indicators to be evaluated, the fact that distribution effects are often ignored, and the ignorance of the process of *ex ante* evaluation. Based on Chapter 3, a checklist was developed that could be used for the application of theoretical insights into the area of transport. As is the general case in the area of applied ethics, the selection of ethical theories to be used for a specific transport related evaluation purpose is case specific, and there is no general recipe for making related choices. The checklist aims nevertheless to give some guidance, if one wants to apply ethical theories in the area of the *ex ante* evaluation of transport policy options.

Partly based on the checklist of Chapter 3, Chapters 4–6 focus on the *what*-question: what are the ethical aspects of specific subjects? Chapter 4 discusses social exclusion, an important concept strongly related to the concept of accessibility. It shows that social exclusion related aspects could be very relevant for specific transport policy options, but that CBA has severe limitations as a tool to evaluate such policy options. Chapter 5 discusses environmental issues. A major conclusion is that long-term sustainability is poorly addressed in current CBA practice, mainly because, due to discounting, long-term effects hardly have any relevance in net present values. Chapter 6 discusses safety, showing that pricing (statistical) lives is not without dispute, and includes several ethically relevant issues.

Chapters 7 and 8 focus on the *how* question: how to do research from an ethical perspective? Chapter 7 discusses the ethics of doing research. It shows that codes of conduct give some guidance for the ethical behaviour of researchers, although several of the persons interviewed for understanding the ethics of doing research in practice (see Chapter 7) do not, or hardly know, about them. Chapter 8 discusses the specific (research) case of modelling transport (as a subcategory of the ethics of doing research) from an ethical perspective, showing that the use of models for *ex ante* evaluations of projects and policies includes making several ethically relevant choices.

This chapter gives some final reflections, based on the preceding chapters. It is important to realize that the reflections are those of a researcher in the area of transport who studied ethics, not those of a philosopher that studied transport. As a result, the contribution of these reflections primarily relates to the relevance of this book for the transport community.

A first reflection is to some extent also included in Chapter 3: the major question of *how useful is CBA for the* ex ante *evaluation of transport policy projects and policies?* This book could easily give the impression that I think, from an ethical perspective, that CBA is not (or hardly) of any use for such purposes. This is because of the many limitations as discussed in Chapters 3 and 4–6, a very important one being that CBA is strongly related to one ethical theory only: utilitarianism. But I think we should be careful about being too sceptical. If one takes the perspective (as I do) that for the quality of public decision making it is important that decision makers are well informed, one can assume (as explained in Chapter 3) that the quality of decision making is higher if the decision makers make the choice they would have made: (1) if they were to have all (from their perspective) potentially relevant choice options available; (2) if they were fully informed; and (3) if they were able to evaluate different choice options (i.e. weight the pros and cons of choice options). This could be a valid rule of thumb under the conditions of a high level of democracy. Then the question becomes: which methodology for *ex ante* evaluations of transport projects and policies is 'best'? One could argue that it is important to evaluate the pros and cons of relevant choice options, but that an *analysis* of these pros and cons is not needed. In that case, a simple score card could do the job. (Note that a major advantage of CBA and MCA is that a list of important pros and cons is presented in both methods anyway.) In some cases, this may be true. But in many other cases this is at least risky, mainly because all pros and cons are probably not equally important, not from the decision maker's point of view, nor for the relevant actors in the field, and nor from a broad welfare perspective. Then some form of analysis becomes useful, two main methods being CBA and MCA. The choice between the two methods should, I think, be based on the pros and cons of the options *in a specific case.* The main pro of an MCA is that it allows for the explicit inclusion of actor preferences in weighting relevant outcomes of interest. This also is its main weakness: setting the weights is highly subjective, and can easily (at least: more easily than in the case of a CBA) lead to manipulations. The dominant pros and cons of a CBA are opposite to those of an MCA: it gives less room for specific preferences, but because of its emphasis on (mainly) consumer preferences (expressed in monetary terms), is more neutral. I think that (as explained in Chapter 4), if choice options are more or less comparable, and if the willingness to pay (WTP) of consumers reflects well the values of choice options, the balance of pros and cons of MCA versus CBA supports the use of CBA. But even then, I recommend an explicit check of ethical aspects, as explained in this book. In the case of less comparable choice options, if WTP is a less adequate method to value choice options, or if important ethical aspects are at stake, a hybrid methodology of CBA and MCA might be preferred, or an MCA. The limitations of CBA, as far as ethical issues are concerned, are related to, among other factors (as explained above), social exclusion issues, distribution issues, and effects that occur in the long term, such as long-term intergenerational justice. I hope this book has provided some guidance on the cases in which the use of CBA (only) might be relatively cumbersome. I do not aim to give a blueprint for what exactly to do in such cases. A general recommendation is that if ethical issues could be of importance for the *ex ante* evaluation of transport projects and policies, it is recommended to at least add sensitivity analyses to a standard CBA, addressing questions like: how would policy options be evaluated using other (additional or alternative) assumptions on the indicator(s) to be considered; other than utility, what would be the impact of adding different assumptions on valuing distribution effects; what if the value of CO_2 were to increase according to the discount rate; what if one were to use an equity based value of time; what if the value of a statistical life were to be income independent, etc.?

In some cases, the choice would not be between CBA and MCA, but between either CBA or MCA and cost-effectiveness analysis (CEA). Especially when choices need to be made between options with a specific aim such as reducing CO_2 emissions or road fatalities, and when not many (relevant) effects are important other than those reductions and the costs of the options, a CEA could do the job. In this case, potential ethical dimensions probably do not play a role.

A second reflection relates to the *importance of the concept of accessibility*. Some, but not all, of the equity related aspects that might be relevant for the *ex ante* evaluation of transport projects and policies relate to accessibility, social exclusion being maybe the most important subject. Also the more general equity related issue of possibilities to participate in (outdoor) activities is strongly related to accessibility, as are some of the distribution issues related to having these possibilities to participate.

A third reflection relates to the *limitations of market based 'solutions'*. Even if markets were to perform perfectly, there are equity relevant issues that might make one not over-optimistic about market based 'solutions'. This could especially be the case if income related equity issues are at stake, such as in the case of the willingness to pay for travel for low income groups (and related social exclusion), or the use of a cap-and-trade system to reduce the emission of greenhouse gasses.

Fourthly, in my opinion a very important question is *to what extent can transport be dealt with as a separate sector in the case of discussions on ethics*? In several cases, this may be cumbersome. Firstly, although this book dealt with transport only, transport is strongly interwoven with society, because a large majority of transport is a means to participate in activities, not a goal in itself. This implies that reflections on transport and ethics could be relevant for ethical considerations related to activities. One can think of impacts on different shops in the case of policies to reduce social exclusion: people might change the shops (or services or schools and many other places) they visit as a result of such policies, which could have equity implications for those activities and related actors. Secondly, as far as income is concerned, it is at least questionable if a partial focus (such as on transport only) is straightforward. Can one conclude that people face a lack of options to participate in activities because their income is too low to pay for the transport needed? Expenditures on transport compete with other categories of goods (and services), such as housing, food or ICT. If one wants to improve the quality of life of persons for ethical reasons, a focus on transport only might be too limited. Related to this point, is the third reason why a focus on transport only might be cumbersome: if one were to prefer to focus on quality of life related indicators for *ex ante* evaluations, such as happiness, it is important to realize that not only transport is relevant for the quality of life. Consequently, one should at least recognize the limited scope in the case of studying transport only. In addition, transport and other aspects relevant to the quality of life (such as social contacts, health, or education) are related to the transport system and options for persons to travel. All in all, despite the limited scope of this book, I think one should be careful to judge ethical issues of transport separately.

Finally, I think that what is fair or more generally ethically 'right' or 'wrong' could be strongly related to *context*, more particularly in terms of place and time. What is considered to be fair nowadays might differ from some decades ago, or some decades in the future. This of course applies to many subjects in society, but probably also to transport. At the time of introducing paid parking in central urban areas in the 1960s and 1970s, a lot of opposition originated from perceptions of fairness, whereas now hardly anybody would consider it as unfair that one has to pay for parking in such areas. An example of the importance of place is given by Levinson (2010), in the context of road pricing: what is acceptable in Europe may not be in North America, or vice versa. Pay lanes in the USA have been derided as 'Lexus lanes' whereas, to the best of my knowledge, comparable labels do not exist for the French toll roads. On the other hand, the high speed rail line (TGV) from Paris to the south of France has been nicknamed the 'brown ass express': it is supposed to be popular amongst high income yuppies in Paris, who take the TGV for short trips to the Mediterranean coast, at the cost of those living near the rail line. The importance of context, including place and time, is generally acknowledged in the literature in the area of ethics; for example, in her book on the ethics of research Beach (1996) states that there is 'a strong relationship between religious, cultural, political and economic values, and scientific judgement'. Such relationships are also emphasized by Resnik (1998).

Although Chapters 4–6 deal with the three most important categories of evaluation criteria for transport policies: accessibility, the environment and safety, the chapters do not cover *all* output categories that could be relevant from an ethics perspective. Within the areas of accessibility, the environment and safety, not all ethically relevant issues are discussed. In addition, the criteria of accessibility, the environment and safety do not cover *all* impacts that could be relevant from an ethical perspective; for example, privacy and security can in some cases be important as well. In a similar manner, policies to increase security can have penalties in the area of other values, such as privacy (and costs) – see, for example, Potoglou et al. (2010) who carried out a stated choice study on the security of the UK rail network. Overall, therefore, I do not claim that the book gives a more or less complete overview of issues in the area of *ex ante* evaluations of transport projects and policies that are ethically relevant.

Chapters 4–6 discuss accessibility, the environment and safety separately. A complication might occur because *some policy options might have an impact on two of these three categories, or even all three.* For example, a new bus or rail line might reduce social exclusion, but also reduce environmental pressure and accidents. If so, some of the effects could be included in a CBA relatively easily (environmental and safety effects), others (social exclusion) not. If a CBA were to be used for the *ex ante* evaluations of options for the new bus or rail line, at least an explicit evaluation of social exclusion effects (which are difficult to evaluate using a CBA framework – see above) is probably needed, in addition to those effects included in the CBA.

Next, this chapter compares the application of the checklist in Section

3.6 to the subjects of Chapters 4–6. Table 9.1 gives an overview of this comparison.

Table 9.1 shows that explicitly applying the checklist results in several (additional) issues of ethical importance. I conclude that, at least for the subjects discussed in Chapters 4–6, the checklist is very useful. It is important to realize that some of the cells are discussed in the sections preceding those on applying the checklist, so Table 9.1 does not give a full overview of all relevant issues, but those that are additional to the preceding sections.

In addition, this book takes the perspective of *ex ante* evaluations, which certainly is *not the only perspective that can be chosen in the area of transport and ethics*. An important alternative could be the perspective of design (of parts of the transport system or policy design). Design and evaluation are of course strongly related: evaluation criteria are often design criteria. But the point of departure differs. If one starts from the perspective of designing policies, important questions could be: which are the ethically relevant aspects of a specific policy? Here, I discuss an example: a specific (road) pricing policy scheme. Depending on the scheme, important ethical aspects could be privacy and distribution effects – distribution and equity effects related to both (road) users and non-users (e.g. those exposed to noise or pollutants), and related to both process and outcomes (Levinson, 2010). Distribution and related equity effects have been studied already by several authors (e.g. McMullen et al., 2010; see for an overview Levinson, 2010). Distribution effects can strongly relate to revenue use: for distribution effects of, for example, a road pricing scheme, it really matters if the revenues are used for building more motorways, or for reducing taxes for low income categories. They can be addressed with intelligent designs (Levinson, 2010). Related to this: acceptability of such policies is strongly related to revenue use (Schuitema and Steg, 2008). One can explicitly try to design policies, having equity (or more general: ethical) aspects in mind. Again, using pricing policies as an example, Schuitema et al. (2011) found that, overall, fairness and acceptability of pricing policies was higher when respondents believed that future generations, nature and the environment were protected (reflecting environmental justice), irrespective of absolute differences in overall fairness and acceptability of the policies. Also De Groot and Steg (2009) and Eriksson et al. (2008) (cited in Schuitema et al., 2011) found collective considerations to be important for acceptability of pricing policies.

Next, an important question is: how to deal with ideas of justice in the area of *ex ante* evaluations in transport? Would it be possible to *develop a common approach to deal with justice in the area of transport*, as a general point of departure? Answering such questions probably

Table 9.1   An overview of applying the checklist in Section 3.6

	Social exclusion	Long-term sustainability	Pricing lives
What is the problem or the challenge?	Importance of social exclusion. Importance of minimum levels of participation. Importance of voluntary versus non-voluntary choices. Is policy the cause of social exclusion?	Depletion of fossil fuels poorly addressed	Safety may be undervalued due to decreasing trends in fatalities
What are the choice options?	Choice for policy can work out differently for different groups of people	(Very) long-term issues ignored	'Very safe choice options' overlooked
What are all the important pros and cons of the choice options?			Adaptation of travel behaviour and activities ignored
Who are the winners and losers?		Future generations can be losers	Poor attention paid to victims
Can losers be compensated, and will they be compensated?	Maybe, by specific social exclusion policies or by ICT	Yes, substitutes	Partly, but not in the case of fatalities
Are there particular trade-offs?	Maybe between categories of socially excluded persons	Yes, between generations	Sure. Monetary and other costs versus safety
Do irreplaceable things exist or not?	Probably not	Yes, depletion of fossil fuels, impacts of climate change	Depends on ethical perspective
Maximization or not?	Minimum levels are more important than maximization	Cap-and-trade (only) can result in 'unfair' outcomes	Maximization results in too high costs

Table 9.1 (continued)

	Social exclusion	Long-term sustainability	Pricing lives
Does closed partiality occur?	Yes, this can happen	Yes, by ignoring future generations	Yes, for example children
Are additional values affected, and, if so which, for whom, and in which way?	Risk of violation freedom of choice, paternalism	Those of future generations	Freedom to move and to participate in activities
Do (additional) considerations with respect to equity, justice or equality exist?	No additional issues	No additional issues	No additional issues
Are commitments or duties at stake?	Political commitments	No additional issues	Political commitments
Is a choice needed?	Could be	Yes	Yes

requires the knowledge of an educated philosopher with a lot of experience in the field of applied ethics. It is way beyond my ambition to answer these questions. Yet, I feel attracted to a paper written by my colleague Neeke Doorn (2009). She discusses the ideas that Rawls labelled 'Wide Reflective Equilibrium' and 'overlapping consensus'. Rawls' ideas aim 'to find a balance between considered judgements and intuitions, concerning particular cases on the one hand, and general principles and theories on the other' (Doorn, 2009: 127). Based on Rawls, Doorn (2009: 129) states that an equilibrium exists if three different types of considerations 'cohere and are mutually supportive': (1) considered moral judgements about particular cases or situations; (2) moral principles; and (3) descriptive and normative background theories. 'Reflective' means that 'the equilibrium is arrived at by working back and forth between the different considerations and all are appropriately adjustable in the light of new situations or points of views'. 'Wide' means that 'coherence is achieved between all three levels of considerations . . . and not only the considered judgements and moral principles'. The concept of 'overlapping consensus' means that 'people are able to live together despite conflicting moral values and ideals as long as people share a moral commitment to society's basic structure' (Doorn, 2009: 130). The method is a political method. Based on an analysis of 12 applications of these Rawlsian approaches, Doorn concludes that these applications mainly originate from the political domain, despite the fact that several authors have suggested using this method in other domains. Another conclusion is that obstacles for applying the approaches, firstly, are related to inclusiveness: all relevant actors should be included, and they can equally participate in the debate. Secondly, people should be detached from their personal life in the case of non-individual applications of the method. There might be a long way to go before such an approach could be developed, accepted and applied satisfactory. The outcomes of the approach will also very likely, at least to some extent, be country specific; firstly because ideas of justice vary over time and place, and secondly because guidelines and practices related to the *ex ante* evaluation of transport policy options (such as infrastructure plans) vary between countries. Nevertheless, the eclectic approach – combining multiple theories to come to a practically applicable approach – would certainly match the eclectic approaches that are often used in studying transport and its impacts on society. It is generally acknowledged that the transport system and its effects on society are best understood if the insights of several disciplines are combined (see Chapter 1).

Maybe these Rawlsian approaches could be used as a point of departure in order to develop a common approach to deal with the idea of justice in the area of transport. I think that in that case it is important to realize that the approaches are primarily developed to be applied at the individual level, whereas in transport related discussions, other actors, such as environmental interest groups or transport companies, matter as well. Secondly, it may be problematic for some people to become detached from their personal life, because people can easily relate their own life (e.g. in their role as traveller or as citizen living at a specific location) to the policy question and related policy options at stake.

Finally, the points of departure, demarcations and assumptions of this book could be of relevance for the use of its contents (see Chapter 1). A major point of departure relates to the scope of the *ex ante* evaluation of transport projects and policies. There is more to be said on transport and ethics related to this subject. In addition, not only do I take the perspective of democracy for decision making on transport, but I also assume a *high democratic level of society*, an assumption that probably is not always applicable. If the level of democracy (see Chapter 3 for a discussion) is not that high, the role of research in informing the decision maker could be placed in a different perspective. It is beyond the scope of this book to further discuss this issue.

Notes

PREFACE AND ACKNOWLEDGEMENTS

1. In the transport community equity, fairness, and justice are usually used interchangeably, depending on the context (Baron, 2000, cited by Thomopoulos et al., 2009).
2. Trudie retired 1 October 2010.

CHAPTER 1

1. Date of last search: 19 May 2010.
2. See, e.g., Friedman et al., 2002; Van de Poel, 2009.
3. In some cases however, this choice can include moral aspects. Consider, for example, the idea that only one of two stations can be built, for instance because of train timetable limitations. Suppose the political promise is made to a local community that, before a certain year, a railway station will be built in their community, to compensate for another political choice, for instance the choice not to build a motorway exit connecting the local community to the motorway system. In that case, the political promise introduces a moral obligation that is relevant for the decision.

CHAPTER 2

1. I have the impression that social exclusion is, relatively often, studied by women. My impression is, firstly, mainly based on the gender of authors of papers in this area. A second indication is the attendance of special sessions at conferences; for example. the first session on social exclusion at the World Conference on Transport Research, Lisbon, July 2010, was visited by 32 persons, of which 17 were women, whereas a large majority of the participants of the conference were male. Gender was not asked for in the original questionnaire because I personally know all respondents.

2. Some people explicitly referred to the announcement in *Verkeerskunde* or *Verkeer in Beeld*, or to persons who forwarded the email, but six persons did not.

CHAPTER 3

1. E.g. Geurs et al., 2006, 2009; Melkert and Van Wee, 2009; Nijland and Van Wee, 2008; Priemus et al., 2008; Rietveld and Van Wee, 2008; Van Wee, 2007b; Van Wee and Tavasszy, 2008. See its underlying concepts such as the valuation of travel time savings (e.g. Van Wee and Rietveld, 2008; Van Wee et al., 2006), and procedures related to the use of CBA (e.g. Annema et al., 2007; De Jong and Van Wee, 2007).
2. This section is partly based on Van Wee and Tavassy (2008). This section focuses on CBA for potential new transport infrastructure projects. However, CBA can also be used for th*e ex ante* evaluation of other transport policies, for example with respect to road pricing.
3. For a discussion on speeding and criminalization, see Fahlquist (2009).
4. Two categories of travellers in the situation of a new infrastructure project can be distinguished: those who would also travel without the new project, and those who travel only in the case of the new project. The sum of benefits for the first category equals the number of persons multiplied by the value of the travel time gains (time multiplied by the marginal value of time). For the second category (new travellers), the sum is half of the total product by the number of persons multiplied by the value of the travel time gains. This is because some of those people would start travelling even after a very small decrease in travel time, whereas others would only do so after the final minutes of travel time gains. Assuming a linear demand curve expressing demand as a function of travel time gains (or better: a reduction in so-called Generalized Transport Costs including time, money, and effort), the sum of benefits can be calculated by multiplying the product of the number of new travellers times the value of the travel time gains, by 0.5. This rule does not only apply to passenger transport, but also to freight transport.
5. This applies to outcomes of interest that are (only) relevant for consumers. In the case of other outcomes of interest, such as CO_2 emissions, the consumers' perspective is not the best basis.
6. For a discussion on multi-actor systems and ethics, see Pruyt (2010).

CHAPTER 4

1. Note that increasing the number of activities which are accessible, and flexible, relates to the value of 'freedom' as discussed in Chapter 3.

CHAPTER 5

1. This introduction is partly based on Van Wee (2011).
2. This section is based on Van Wee (2010).
3. Currencies are as presented in the paper. The euro–dollar exchange rates have varied significantly over the period of the construction of the infrastructure lines that are included in the range as presented. Using, for example, the current exchange (dollar–euro) rate would therefore be misleading.
4. For a discussion on these options, see Heyd (2009) – it is beyond the scope of this chapter to elaborate on this discussion.
5. Nevertheless, utilitarianism is criticized because it would fail to deal with the problem of intergenerational justice (e.g. Wallack, 2006). In my opinion these critiques relate to the way utilitarianism has often dealt with the subject of discounting, but do not convincingly show that utilitarianism by definition is incapable of dealing with intergenerational justice.
6. The text on the economic line of reasoning is based on Koopmans (2009).

CHAPTER 6

1. This section is partly based on Van Wee (2011).
2. To some extent these costs could be partly distance dependent: if people buy a (perceived) safer car because they drive a lot, there is a distance dependent component in the choice.
3. For an overview of the ethics of (technological) risk, see Asveld and Roeser (2009). For a discussion on the incommensurability of several risk categories, see Espinoza (2009).
4. Intelligent Speed Adaption (ISA) is a system (forced or voluntary) to control the speed of motor vehicles: the driver of a motor vehicle gets a warning if she speeds, or it is even technically impossible to speed. Such systems could be made dynamic; for example, at the time children travel to and from schools the maximum speed on neighbouring roads could be lower compared to other times.

CHAPTER 7

1. Experimental design is the term Resnik uses. More generally speaking, money can influence research design (which is much broader than experimental design).
2. Note that the last two bullet points (above) also specifically relate to scientific research (Bullock and Panicker, 2003).
3. According to Resnik (2007: 111) 'a researcher has a conflict of interest if and only if he or she has personal financial, professional, or political interests that have a significant chance of compromising the judgment of the average scientist in the conduct of research'.
4. The prisoner's dilemma is a fundamental problem in game theory that demonstrates why two people might not cooperate even if it is in both their interests to do so (see http://en.wikipedia.org/wiki/Prisoner%27s_dilemma).
5. This section is an updated and condensed version of a paper published in *Environment and Planning B* (Van Wee, 2007a) based on research, partly carried out by Delft University of Technology for the Dutch Parliamentary Commission Infrastructure Projects (TCI, 2004), a highly influential commission that recently analysed the quality of decision making with respect to large infrastructure projects and in particular the role of parliament in this.
6. Several of the authors reviewed do not explicitly present a definition of 'large' projects or 'megaproject'. Here I limit myself to infrastructure projects. These include roads, rail lines, channels, (extensions of) airports and harbours, bridges and tunnels. I limit myself to hardware only, excluding software, projects related to deregulations, liberalization, privatization, etc. An important question then is: what is the minimum cost level to label an infrastructure project as 'large'? The authors of the literature reviewed do not present a (generally accepted) minimum level. The 'cheapest' project in the database of Flyvbjerg et al. (2003a) is US$1.5 million, typically being stretches of roads in larger road schemes. I would not define such projects as megaprojects. Intuitively, I assume the minimum cost level to be some €500 million.
7. The authors use the word 'value'. They probably mean costs or expenditure, the value (in economic terms) may of course be lower or higher.
8. The analysis was carried out using SPSS, the rotation method is Oblimin with Kaiser Normalization.
9. The Dutch OEI guidelines explain that in the case of the *ex ante*

evaluation of large transport infrastructure projects a CBA should be made, and gives guidance on how to do this.

10. The issue of conflicts between values or codes is widely discussed in the literature – see, for example, Resnik (1998).

11. Here I do not discuss if it is 'right' that the calculated concentrations play a huge role in decision making of such policy options – this role is often criticized because of the high level of uncertainty of the calculated concentrations. I only use the example to illustrate the importance of the use of research.

CHAPTER 8

1. For a discussion on the ethical aspects of engineering models, see Murphy et al. (2010).

Bibliography

Ackerman, F., L. Heinzerling (2003), *Priceless: On Knowing the Price of Everything and the Value of Nothing*. New York: New Press.

Akerlof, G.A., R.J. Shiller (2009), *Animal Spirits: How Human Psychology Drives the Economy, and Why it Matters for Global Capitalism*. Princeton and Oxford: Princeton University Press.

Allison, J., A. Chames, W.W. Cooper, T. Sueyoshi (1994), How do the construction and/or interpretation of models affect our decisions? In: Wallace, W.A. (ed.), *Ethics in Modeling*. Oxford: Pergamon.

Anand, P., A. Wailoo (2000), Utilities versus rights to publicly provided goods: arguments and evidence from health care rationing, *Economica*, **6**, 543–77.

Annema, J.A., C. Koopmans, B. van Wee (2007), Evaluating transport infrastructure investments: the Dutch experience with a standardized approach, *Transport Reviews*, **27** (2), 125–50.

Arneson, R. (1989), Equality of opportunity for welfare, *Philosophical Studies*, **56**, 77–93.

Arneson, R. (1990a), Libertarism, distributive subjectivism, and equal opportunity for welfare, *Philosophy & Public Affairs*, **19**, 159–94.

Arneson, R. (1990b), Primary goods reconsidered, *NOÛS*, **24**, 429–54.

Arneson, R. (1991), Lockean self-ownership: towards a demolition, *Political Studies*, **39**, 36–54.

Arrhenius, G. (2009), Egalitarianism and population change. In: Gosseries, A., L.H. Meyer (eds), *Intergenerational Justice*. Oxford: Oxford University Press, pp. 323–46.

Asveld, L., S. Roeser (2009), *The Ethics of Technological Risk*. London and Sterling, VA: Earthscan.

Attas, D. (2009), A transgenerational difference principle. In: Gosseries, A., L.H. Meyer (eds), *Intergenerational Justice*. Oxford: Oxford University Press, pp. 189–218.

Audi, R. (2007), *Moral Value and Human Diversity*. Oxford and New York: Oxford University Press.

Auditor General of Sweden (1994), *Riksrevisionsverket. Infrastruktur-investingar: en kostnadsjamorelse mellan poan of utyfall i 15 storre prosjekt innom vagverket of banverket*. RVV 1994: 23.

Barabba, V.P. (1994), The role of models in managerial decision making – never say the model says. In: Wallace, W.A. (ed.), *Ethics in Modeling*. Oxford: Pergamon, pp. 145–60.

Baron, J. (2000), *Thinking and Deciding* (3rd edn). Cambridge: Cambridge University Press.

Bass, R. (1998), Evaluating environmental justice under the national environmental policy act, *Environmental Impact Assessment Review*, **18**, 83–92.

Battellino, H. (2009), Transport for the transport disadvantaged: a review of service delivery models in New South Wales, *Transport Policy*, **16**, 123–29.

Baumol, W.J., W.E. Oates (1988), *The Theory of Environmental Policy* (2nd edn). Cambridge: Cambridge University Press.

Beach, D. (1996), *The Responsible Conduct of Research*. New York, Basel, Cambridge and Tokyo: Weinheim.

Beauchamp, T.L. (2003), The nature of applied ethics. In: Frey, R.G., C. Heath Wellman (eds), *A Companion to Applied Ethics*. Oxford: Blackwell Publishing Ltd, pp. 3–16.

Beckerman, W. (2006), The impossibility of a theory of intergenerational justice. In: Tremmel, J.C. (ed.), *Handbook of Intergenerational Justice*. Cheltenham, UK and Northampton, MA, USA: Edward Elgar, pp. 53–71.

Beckmann, J. (2001), Automobility – a social problem and theoretical concept, *Environment and Planning D*, **19** (5), 593–607.

Bennett, D.H., T.E. McKone, J.S. Evans, W.W. Nazaroff, M.D. Margni, O. Jolliet, K.R. Smit (2002), Defining intake fraction, *Environmental Science & Technology*, May, 3–7.

Bergman, S., T. Sager (eds) (2008), *The Ethics of Mobilities*. Aldershot, UK and Burlington, USA: Ashgate.

Beuthe, M. (2002), Transport evaluation methods: from Cost–Benefit Analysis to Multicriteria Analysis and the decision framework. In: L. Giorgi et al. (eds), *Project and Policy Evaluation in Transport*. Farnham: Ashgate Publishing Ltd, pp. 209–41.

Birnbacher, C. (2006), Principles of intergenerational justice. In: Tremmel, J.C. (ed.), *Handbook of Intergenerational Justice*. Cheltenham, UK and Northampton, MA, USA: Edward Elgar, pp. 23–38.

Blauwens, G., P. De Baere, E. Van de Voorde (2008), *Transport Economics* (3rd edn). Antwerpen: De Boeck.

Bognar, G. (2009), Welfare judgements and risk. In: Asveld, L., S. Roeser (eds), *The Ethics of Technological Risk*. London and Sterling, VA: Earthscan, pp. 144–60.

Brainard, J.S., A.P. Jones, I.J. Bateman, A.A. Lovett, P.J. Fallon (2002),

Modelling environmental equity: access to air quality in Birmingham, England, *Environment and Planning A*, **34**, 695–716.

Bristow, A., J. Nellthorp (2000), Transport project appraisal in the European Union, *Transport Policy*, **7** (1), 51–60.

Bromley, D.W. (1989), Entitlements, missing markets, and environmental uncertainty, *Journal of Environmental Economics and Management*, **17** (2), 181–94.

Broome, J. (2005), Should we value population? *The Journal of Political Philosophy*, **13** (4), 399–413.

Broome, J. (2008), The ethics of climate change, *Scientific American*, June, 97–102.

Brown, D.A. (n.d.), Ethical issues in the use of cost-benefit analysis of climate change programs, available at: http://climateethics.org/?p=36 (accessed 18 May 2010).

Bruzelius, N., B. Flyvbjerg, W. Rothengatter (2002), Big decision, big risks: improving accountability in mega projects, *Transport Policy*, **9** (2), 143–54.

Bullock, M., S. Panicker (2003), Ethics for all: differences across scientific society codes, *Science and Engineering Ethics*, **9**, 159–70.

Bureau, B., M. Glachant (2008), Distributional effects of road pricing: assessment of nine scenarios for Paris, *Transportation Research Part A*, **42**, 995–1008.

Burgess, A. (2004), *Cellular Phones, Public Fears, and a Culture of Precaution*. Cambridge: Cambridge University Press.

Button, K. (2003), *Recent Developments in Transport Economics*. Cheltenham, UK and Northampton, MA, USA: Edward Elgar.

Button, K.J. (2010), *Transport Economics* (3rd edn). Cheltenham, UK and Northampton, MA, USA: Edward Elgar.

Bykvist, K. (2009), Preference-formation and intergenerational justice. In: Gosseries, A., L.H. Meyer (eds), *Intergenerational Justice*. Oxford: Oxford University Press, pp. 301–22.

Campos, J., G. De Rus (2009), Some stylized facts about high-speed rail: A review of HSR experiences around the world, *Transport Policy*, **16**, 19–28.

Cartmel, F., A. Furlong (2000), Youth unemployment in rural areas, available at: http://www.jfr.org.uk.

Church, A., M. Frost, K. Sullivan (2000), Transport and social exclusion in London, *Transport Policy*, **7** (3), 195–205.

Cohen, G.A. (1986), Self-ownership, world-ownership and equality. In: Lucash, F. (ed.), *Justice and Equality Here and Now*. Ithaca: Cornell University Press.

Cohen, G.A. (1989), On the currency of egalitarian justice, *Ethics*, **99**, 906–44.

Cohen, G.A. (1993), Equality of what? On welfare, goods, and capabilities. In: Nussbaum, M, A. Sen, *The Quality of Life*. Oxford: Clarendon Press, pp. 95–139.

Cohen, G.A. (1995), *Self-ownership, Freedom, and Equality*. Cambridge: Cambridge University Press.

Cookson, R., P. Dolan (2000), Principles of justice in health care rationing, *Journal of Medical Ethics*, **26**, 323–9.

Cranor, C. (2009), A plea for a rich conception of risks. In: Asveld, L., S. Roeser, *The Ethics of Technological Risk*. London and Sterling, VA: Earthscan, pp. 27–39.

Currie, G., T. Richardson, P. Smyth, D. Vella-Brodrick, J. Hine, K. Lucas, J. Stanley, J. Morris, R. Kinnear, J. Stanley (2009), Investigating links between transport disadvantage, social exclusion and well-being in Melbourne – preliminary results, *Transport Policy*, **16**, 97–105.

Daly, H.E. (2007), *Ecological Economics and Sustainable Development, Selected Essays of Herman Daly*, Cheltenham, UK and Northampton, MA, USA: Edward Elgar.

Darwall, S.L. (2003), Theories of ethics. In: Frey, R.G., C. Heath Wellman (eds), *A Companion to Applied Ethics*. Malden, MA, Oxford and Carlton, Victoria: Blackwell Publishing Ltd, pp. 17–37.

David, S.C., S.W. Diegel, R.G. Boundy (2009), *Transportation Energy Data Book. Edition 28*. Oak Ridge, TN: Oak Ridge National Laboratory/US Department of Energy.

Davidson, M.D. (2009), Acceptable risk to future generations. In: L. Asveld and S. Roeser (eds), *The Ethics of Technological Risk*. London and Sterling, VA: Earthscan, pp. 77–91.

Davis, S.C., S.W. Diegel, R.G. Boundy (2010), *Transportation Energy Data Book*. Oak Ridge, TN: Oak Ridge National Laboratory.

De Blaeij, A.T. (2003), *The Value of a Statistical Life in Road Safety: Stated Preference Methodologies and Empirical Estimates for the Netherlands*. Tinbergen Institute Research Series, Vrije Universiteit, Amsterdam.

De Blaeij, A.T., R.J.G.M. Florax, P. Rietveld, E. Verhoef (2003), The value of statistical life in road safety: a meta-analysis, *Accident Analysis and Prevention*, **35** (6), 973–86.

De Dios Ortúzar, J., L.G. Willumsen (2001), *Modelling Transport* (3rd edn). Chichester, UK: Wiley.

De Groot, J.I.M., L. Steg (2009), Mean or green: which values can promote stable pro-environmental behaviour? *Conservation Letters*, **2**, 61–6.

De Jong, G., A. Daly, M. Pieters, T. Van der Hoorn (2007), The logsum as an evaluation measure: review of the literature and new results, *Transportation Research Part A*, **41** (9), 874–89.

De Jong, W.M., G.P. Van Wee (2007), A new guideline for 'ex ante' evaluation of large infrastructure projects in the Netherlands. In: Haezendonck, E. (ed.), *Transport Project Evaluation*. Cheltenham, UK and Northampton, MA, USA: Edward Elgar, pp. 151–67.

Department for Transport (2002), *Social Exclusion and the Provision and Availability of Public Transport*, available at: https://www.liftshare.com. business/pdfs/Dft-social%20exclusion.pdf.

DETR (1997), *Perceptions of Safety from Crime on Public Transport*. London: Crime Concern and Transport and Travel Research.

Dionne, G., P. Lanoie (2004), Public choice and the value of a statistical life for cost–benefit analysis: the case of road safety, *Journal of Transport Economics and Policy*, **38** (2), 247–74.

DOI (Department of Infrastructure) (2003), *Metropolitan Bus Plan. Final Report*. DOI: Melbourne, Australia.

Doorn, N. (2009), Applying Rawlsian approaches to resolve ethical issues: inventory and setting of a research agenda, *Journal of Business Ethics*, **92**, 127–43.

Dorland, C., H.M.A. Jansen (1997), *ExternE Transport – the Netherlands. Dutch Case Studies on Transport Externalities*. Institute for Environmental Studies (IVM), Free University, Amsterdam.

Douglas, H.E. (2009), *Science, Policy and the Value-free Ideal*. Pittsburgh, PA: University of Pittsburgh Press.

Dupuit, J. (1844), On the measurement of the utility of public works, *Annales de pont et chaussees*, 2nd ser. 8.

Dworkin, R. (1981a), What is equality? Part 1: equality of welfare. *Philosophy & Public Affairs*, **10**, 185–246.

Dworkin, R. (1981b), What is equality? Part 2: equality of resources, *Philosophy & Public Affairs*, **10**, 283–345.

Easterlin, R.A. (1973), Does money buy happiness? *Public Interest*, **30** (30), 3–10.

Easterlin, R.A. (1974), Does economic growth improve the human lot? In: David, P.E., W.E. Melvin (eds), *Nations and Households in Economic Growth*. Palo Alto, CA: Stanford University Press, pp. 89–125.

Eijgenraam, C.J.J., C.C. Koopmans, P.J.G. Tang, A.C.P Verster (2000), *Evaluation of Infrastructural Projects; Guide for Cost–Benefit Analysis, Sections I and II*, The Hague: CPB, Rotterdam: NEI (changed name to ECORYS).

Eliasson, J., L.-G. Mattson (2006), Equity effects of congestion pricing: quantitative methodology and a case study for Stockholm, *Transportation Research Part A*, **40**, 602–20.

Elvebakk, B., T. Steiro (2009), First principles, second hand: perceptions and interpretations of Vision Zero in Norway, *Safety Science*, **47**, 958–66.

Elvik, R. (1999), Can injury prevention efforts go too far? Reflections on some possible implications of Vision Zero for road accident fatalities, *Accident Analysis and Prevention*, **31** (3), 265–86.

Elvik, R. (2002), Cost–benefit analysis of ambulance and rescue helicopters in Norway: reflections on assigning a monetary value to saving a human life, *Applied Health Economics and Health Policy*, **1** (2), 55–63.

Eriksson, L., J. Garvill, A.M. Norland (2008), Acceptability of single and combined transport policy measures: the importance of environmental and policy specific beliefs, *Transportation Research Part A*, **42**, 1117–28.

Espinoza, N. (2009), Incommensurability: the failure to compare risks. In: Asveld, L. and S. Roeser (eds), *The Ethics of Technological Risk*. London/Sterling, VA: Earthscan, pp. 128–43.

European Union (2006), *Energy & Transport in Figures, 2006. Part 3: Transport*. Brussels: European Commission, available at: http://ec. europa.eu/dgs/energy_transport/figures/pocketbook/doc/2006/2006_tra nsport_en.pdf.

European Union (2008), http://www.irfnet.eu/media/press_release/ statistics/erfeuropean_road_statistics_2008_booklet_150x210mm_v08_ press_safety.pdf (accessed 15 September 2008).

Evans, J.S., S.K. Wolff, K. Phonboon, J.I. Levy, K.R. Smith (2002), Exposure efficiency: an idea whose time has come? *Chemosphere*, **49**, 1075–91.

Eyre, N.J., E. Ozdemiroglu, D.W. Pearce, P. Steele (1997), Fuel and location effects on the damage costs of transport emissions, *Journal of Transport Economics and Policy*, **31** (1), 5–24.

Fahlquist, J.N. (2006), Responsibility ascriptions and Vision Zero, *Accident Analysis and Prevention*, **38**, 1113–8.

Fahlquist, J.N. (2009), Saving lives in road traffic – ethical aspects, *Journal of Public Health*, **17**, 385–94.

Feinberg, J. (1986), Wrongful life and the counterfactual element in harming, *Philosophy and Social Policy*, **4** (1), 145–78.

Feitelson, E. (2002), Introducing environmental equity dimensions into the sustainable transport discourse: issues and pitfalls, *Transportation Research Part D*, **7** (2), 99–118.

Flyvbjerg, B., N. Bruzelius, W. Rothengatter (2003a), *Megaprojects and Risk: An Anatomy of Ambition*. Cambridge: Cambridge University Press.

Flyvbjerg, B., N. Bruzelius, B. van Wee (2008), Comparison of capital costs per route-kilometre in urban rail, *European Journal of Transport and Infrastructure Research*, **8** (1), 17–30.

Flyvbjerg, B., M.K. Skamris Holm, S.L. Buhl (2003b), How common and how large are cost overruns in transport infrastructure projects? *Transport Reviews*, **23** (1), 71–88.

Flyvbjerg, B., M.K. Skamris Holm, S.L. Buhl (2004), What causes cost overrun in transport infrastructure projects? *Transport Reviews*, **24** (1), 3–18.

Flyvbjerg B., M.K. Skamris Holm, S.L. Buhl (2005), How (in)accurate are demand forecasts in public works projects? The case of transportation, *Journal of the American Planning Association*, **71** (2), 131–46.

Frey, R.G., C. Heath Wellman (eds) (2003), *A Companion to Applied Ethics*. Oxford: Blackwell Publishing Ltd.

Friedman, B., P.H. Kahn Jr., A. Borning (2002), *Value Sensitive Design: Theory and Methods*. University of Washington Computer Science & Engineering Technical Report 02-12-01, December.

Gardiner, S.M. (2006), Protecting future generations: intergenerational buck-passing, theoretical ineptitude and a brief for a global core precautionary principle. In: Tremmel, J.C. (ed.), *Handbook of Intergenerational Justice*. Cheltenham, UK and Northampton, MA, USA: Edward Elgar, pp. 148–169.

Gass, S.I. (1994), Ethical concerns and ethical answers. In: Wallace, W.A. (ed.), *Ethics in Modeling*. Oxford: Pergamon.

Gert, B. (1982), Licensing professionals, *Business and Professional Ethics Journal*, **1**, 51–60.

Geurs, K.T., J. Ritsema van Eck (2001), *Accessibility Measures: Review and Applications. Evaluation of Accessibility Impacts of Land-use Transportation Scenarios, and Related Social and Economic Impacts*. RIVM report 408505006. Bilthoven: Rijksinstituut voor Volksgezondheid en Milieu.

Geurs, K., J. Ritsema van Eck (2004), Editorial. Special issue: Land use transport interaction modelling, *European Journal of Transport and Infrastructure Research*, **4** (3), 247–9.

Geurs, K.T., B. van Wee (2004a), Accessibility evaluation of land-use and transport strategies: review and research directions, *Transport Geography*, **12**, 127–40.

Geurs, K., B. van Wee (2004b), Backcasting as a tool for sustainable transport policy making: the Environmental Sustainable Transport study in the Netherlands. *European Journal of Transport and Infrastructure Research*, **4** (1), 47–69.

Geurs, K.T., W. Boon, B. van Wee (2009), Social impacts of transport: literature review and the state of the practice of transport appraisal in the Netherlands and the United Kingdom, *Transport Reviews*, **29** (1), 69–90.

Geurs, K., R. Haaijer, B. van Wee (2006), Option value of public transport: methodology for measurement and case study for regional rail links in the Netherlands, *Transport Reviews*, **26** (5), 613–43.

Gilbert, R., A. Perl (2008), *Transport Revolutions: Moving People and Freight Without Oil*. London: Earthscan.

Glaser, B.G., A.L. Strauss (1967), *The Discovery of Grounded Theory: Strategies for Qualitative Research*, Hawthorne, NY: Aldine de Gruyter Press.

Gordon, D., L. Adelman, K. Ashworth, J. Bradshaw, R. Levitas, S. Middleton, C. Pantazis, D. Patsios, S. Payne, P. Townsend, J. Williams (2000), *Poverty and Social Exclusion in Britain*. York: Joseph Rowntree Foundation.

Gosseries, A. (2001), What do we owe the next generation(s), *Loyola of Los Angeles Law Review*, **35**, 293–355.

Gosseries, A. (2009), Three models of intergenerational reciprocity. In: Gosseries, A., L.H. Meyer (eds), *Intergenerational Justice*. Oxford: Oxford University Press, pp. 119–48.

Gosseries, A., L.H. Meyer (eds) (2009), *Intergenerational Justice*. Oxford: Oxford University Press.

Graham, D.J., S. Glaister (2004), Road traffic demand elasticity estimates: a review, *Transport Reviews*, **24** (3), 261–74.

Grant-Muller, S.M., P. MacKie, J. Nellthorp, A. Pearman (2001), Economic appraisal of European transport projects: the state-of-the-art revisited, *Transport Reviews*, **21** (2), 237–61.

Grieco, M., L. Pickup, R. Whipp (1989), *Gender, Transport and Employment*. Avebury: Aldershot.

Gunn, H. (2001), Spatial and temporal transferability of relationships between travel demand, trip cost and travel time, *Transportation Research E*, **37**, 163–89.

Gutmann, A., D. Thompson (1996), *Democracy and Disagreement*. Cambridge, MA: Harvard University Press.

Hamilton, K., L. Jenkins (2000), A gender audit for public transport: a new policy tool in the tackling of social exclusion, *Urban Studies*, **37** (10), 1793–800.

Hamilton, K., L. Jenkins, A. Gregory (1991), *Woman and Transport: Bus Deregulation in West Yorkshire*. Bradford: Leeds University Press.

Hammitt, J.K. (2002), QALYs versus WTP, *Risk Analysis*, **22**, 985–1001.

Hammitt, J.K. (2007), Valuing changes in mortality risk: lives saved versus life years saved, *Review of Environmental Economics and Policy*, **1** (2), 228–40.

Hanemann, M. (1991), Willingness to pay and willingness to accept: how much can they differ? *American Economic Review*, **81** (3), 635–47.

Hanley, N., E.B. Barbier (2009), *Pricing Nature: Cost–Benefit Analysis and Environmental Policy*. Cheltenham, UK and Northampton, MA, USA: Edward Elgar.

Hansson, S.O. (2007), Philosophical problems in cost-benefit analysis, *Economics and Philosophy*, **23**, 163–83.

Hansson, S.O. (2009), An agenda for the ethics of risk. In: Asveld, L., S. Roeser (eds), *The Ethics of Technological Risk*. London/Sterling, VA: Earthscan, pp. 11–24.

Hausman, D.M., M.S. McPherson (2006), *Economic Analysis, Moral Philosophy, and Public Policy* (2nd edn). Cambridge: Cambridge University Press.

Hayashi, Y., H. Morisugi (2000), International comparison of background concept and methodology of transportation project appraisal, *Transport Policy*, **7**, 73–88.

Heinen, E., B. van Wee, K. Maat (2009), Commuting by bicycle: an overview of literature, *Transport Reviews*, **30** (1), 59–96.

Hensher, D.A., K.J. Button (2000), *Handbook of Transport Modelling*. New York: Elsevier.

Heyd, D. (2009), A value or an obligation? In: Gosseries, A., L.H. Meyer (eds), *Intergenerational Justice*. Oxford: Oxford University Press, pp. 167–88.

Hicks, J. (1939), The foundations of welfare economics, *Economic Journal*, **49**, 696–712.

Hine, J. (2003), Editorial. Social exclusion and transport systems, *Transport Policy*, **10**, 263.

Hine, J., M. Grieco (2003), Scatters and clusters in time and space: Implications for delivering integrated and inclusive transport, *Transport Policy*, **10** (4), 299–306.

Hine, J., F. Mitchell (2001), Better for everyone? Travel experiences and transport exclusion, *Urban Studies*, **38** (2), 319–32.

Hodgson, F.C., J. Turner (2003), Participation not consumption: the need for new participatory practices to address transport and social exclusion, *Transport Policy*, **10**, 265–72.

Hoel, M., T. Sterner (2007), Discounting and relative prices, *Climate Change*, **84**, 265–80.

Hood, R. (2003), Global warming. In: Frey, R.G., C. Heath Wellman (eds), *A Companion to Applied Ethics*. Oxford: Blackwell Publishing Ltd, pp. 674–84.

Hüttenmoser, M. (1995), Children and their living surroundings: empirical investigations into the significance of living surroundings for the everyday life and development of children, *Children's Environments*, **12** (4), 403–13.

Jamieson, D. (2003), Values in nature. In: Frey, R.G., C. Heath Wellman (eds), *A Companion to Applied Ethics*. Oxford: Blackwell Publishing Ltd, pp. 650–61.

Johansson-Stenman, O., P. Martinsson (2008). Are some lives more valuable? An ethical preferences approach, *Journal of Health Economics*, **27** (3), 739–52.

Jones, P. (2001), *Addressing Equity Concerns in Relation to Road User Charging*. CUPTD position paper CUPID-PROGRESS workshop Trondheim, available at: http:/www.transport-pricing.net/reports4.html

Jones, S.C., M. Lynch (2007), Non-advertising alcohol promotions in licensed premises: does the Code of Practice ensure responsible promotion of alcohol? *Drug and Alcohol Review*, **26** (5), 477–85.

Kahneman, D., J.L. Knetsch (1992), Valuing public goods: the purchase of moral satisfaction, *Journal of Environmental Economics and Management*, **22**, 57–70.

Kahneman, D., A. Tversky (2000), *Choices, Values and Frames*. Cambridge: Cambridge University Press.

Kahneman, D., I. Ritov, D. Schkade (1999), Economic preferences or attitude expressions? An analysis of dollar responses to public issues, *Journal of Risk and Uncertainty*, **19**, 203–35.

Kahneman, D., P. Slovic, A. Tversky (1982), *Judgement under Uncertainty: Heuristics and Biases*. Cambridge: Cambridge University Press.

Kaldor, N. (1939), Welfare propositions of economics and interpersonal comparisons of utility, *Economic Journal*, **49**, 549–52.

Kaptein, M. (2004), Business codes of multinational firms: what do they say? *Journal of Business Ethics*, **50**, 13–31.

Keeler, E.B., S. Cretin (1983), Discounting of life-saving and other non-monetary effects, *Management Science*, **29**, 300–306.

Kenyon, S., G. Lyons, J. Rafferty (2002), Transport and social exclusion: investigating the possibility of promoting inclusion through virtual mobility, *Journal of Transport Geography*, **10**, 207–19.

Khisty C.J., U. Zeitler (2001), Is hypermobility a challenge for transport ethics and systemicity? *Systemic Practice and Action Research*, **14** (5), 597–613.

Koopmans, C. (2009), *Literatuurverkenning veranderende preferenties. Note 9-12-2009*, Amsterdam: Stichting voor Economisch Onderzoek.

Koopmans, C.C. (2010), *Van zacht naar hard: milieueffecten in kosten-batenanalyses*. Amsterdam: Vrije Universiteit Amsterdam.

Krumdieck, S., S. Page, A. Dantas (2010), Urban form and long-term fuel supply decline: A method to investigate the peak oil risks to essential activities, *Transportation Research Part A*, **44** (5), 306–22.

Kumar, R. (2009), Wronging future people: a contractualist proposal. In: Gosseries, A., L.H. Meyer (eds), *Intergenerational Justice*. Oxford: Oxford University Press, pp. 251–71.

Lahdelma, R., P. Salkminen, J. Hokkanen (2000), Using multicriteria methods in environmental planning and management, *Environmental Management*, **26** (6), 595–605.

Leung, J., J. Guria (2006), Value of statistical life: adults versus children, *Accident Analysis & Prevention*, **38**, 1208–17.

Levine, J., Y. Garb (2002), Congestion pricing's conditional promise: promotion or accessibility of mobility? *Transport Policy*, **9** (3), 179–88.

Levinson, D. (2010), Equity effects of road pricing: a review, *Transport Reviews*, **30** (1), 33–57.

Light, A. (2003), Environmental ethics. In: Frey, R.G., C. Heath Wellman (eds), *A Companion to Applied Ethics*. Oxford: Blackwell Publishing Ltd, pp. 633–49.

Litman, T.A. (2001), What's it worth? Economic evaluation for transportation decision-making. Internet symposium on benefit–cost analysis. Ottawa: Transportation Association of Canada.

Litman, T. (2002), Evaluating transportation equity, *World Transport Policy & Practice*, **8** (2), 50–65.

Litman, T. (2006), Community cohesion as a transport planning objective, paper 07-0550 for presentation at the Transportation Research Board 2007 Annual Meeting.

Little, J.D.C. (1994), On model building. In: Wallace, W.A. (ed.), *Ethics in Modeling*. Oxford: Pergamon, pp. 167–83.

Loader, C., J. Stanley (2009), Growing bus patronage and addressing transport disadvantage – the Melbourne experience, *Transport Policy*, **16**, 106–14.

Lorenzo, O., P. Esqueda, J. Larson (2010), Safety and ethics in the global workplace: asymmetries in culture and infrastructure, *Journal of Business Ethics*, **92**, 87–106.

Lucas, K. (ed.) (2004), *Running on Empty: Transport, Social Exclusion and Environmental Justice*. Bristol: Policy Press.

Lucas, K. (2006), Providing transport for social inclusion within a framework for environmental justice in the UK, *Transportation Research Part A*, **40**, 801–9.

Lucas, K., T., Grosvenor, R. Simpson (2001), *Transport, the Environment and Social Exclusion*. New York: Joseph Rowntree Foundation/York Publishing Ltd.

Lucas, K., S. Tylers, G. Christodoulou (2009), Assessing the 'value' of new transport initiatives in deprived neighbourhoods in the UK, *Transport Policy*, **16** 115–22.

Luxton, M. (2002), *Feminist Perspectives on Social Inclusion and Children's Well-Being*. Toronto: Laidlaw Foundation.

Lyons, G. (2003), The introduction of social exclusion into the field of travel behaviour, *Transport Policy*, **10**, 339–42.

Macharis, C., E. van Hoeck, E. Perkin, T. van Lier (2010), A decision analysis framework for intermodal transport: comparing fuel price increases and the internalisation of external costs, *Transportation Research Part A*, **44** (7), 550–61.

Mackett, R.L., K. Achuthan, H. Titheridge (2008), AMELIA: A tool to make transport policies more socially inclusive, *Transport Policy*, **15** (6), 372–8.

Mackie, P., J. Preston (1998), Twenty-one sources of error and bias in transport appraisal, *Transport Policy*, **5** (1), 1–7.

Mackie, P.J., M. Wardman, A.S. Fowkes, G.A. Whelan, J. Nellthorp, J.J. Bates, (2003), Value of travel time savings in the UK, paper prepared for the Department for Transport, Leeds: Institute for Transport Studies, University of Leeds/John Bastes Services.

MacLean, D. (2009), Ethics, reason and risk analysis. In: Asveld, L. and S. Roeser (eds), *The Ethics of Technological Risk*. London/Sterling, VA: Earthscan, pp. 115–27.

Mandeloff, M., R. Kaplan (1989), Are large differences in lifesaving costs justified? A psychometric study of the relative value placed on preventing deaths, *Risk Analysis*, **9**, 349–63.

Marshall, J.D., T.E. McKone, E. Deaking, W.W. Nazaroff (2005), Inhalation of motor vehicle emissions: effects of urban population and land area, *Atmospheric Environment*, **39**, 283–95.

Marshall, J.D., W.J. Riley, Th. E. McKone, W. Nazaroff (2003), Intake fraction of primary pollutants: motor vehicle emissions in the South Coast Air Basin, *Atmospheric Environment*, **37**, 3455–68.

Martens, K. (2006), Basing transport planning on principles of social justice, *Berkeley Planning Journal*, 19 (www-dcrp.ced.berkeley.edu/bpj).

Martens, K., E. Hurvitz (2011), Distributive impacts of demand-based modelling, *Transportmetrica*, 181–200.

Mason, R.O. (1994), Morality and models. In: Wallace, W.A. (ed.), *Ethics in Modeling*. Oxford: Pergamon, pp. 183–94.

McKay, R. (2000), Applying ethical principles to the decision to build the Red Hill Creek Expressway, *International Journal of Public Sector Management*, **13** (1), 58–67.

McMullen, B.S., L. Zhang, K. Nakahara (2010), Distribution impacts of changing from a gasoline tax to a vehicle-mile tax for light vehicles: a case study of Oregon, *Transport Policy*, **17**, 359–66.

Meadows, D.H., D.L. Meadows, J. Randers, W.W. Behrens (1972), *The*

Limits to Growth – A Report for the Club of Rome Project. New York: Universe Books.

Meijers, A. (ed.) (2009), *Handbook of the Philosophy of Science. Volume 9: Philosophy of Technology and Engineering Sciences*. Oxford: Elsevier.

Melkert, J., B. van Wee (2009), Assessment of innovative transport concepts using cost–benefit analysis, *Transportation Planning and Technology*, **32** (6), 545–71.

Meyer, L.H., D. Roser (2009), Enough for the future. In: Gosseries, A., L.H. Meyer (eds), *Intergenerational Justice*. Oxford: Oxford University Press, pp. 219–48.

Mokhtarian, P., C. Chen (2004), TTB or not TTB that is the question: a review and analysis of the empirical literature on travel time (and money) budgets, *Transportation Research Part A*, **38** (9–10), 643–75.

Morisugi, H., Y. Hayashi (2000), Editorial, *Transport Policy*, **7** (1), 1–2.

Morton, A. (1991), *Disaster and Dilemmas: Strategies for Real-life Decision Making*. Oxford: Basil Blackwell Ltd.

Mulvey, J.M. (1994), Models in the public sector: success, failure and ethical behaviour. In: Wallace, W.A. (ed.), *Ethics in Modeling*. Oxford: Pergamon, pp. 58–74.

Murphy, C., P. Gardoni, C.E. Harris Jr (2010), Classification and moral evaluation of uncertainties in engineering modeling, *Science and Engineering Ethics*. DOI 10.1007/s11948-010-9242-2.

Nagel, T. (1987), The fragmentation of value. In: C.W. Gowans (ed.), *Moral Dilemmas*. New York and Oxford: Oxford University Press, pp. 128–41.

Newton, P.N. (ed.) (1997), *Reshaping Cities for a More Sustainable Future – Exploring the Link between Urban Form, Air Quality, Energy and Greenhouse Gas Emissions*. Research Monograph 6, Melbourne: Australian Housing and Research Institute (AHURI) (http://www. ea.gov.au/atmosphere/airquality/urban-air/urban air docs.html).

Ng, Y.-K. (1992), The older the more valuable: divergence between utility and dollar values of life as one ages, *Journal of Economics*, **55**, 1–16.

Nijkamp, P., B. Ubbels (1999), How reliable are estimates of infrastructure costs? A comparative analysis, *International Journal of Transport Economics*, **26** (1), 23–53.

Nijland, H., G.P. van Wee (2005), Traffic noise in Europe: a comparison of calculation methods, noise indices and noise standards for road and railroad traffic in Europe, *Transport Reviews*, **25** (5), 591–612.

Nijland, H., B. van Wee (2008), Noise valuation in ex-ante evaluation of major road and railroad projects, *European Journal of Transport and Infrastructure Research*, **8** (3), 216–26.

Nilsen, P., D.S. Hudson, A. Kullberg, T. Timpka, R. Ekman, K. Lindqvist (2004), *Making Sense of Safety*, Injury Prevention, **10**, 71–3.

Nozick, K. (1974), *Anarchy, State, and Utopia*. New York: Basic Books.

Odeck, J. (2004), Cost overruns in road construction – what are their sizes and determinants? *Transport Policy*, **11** (1), 43–53.

Odgaard, T., C. Kelly, J. Laird (2005), Current practice in project appraisal in Europe, HEATCO research project (Harmonised European Approaches for Transport Costing and Project Assessment).

OECD/IEA (2009), *Transport, Energy and CO$_2$*. Paris: OECD/IEA.

Ohnmacht, T., H. Maksim, M.M. Bergman (eds) (2009a), *Mobilities and Inequality*. Aldershot, UK and Burlington, USA: Ashgate.

Ohnmacht, T., H. Maksim, M.M. Bergman (2009b), Mobilities and inequality – making connections. In: Ohnmacht, T., H. Maksim, M.M. Bergman (eds), *Mobilities and Inequality*. Aldershot, UK and Burlington, USA: Ashgate, pp. 7–26.

Olsson, N.O.E., H.P. Krane, A. Rolstadåsb, M. Veisethc (2010), Influence of reference points in ex post evaluations of rail infrastructure projects, *Transport Policy*, **17** (4), 251–8.

Parfit, D. (1984), *Reasons and Persons*. Oxford: Clarendon Press.

Pearce, D.W. (ed.) (2007), *Environmental Valuation in Developed Countries*. Cheltenham, UK and Northampton, MA, USA: Edward Elgar.

Perman, R., Y. Ma, J. McGilvray, M. Common (2003), *Natural Resource and Environmental Economics*. Gosport: Pearson Education Ltd and Ashford Colour Press Ltd.

Pickrell, D.H. (1990), *Urban Rail Transit Projects: Forecasts Versus Actual Ridership and Costs*. Washington, DC: US Department of Transportation.

Pickrell, D.H. (1992), A desire named streetcar – fantasy and fact in rail transit planning, *Journal of American Planning Association*, **58** (2).

Portney, P.R., J.P. Weyant (eds) (1999), *Discounting and Intergenerational Equity*. Washington, DC: Resources for the Future.

Posner, R.A. (2004), *Catastrophe: Risk and Response*. New York: Oxford University Press.

Potoglou, D., N. Robinson, C.W. Kim, P. Burge, R. Warnes (2010), Quantifying individuals' trade-offs between privacy, liberty and security: the case of rail travel in UK, *Transportation Research Part A*, **44**, 169–81.

Preston, J. (2009), Epilogue: transport policy and social exclusion – some reflections, *Transport Policy*, **16**, 140–42.

Priemus, H., B. Flyvbjerg, B. van Wee (eds) (2008), *Decision-Making on Mega-Projects: Cost–benefit Analysis, Planning and Innovation*. Cheltenham, UK and Northampton, MA, USA: Edward Elgar.

Priya, T., A. Uteng (2009), Dynamics of transport and social exclusion: effects of expensive driver's license, *Transport Policy*, **16**, 130–39.

Pruyt, E. (2010), Multi-actor systems and ethics, *International Transactions in Operational Research*, **17** (4), 507–20.

Raad voor Verkeer en Waterstaat, VROM-Raad, Algemene Energieraad (2008), *Een prijs voor elke reis. Een reductiestrategie voor CO₂-reductie in verkeer en vervoer*. Den Haag: Raad voor Verkeer en Waterstaat, VROM-Raad, Algemene Energieraad (in Dutch).

Rajé, F. (2003), The impact of transport on social exclusion processes with specific emphasis on road user charging, *Transport Policy*, **10**, 321–38.

Rawls, H. (1982), Social unity and primary goods. In: Sen, A., B. Williams (eds), *Utilitarianism and Beyond*. Cambridge, MA: Cambridge University Press, pp. 159–85.

Rawls, J. (1971), *A Theory of Justice*. Boston, MA: Harvard University Press.

Resnik, D.B. (1998), *The Ethics of Science: An Introduction*. London and New York: Routledge.

Resnik, D.B. (2007), *The Price of Truth: How Money Affects Norms of Science*. Oxford: Oxford University Press.

Rietveld, P. (2003), Winners and losers in transport policy: on efficiency, equity, and compensation. In: Hensher, D.A., K.J. Button (ed.), *Handbook of Transport and the Environment* (Handbooks in Transport, 4). Amsterdam: Elsevier, pp. 585–602.

Rietveld, P., B. van Wee (2008), Ex ante evaluation of railway station development projects: issues still to be solved. In: Bruinsma, F., H. Priemus, P. Rietveld, B. Van Wee (eds), *Railway Development: Impacts on Urban Dynamics*. Heidelberg: Physica Verlag, pp. 147–70.

Rietveld, P., J. Rouwendal, A.J. Vlist van der (2007), Equity issues in the evaluation of transport policies and transport infrastructure projects. In: Geenhuizen van, M., A. Reggiani, P. Rietveld (eds), *Policy Analysis of Transport Networks*. Aldershot: Ashgate, pp. 19–36.

Roemer, J.E. (1996), *Theories of Distributive Justice*. Cambridge, MA and London: Harvard University Press.

Roeser, S. (2009), The relation between cognition and affect in moral judgments about risks. In: Asveld L., S. Roeser (eds), *The Ethics of Technological Risk*. London / Sterling, VA: Earthscan, pp. 182–201.

Saelensminde, K. (2004), Cost–benefit analyses of walking and cycling track networks taking into account insecurity, health effects and external costs of motorized traffic, *Transportation Research Part A: Policy and Practice*, **38** (8), 593–606.

Sagoff, M. (1988), *The Economy of the Earth*. New York: Cambridge University Press.

Sanchez, T.W. (2008), Poverty, policy, and public transportation, *Transportation Research Part A*, **42**, 833–41.

Sarewitz, D., R. Pielke, M. Keykhah (2003), Vulnerability and risk: some thoughts from a political and policy perspective, *Risk Analysis*, **23** (4), 805–10.

Scanlon, T. (1986), Equality of resources and equality of welfare: a forced marriage? *Ethics*, **97**, 111–18.

Scanlon, T. (1988), The significance of choice. In: McMurrin, S. (ed.), *The Tanner Lectures on Human Values. Vol. 8*. Salt Lake City: University of Utah Press.

Schafer, A., D. Victor (1997), The past and future of global mobility, *Scientific American*, **227** (4), 36–9.

Schafer, A., J.B. Heywood, H.D. Jacoby, I.A. Waitz (2009), *Transportation in a Climate-Constrained World*. Boston: MIR Press.

Schönfelder, S., K.W. Axhausen (2003), Activity spaces: measures of social exclusion? *Transport Policy*, **10** (4), 273–86.

Schuitema, G., L. Steg (2008), The role of revenue use in the acceptability of transport pricing policies, *Transportation Research Part F*, **11**, 221–31.

Schuitema, G., L. Steg, M. van Kruining (2011), When are transport pricing policies fair and acceptable? The role of six fairness principles. *Social Justice Research*, **24** (1), 66–84.

Schuurbiers, D., P. Osseweijer, J. Kinderlerer (2009), Implementing the Netherlands code of conduct for scientific practice – a case study, *Science Engineering Ethics*, **15**, 213–31.

Schwanen, T., M.-P. Kwan, (2008), The internet, mobile phone and space-time constraints, *GeoForum*, **39** (3), 1362–77.

Schwartz, T. (1978), Obligations to posterity. In: Sikora, I., B. Barry (eds), *Obligations to Future Generations*. Philadelphia: Temple University Press, pp. 3–13.

Scott, D.M., M.W. Horner (2008), The role of urban form in shaping access to opportunities, *Journal of Transport and Land Use*, **1** (2), 89–119.

Sen, A. (1980), Equality of what? In: McMurrin, S. (ed.), *The Tanner Lectures on Human Values. Vol. 1*. Salt Lake City: University of Utah Press, pp. 353–69.

Sen, A. (1992), *Inequality Reexamined*. Oxford: Oxford University Press.

Sen, A. (2009), *The Idea of Justice*. London: Allen Lane.

Serageldin, I., A. Steer, (1994), *Making Development Sustainable: From Concepts to Action*. Washington, DC: The World Bank.

Shepard, D.S., R.J. Zeckhauser (1984), Survival versus consumption, *Management Science*, **30**, 423–39.

Skamris, M.K., B. Flyvbjerg (1997), Inaccuracy of traffic forecasts and cost estimates on large transport projects, *Transport Policy*, **4** (3), 141–6.

Slovic, P., B. Fischhoff, S. Lichtenstein (1985), Regulation of risk: a psychological perspective. In: R. Noll (ed.), *Regulatory Policy and the Social Sciences, California Series on Social Choice and Political Economy*. Berkeley and London: University of California Press.

Smith, K.R. (1993a), Fuel combustion, air pollution, and health: the situation in developing countries, *Annual Review of Energy and the Environment*, **18**, 529–66.

Smith, K.R. (1993b), Taking the true measure of air pollution, *EPA Journal*, **19** (4), 6–8.

Spinney, J.E.L., D.M. Scott, K.B. Newbold (2009), Transport mobility benefits and quality of life: a time-use perspective of elderly Canadians, *Transport Policy*, **16**, 1–11.

Stanford Encyclopedia of Philosophy (n.d.), http://plato.stanford.edo/.

Stanley, J., K. Lucas (2009), Editorial. Special issue of the *Journal of Transport Policy* focusing on international perspectives on transport and social exclusion, *Transport Policy*, **16**, 89.

Stanley, J.R., J.K. Stanley (2007), Public transport and social policy goals, *Road & Transport Research*, **16** (1), 20–30.

Stanley, J., D. Vella-Brodrick (2009), The usefulness of social exclusion to inform social policy in transport, *Transport Policy*, **16**, 90–96.

Steiner, H., P. Vallentyne (2009), Libertarian theories of intergenerational justice. In: Gosseries, A., L.H. Meyer (eds), *Intergenerational Justice*. Oxford: Oxford University Press, pp. 50–76.

Sterner, T., U.M. Persson (2008), An even Sterner review: introducing relative prices into the discounting debate, *Review of Environmental Economics and Policy*, **2** (1), 61–76.

Subramanian, U., M. Cropper (2000), Public choices between life saving programs: the tradeoff between qualitative factors and lives saved, *Journal of Risk and Uncertainty*, **21**, 117–49.

Sunstein, C.R. (2005), Cost–benefit analysis and the environment, *Ethics*, **115**, 351–85.

Swierstra, T., K. Jelsma (2006), Responsibility without moralism in technoscientific design practice, *Science, Technology & Human Values*, **31** (3), 309–32.

Szalai, A. (ed.) (1972), *The Use of Time: Daily Activities of Urban and Suburban Populations in Twelve Counties*. The Hague: Mouton.

Taebi, B. (2010), Nuclear power and justice between generations: a moral analysis of fuel cycles, PhD thesis, Delft University of Technology/3 TU Centre for Ethics and Technology.

Thomopoulos, N., S. Grant-Muller, M.R. Tight (2009), Incorporating equity considerations in transport infrastructure evaluation: current practice and a proposed methodology, *Evaluation and Program Planning*, **32** (4), 351–9.

Thompson, J. (2009), Identity and obligation in a transgenerational policy. In: Gosseries, A., L.H. Meyer (eds), *Intergenerational Justice*. Oxford: Oxford University Press, pp. 25–49.

Tijdelijke Commissie Infrastructuurprojecten (TCI) (2004), *Grote projecten uitvergroot. Een infrastructuur voor besluitvorming, Tweede Kamer, 2004–2005, 29.283 nrs. 5-6*, The Hague (Sdu Uitgevers).

Tingvall, C., N. Haworth (1999), Vision zero – an ethical approach to safety and mobility, paper presented to the 6th ITE Conference on Road Safety and Traffic Enforcement: Beyond 2000. Melbourne, 6–7 September.

Tremmel, J.C. (ed.) (2006), *Handbook of Intergenerational Justice*. Cheltenham, UK and Northampton, MA, USA: Edward Elgar.

Trujillo, L., E. Quinet, A. Estache (2002), Dealing with demand forecasting games in transport privatization, *Transport Policy*, **9** (4), 325–34.

Turner, J., N. Apt, M. Grieco, E.A. Wakaye (1998), Users not losers: gender representation in transport design and operation, paper presented at WCTR, Antwerp, July.

Urry, J. (2004), The 'system' of automobility, *Theory, Culture & Society*, **21** (4–5), 25–39.

Van de Poel, I. (2009), Values in engineering design. In: Meijers, A. (ed.), *Handbook of the Philosophy of Science. Volume 9: Philosophy of Technology and Engineering Sciences*. Oxford: Elsevier, pp. 973–1006.

Van de Poel, I., L. Royakkers (2010), *Ethics, Engineering and Technology*. Oxford: Blackwell.

Van Wee, B. (2007a), Large infrastructure projects: a review of the quality of demand forecasts and cost estimations, *Environment and Planning B*, **34** (4), 611–25.

Van Wee, B. (2007b), Rail infrastructure: challenges for cost–benefit analysis and other *ex ante* evaluations, *Transportation Planning and Technology*, **30** (1), 31–48.

Van Wee, B. (2009), Traffic and transport: an introduction. In: van Wee, B. and J.A. Annema (eds), *Traffic and Transport in Main Lines (Verkeer en vervoer in hoofdlijnen)*. Bussum: Coutinho (in Dutch).

Van Wee, B. (2010), Systems and actors: the transport system, *Journal of Design Research*, **8** (4), 434–58.

Van Wee, B. (2011), Urban transport and sustainability. In: van Bueren, E., H. van Bohemen, L. Itard, H. Visscher (eds), *Sustainable Urban Environments: An Ecosystem Approach*, Dordrecht: Springer.

Van Wee, B., P. Rietveld (2008), The myth of travel time saving: a comment, *Transport Reviews*, **28** (6), 688–92.

Van Wee, B., L.A. Tavasszy (2008), Ex-ante evaluation of mega-projects: methodological issues and cost–benefit analysis. In: Priemus, H., B. Flyvbjerg, B. van Wee (eds), *Decision-making on Mega-Projects: Cost–Benefit Analysis, Planning and Innovation*. Cheltenham, UK and Northampton, MA, USA: Edward Elgar, pp. 40–65.

Van Wee, B., M. Hagoort, J.A. Annema (2001), Accessibility measures with competition, *Journal of Transport Geography*, **9**, 199–208.

Van Wee, B., P. Rietveld, H. Meurs (2006), Is average daily travel time expenditure constant? In search of explanations for an increase in average travel time, *Journal of Transport Geography*, **14**, 109–22.

Varian, H. (1992), *Microeconomic Analysis*. New York: W.W. Norton.

Veenhoven, R. (1987), National wealth and individual happiness. In: Grunert, K.G., F. Ölander (eds), *Understanding Economic Behaviour*. Dordrecht, Boston and London: Kluwer Academic Publishers, pp. 9–32.

Veenhoven, R. (1991), Is happiness relative? *Social Indicators Research*, **24** (1), 1–34.

Vickerman, R. (2008), Cost–benefit analysis and the wider economic benefits from mega-projects. In: Priemus, H., B. Flyvbjerg and B. van Wee (eds), *Decision Making on Mega-Projects: Cost–Benefit Analysis, Planning and Innovation*. Cheltenham, UK and Northampton, MA, USA: Edward Elgar, pp. 66–83.

Vlakveld, W.P., Ch. Goldenbeld, Ch. D.A.M. Twisk (2008), *Beleving van verkeersonveiligheid; Een probleemverkenning over subjectieve veiligheid. Report R-2008-15*. Leidschendam: Stichting Wetenschappelijk Onderzoek Verkeersveiligheid SWOV.

VSNU (2004), *The Netherlands Code of Conduct for Scientific Practice: Principles of Good Scientific Teaching and Research*. Amsterdam: VSNU (http://www.vsnu.nl/Media-item/Code-of-conduct-for-scientific-practice-2004.htm).

Wachs, M. (1989), When planners lie with numbers, *APA Journal*, 476, Autumn.

Wachs, M. (1990), Ethics and advocacy in forecasting for public policy, *Business and Professional Ethics Journal*, **9** (1&2), 141–57.

Wallace, W.A. (ed.) (1994a), *Ethics in Modeling*. Oxford: Pergamon.

Wallace, W.A. (1994b), Introduction. In: Wallace, W.A. (ed.), *Ethics in Modeling*. Oxford: Pergamon.

Wallack, M. (2006), Justice between generations: the limits of procedural justice. In: Tremmel, J.C. (ed.), *Handbook of Intergenerational Justice*. Cheltenham, UK and Northampton, MA, USA: Edward Elgar, pp. 86–105.

Walzer, M. (1983), *Spheres of Justice*. New York: Basic Books.

Wardman, M. (2001), A review of British evidence on time and service quality valuations, *Transportation Research Part E*, **37** (2–3), 107–28.

Wegener, M., F. Fürst (1999), *Land-Use Transport Interaction: State of the Art. Deliverable D2a of the project TRANSLAND*. Berichte aus den Insititut für Raumplanung 46, Universität Dortmund, Insititut für Raumplanung, Dortmund.

Weisbrod, G., T. Lynch, M. Meyer (2009), Extending monetary values to broader performance and impact measures: transportation applications and lessons for other fields. *Evaluation and Program Planning*, **32**, 332–41.

Wolf, C. (2003), Intergenerational justice. In: Frey, R.G., C. Heath Wellman (eds), *A Companion to Applied Ethics*. Oxford: Blackwell Publishing Ltd, pp. 279–94.

Wolf, C. (2009), Climate change and climate policies. In: Gosseries, A., L.H. Meyer (eds), *Intergenerational Justice*. Oxford: Oxford University Press, pp. 347–76.

World Business Council for Sustainable Development (WBCSD) (2004), *Mobility 2030: Meeting the Challenges to Sustainability*. Stevenage, UK: WBCSD (http://www.wbcsd.org/web/publications/mobility/mobility-full.pdf).

World Commission on Environment and Development (WCED) (1987), *Our Common Future*. Oxford: Oxford University Press.

Wu, A.M., J.P. Hine (2003), A PTAL approach to measuring changes in bus service accessibility, *Transport Policy*, **10**, 307–20.

Zahavi, Y. (1979), *The UMOT-Project*, Report DOT-RSPA-DPB-2-79-3, Washington, DC: Department of Transportation.

Index